GANGSTERS,
SWINDLERS,
KILLERS, AND
THIEVES

GANGSTERS, SWINDLERS, KILLERS, AND THIEVES

THE LIVES AND CRIMES OF FIFTY AMERICAN VILLAINS

EDITED BY
LAWRENCE BLOCK

OXFORD
UNIVERSITY PRESS
2004

OXFORD

UNIVERSITY PRESS

Oxford   New York
Auckland   Bangkok   Buenos Aires   Cape Town   Chennai
Dar es Salaam   Delhi   Hong Kong   Istanbul   Karachi   Kolkata
Kuala Lumpur   Madrid   Melbourne   Mexico City   Mumbai
Nairobi   São Paulo   Shanghai   Taipei   Tokyo   Toronto

Published by Oxford University Press, Inc.
198 Madison Avenue, New York, New York, 10016
http://www.oup.com/us

Oxford is a registered trademark of Oxford University Press

Library of Congress Cataloging-in-Publication Data
Gangsters, swindlers, killers, and thieves : the lives and crimes of
fifty American villains / Edited by Lawrence Block.
p. cm.
Includes bibliographical references and index.
ISBN 0-19-516952-2 (cloth : alk. paper)
1. Criminals—United States—Biography. 2. United States—Biography—Dictionaries.
I. Block, Lawrence. II. American National Biography. III. Title.
HV6785.G36 2004
364.1'092'273—dc22   2003021073

Designed by Nora Wertz

Grateful acknowledgment is made for permission to reprint lyrics
from "Belle Starr." Words and music by Woody Guthrie. TRO—© Copyright 1963
(Renewed) Ludlow Music, Inc., New York, NY. Used by permission.

Printing number: 9 8 7 6 5 4 3 2 1

Printed in the United States of America
on acid-free paper

Contents

Introduction

Villains. There's something inherently fascinating about them. Sometimes they're bad-bad; the people you love to hate. Sometimes they're good-bad, and you love them and hate yourself for it. Either way they draw your attention and stick in your mind and, more often than not, the heroes who oppose them pale in comparison.

The late Jean Kerr recounted the story of her son's disappointment at landing the role of Adam in the Sunday school play. He'd wanted to play the snake. But Adam was the hero, Kerr told him, and the boy agreed that this was so. But, he countered, the snake had all the lines. And *The Snake Has All the Lines* became the title of Kerr's next book.

> *Back in his room, Keller tried the book again but couldn't keep his mind on what he was reading. He turned on the TV and worked his way through the channels, using the remote control bolted to the nightstand. Westerns, he decided, were like cops and cabs, never around when you wanted them. It seemed to him that he never made a trip around the cable circuit without running into John Wayne or Randolph Scott or Joel McCrea or a rerun of* Gunsmoke *or* Rawhide *or one of those spaghetti westerns with Eastwood or Lee Van Cleef. Or the great villains—Jack Elam, Strother Martin, the young Lee Marvin in* The Man Who Shot Liberty Valance.
>
> *It probably said something about you, Keller thought, when your favorite actor was Jack Elam.*

The passage above appears in *Hit Man*, my own novel about a curiously sympathetic hired killer and, if it does indeed say something about you if your favorite actor is Jack Elam, it very likely says even more if you persist in writing fiction about characters an impartial observer would have to characterize as antisocial. Keller, born in a short story, has gone on to appear

in two novels, with a third on the horizon. Bernie Rhodenbarr, a professional burglar who runs a secondhand bookstore as a hobby, stars in a series
of mysteries that runs to ten volumes. Martin Ehrengraf, who defends criminal cases on a contingency basis, has committed crimes ranging from fraud
and forgery to homicide on his clients' behalf in a dozen short stories.

Even in my books about Matthew Scudder, ex-cop and sober alcoholic
turned private detective, it seems as though the snake gets all the lines.
Scudder's best friend is Mick Ballou, a hoodlum gangleader with gallons
of blood on his hands, and his assistant and surrogate son is a young black
kid with street smarts and little reverence for the law. Scudder himself is
not the traditional private eye with a code; if he ever had one, he's long
since lost the code book, and is a moral relativist who makes it all up as he
goes along.

"I think you're doing something very subversive," a woman told me at a
signing in northern California. "I was reading *Hit List*, and I really like
Keller, although I don't think I should. And at one point I looked up from
the book and said to myself, 'Well, so he kills people. What's so bad about
that?' "

Perhaps it was my predilection for chronicling the adventures of fictional
bad guys that got me the gratifying job of compiling this collection of very
real villains, drawn from a couple hundred years of American history—
and, specifically, from the pages of Oxford University Press's incompara-
ble *American National Biography*. Here, for your enjoyment and edification,
are the life stories of half a hundred thieves, murderers, gangsters, assassins, outlaws, and all-around menaces to civilized society. Each, individ-
ually, has an absorbing story to tell; collectively, they add up to an antisocial
whole that's greater than the sum of its parts, enlarging our sense of just
what it means to be a villain, and what another's villainy means to us.

Some of them make us ache physically with the need to see them punished. Ted Bundy, the clean-cut, handsome boy next door who killed attractive young women for sport, is perhaps the quintessential serial killer of
the twentieth century, and makes the perfect poster boy for capital pun-

ishment—or, if one recoils at the notion of government-sponsored homicide, at the very least for life imprisonment without parole. Ed Gein, whose experiments in taxidermy led to Robert Bloch's and Alfred Hitchcock's *Psycho*, inspires horror more than loathing; we want to see him put away, far away, where we won't have to look at him, or at ourselves.

You'll meet assassins here, three very different men who took the lives of three American presidents. John Wilkes Booth, Lincoln's assassin, saw himself as the last-ditch defender of a lost Confederate cause; Charles Guiteau believed himself to be divinely inspired to shoot James Garfield; Leon Czolgosz's half-digested anarchist sympathies led him to assassinate William McKinley. All three died for what they did, and it was a foregone conclusion that they would; the enormity of their acts, the prominence of their victims pretty much guaranteed their deaths.

You'll encounter quite a few gangsters in this book, including Owney Madden and Al Capone, Bugsy Siegel and Meyer Lansky, Lucky Luciano and Dutch Schultz. "We only kill each other," Siegel told his Hollywood friends, although of course that wasn't always true. One of the guiding principles of Lepke Buchalter's original Murder Incorporated gang was that convictions became unlikely if witnesses disappeared, and no end of witnesses were consequently murdered. The deaths of presumably innocent bystanders were another by-product of the violent side of organized crime, and contemporary drug dealers coined the term *mushrooms* for the passersby caught in drug war crossfire—because they just pop up out of nowhere.

Still, we can overlook the occasional innocent victim as we give ourselves over to the myth of the gangster as it unfolds in fiction like *The Godfather* and *The Sopranos* or in real life. Criminal enterprise, we tell ourselves, is a time-honored way for immigrants to gain a foothold in their new home. They claw their way up, using methods more direct and arguably more honest than those used in climbing the corporate ladder. They may have to kill someone, they may get killed in return, but their sons and daughters will go to college.

If our urban mythology embraces the gangster, the outlaw with the six-gun plays a similar role in our view of the frontier. Here we'll encounter William Clarke Quantrill and a few of the outlaws—Jesse James, Cole Younger—who made their bones in his Civil War guerrilla band. Quantrill's Raiders were vicious murderers or heroic soldiers, depending in part upon your Union or Confederate sympathies, and the ones who turned to crime after the war's end remained heroes to a portion of the population. They and others who robbed banks and trains benefited from a populist sentiment that saw financial institutions and railroads as parasitic exploiters; those who preyed on the predators were quickly cast as latter-day Robin Hoods, although evidence that many of them actually went so far as to give to the poor is hard to come by.

While not every outlaw was so treated in his lifetime, legend continues to burnish images, often with no discernible justification. Tiburcio Vásquez, a Mexican bandit hanged in California, has achieved what may be the most extraordinary posthumous rehabilitation; they've named a medical facility after him in Alameda County.

Vásquez, for all we know, may have been a nice guy, but no one who knew John Wesley Hardin said the same for him. Time and pop music have been kind to Hardin; Bob Dylan, who saw fit to tack on a G and call him John Wesley Harding, portrays him in song as a fair-minded, courageous, socially conscious fellow, a true stand-up guy. That just goes to show what an extra consonant will do for a man, because the real John Wesley Hardin, as you'll see, was an ill-tempered, homicidal, sociopathic racist with no redeeming qualities whatsoever.

The Robin Hood myth, the image of the outlaw as an individual fighting a lone battle against a corrupt and corrupting system, survived the loss of the frontier. The bank robbers of the years between the two world wars achieved that sort of mythic status long before the film *Bonnie and Clyde* made the life look glamorous. John Dillinger, Pretty Boy Floyd, and of course Clyde Barrow and Bonnie Parker, raced their fast cars along country roads and blazed away with their tommy guns, much as Butch Cassidy and the Daltons rode fast horses and fired Colt revolvers. The motorized outlaws of the Dust Bowl and Depression years were in it for the money, but that's not to say that they were unaware of the mythic aspects of their role even as they enacted them. In Dillinger's jail break and Bonnie Parker's poems, we can almost see performers playing consciously to an audience.

One of the things we seem to have trouble believing about those we elevate to mythic status is that they're dead. If we regard them as immortals, how can mortality have its way with them?

It's not only criminals who get this treatment, as the rash of Elvis sightings demonstrates. No one has turned up claiming to be Elvis— unless you want to count all those Vegas lounge acts—but for a while there was a fresh Anastasia popping up every decade or so, and before that poor lady there were all the lost Dauphins of France.

Of our criminals, quite a few have demonstrated a comparable reluctance to stay dead. In one case, that of John Dillinger, a substantial body of evidence exists to suggest that lawmen did indeed shoot another man altogether in front of the Biograph Theater, though what subsequently became of the real John Dillinger is a good question. Butch Cassidy's death is also hard to substantiate; he may have been killed in South America, but he may as well have returned to the U.S. and lived out his life in quiet obscurity.

In other instances, the outlaw's posthumous life represents the triumph of myth over hard fact. The death of Jesse James is probably the best example. Before the body was cold, a broadside ballad had been widely circulated, so that the whole country knew that Robert Ford, the "dirty little coward who shot Mr. Howard," had laid poor Jesse in his grave. The craven betrayal became part of the legend of Jesse James—how he was hanging or straightening a picture on the wall, how Ford shot him in the back, and so on.

With his end so well documented and so widely acknowledged, you'd think Jesse wouldn't have had much trouble staying in his grave. You wouldn't suppose there'd be much opportunity for men claiming to be the living Jesse, nor would you expect the public to pay much attention to such claims. But claims were made and attention was paid, even to the old codger who turned up 103 years after Jesse's birth.

Introductions are a curious literary form. A book like this seems to call for one, yet the whole enterprise strikes me as essentially pointless. While I suppose some people will read these lines, I can't avoid feeling they'll do so largely out of politeness.

Explaining his literary style, novelist Elmore Leonard said he just tries to leave out the parts that people will skip. Introductions, I'm afraid, are frequently skipped, and with good reason. And yet I soldier on.

And, thinking of Elmore Leonard, I find myself struck by the fact that he has written with great success over the years in two genres of popular fiction: the crime novel and the western. (So, coincidentally, has Loren Estleman, and I feel duty-bound to point out that both of these gentlemen live in Detroit. Make of that what you will.)

Few readers of crime fiction read westerns. Few fans of westerns read crime novels. But if you read examples of Leonard's or Estleman's work in both genres, you realize how little difference there is between the two. You meet the same sort of characters, on both sides of the law. The milieu varies, from sagebrush and open range to mean streets. Men ride horses and rustle cattle in one book; in another they hotwire SUVs and deal drugs.

By the same token, the villains you'll meet here, for all their differences, haven't changed that much over the centuries. There are some you may wish you could know, and others you'll be very grateful never to have encountered. Some will inspire grudging admiration, others contempt, still others fear and revulsion. All in all, though, I think you'll be glad to have made their acquaintance. I know I am.

GANGSTERS,
SWINDLERS,
KILLERS, AND
THIEVES

Upon his graduation from Yale in 1911, Thomas Beer planned to study law.

THOMAS BEER

[22 NOVEMBER 1888?–18 APRIL 1940]

Literary forgery is so far removed from the practice of signing another man's name on a check or document that one almost wishes there were a different word for it. Both are criminal, and the literary forger sometimes has profit as a motive—fabricating the Hitler Diaries to sell them to a magazine, for example, or forging spurious manuscripts to be peddled to wealthy collectors. But the literary forger often has more in common with the journalist who invents interviews and attributes statements to nonexistent sources. His crime is embroidery and fabrication. He is creating fiction in nonfiction's realm.

The downfall of Thomas Beer, who had distinguished himself commercially and artistically in both fiction and nonfiction, is one I find particularly poignant. His book on Stephen Crane was his magnum opus, with only one thing wrong with it: a good deal of its content was spurious, the work not of the author's research but of his imagination. He forged letters, made up incidents, and created characters out of the whole cloth. It's hard for me to judge the man harshly, in that I do that sort of thing all the time, but it's different when you pass it off as truth.

Beer's life fell apart a dozen years or so after his work on Crane was published, but it was not until 1988 that Paul Sorrentino and Stanley Wertheim documented the extent of his forgeries. Whether his literary fraud engendered his breakdown, or whether it too derived from his alcoholism, would seem to be moot.

Thomas Beer, writer, was born in Council Bluffs, Iowa, the son of William Collins Beer, a corporate attorney and lobbyist, and Martha Ann Alice Baldwin. Though born in western Iowa, Thomas Beer spent most of his childhood in Yonkers, New York, with summers in Nantucket and on his grandfather's farm in Bucyrus, Ohio. Wealth and position from his father's Wall Street business gave Beer a distinct sense of social superiority, which he manifested in personal relations and cultural criticisms. Despising the bourgeoisie, the working-class masses, and the chic lifestyles of the Jazz Age, Beer projected an image of extreme conservatism and tesselated sophistication. At Yale, class of 1911, he was class poet, friend of the actor Monty Woolley, editor of the literary review, and contributor of twenty stories, essays, and poems. After college he spent five years as a dilatory student in the Columbia law school and as a clerk in his father's law firm, but when his father died at his professional nadir in 1916, Beer turned to letters. His first important short story—"The Brothers"—was published a few months later in the *Century*. He also dated the stimulus for writing *Stephen Crane* to 1916. Soon afterward Beer enlisted in the U.S. Army; first as private, but eventually promoted to first lieutenant, he served in France at the end of World War I.

A prolific writer in his prime, Beer published nearly 140 short stories— an average of more than six a year—between 1917 and 1936. Written expressly for the *Saturday Evening Post*, most of these bittersweet comedies celebrate the wholesomeness of the American heartland. Beer's settings are generally farms and small towns in upstate New York or Ohio; his prototypic hero, Adam Egg, is a muscular, laconic youth who serves as moral arbiter in resolving domestic or communal unrest. Beer's formulaic plots usually contain hints of Oedipal conflicts and sibling rivalries, but they are always agreeably resolved. His stories, like Norman Rockwell's artwork, appealed strongly to the *Post* readership in affirming the innate wisdom of common folk.

This self-proclaimed "desolating literary prostitution" earned Beer a modest fortune. His potboilers sold for as much as $3,000 each; in 1931 he earned more than $31,000. Nevertheless, success by this means embarrassed him. Beer's deportment and tastes diverged sharply from the fictional world that made him popular. A closet homosexual, he cultivated a studied urbanity and a loathing of the vulgar and the provincial. Like Petronius, his favorite Latin author, Beer sneered at convention and promoted style above morality. Alfred Kazin ranked him with other "Exquisites"—James Branch Cabell, Joseph Hergesheimer, and Elinor Wylie—who cultivated an "elaborate decadence and estheticism."

Alfred Knopf, Beer's publisher and patron, encouraged him to excel. "I have—for reasons I can hardly explain—great confidence in you," Knopf wrote, responding to the submission of Beer's first novel in 1921, "and feel that your work is going to count." The three novels did not, however, live up to the publisher's expectation. *The Fair Rewards* (1922) and *Sandoval* (1924) are studies of bygone manners projected against the background of New York City in the nineteenth century. First admired for their ornate virtuosity, these novels pale when compared with the more innovative modernism of Ernest Hemingway, F. Scott Fitzgerald, and Sinclair Lewis. *The Road to Heaven* (1928), a philosophically ambitious novel, suggests a Spenglerian analysis of culture through the cousins Abner and Lamon Coe—one typifying decadent urbanity; the other, rustic vitality.

Beer's best writing is found in his nonfiction, where he displayed remarkable ability as a biographer, historian, and cultural critic. *The Mauve Decade: American Life at the End of the Nineteenth Century* (1926), an anecdotal tour de force, derives its title from James Whistler, who supposedly observed that "Mauve is just pink trying to be purple." Flamboyant, nostalgic, impudent, and cynical, *The Mauve Decade* illustrates Beer's style at its height. What the book lacks in historical accuracy is redeemed by its vivid, incisive images of America in the 1890s. In a similar manner, *Hanna* (1929), an impressionistic biography of Mark Hanna, explores politics in the Gilded Age. Members of Beer's family were powers in the Republican party in Ohio; his father served Hanna and William McKinley as an undercover agent and campaign manager. Parts of *The Mauve Decade* and *Hanna* constitute a history of the Beer family, deriving from family papers and memories, real and invented.

Beer's principal yet most problematic work is his *Stephen Crane: A Study in American Letters* (1923), the first biography of Stephen Crane and unfortunately the basis of future scholarship. Reviewers greeted Beer's *Crane* with enthusiasm, stating that it set an example for a new type of life history, devoid of hagiography and replete with dramatic appeal. However, later biographers found the book evasive and inaccurate, particularly in its misrepresentation of Crane's "marriage" to the nightclub manager and madam who called herself Cora "Taylor." Worse still, it now appears that the excerpts from approximately seventy of Crane's letters that Beer published in *Stephen Crane* and elsewhere were forgeries, and that many of the episodes and persons named in his book and essays on Crane do not, in fact, exist. Once trusted as a source for Stephen Crane studies, Thomas Beer is now wholly discredited.

Beer's career came to an abrupt halt in July 1937 when he broke down and was confined for fourteen months to the Hartford Retreat, a neuropsychiatric clinic, where he was treated for hypertension, insomnia, vertigo, obesity, and depression. Unmentioned in clinical records, though doubtless a major contributing factor, was alcoholism. When he was discharged in September 1938, Beer had two contracts pending with Knopf, but he could no longer write. Unable to earn a living, he sold his property—including his books and art collection at a devastating loss—and moved to an apartment in Manhattan. He died at the Albert Hotel in Greenwich Village, New York City, officially of a heart attack, but most likely a suicide.

J.C.

BILLY THE KID

[15 SEPTEMBER 1859–14 JULY 1881]

The legends collide. He was a lightning marksman, able to outdraw virtually anyone and fire his six-gun with deadly accuracy. He was a cowardly psychopath who shot most of his victims in the back, or from ambush. He was yet another latter-day Robin Hood, fighting the powerful interests on behalf of the oppressed. He was a hired gun, available to the highest bidder. He killed twenty-one men before his twenty-first birthday. He killed half a dozen men, if that.

Oddly, given all the myth that sprang up around him, there were no rumors holding that the Kid survived that final encounter with Pat Garrett. Perhaps this particular legend required an early death. Still, you have to wonder how the Kid might have turned out.

Incidentally, Lew Wallace, the governor of New Mexico who tried to gain amnesty for the Kid, is the same fellow who wrote Ben-Hur.

Billy the Kid, western outlaw and legendary figure in international folklore, was born Henry McCarty, probably in Brooklyn, New York, probably on the date given, and probably of Irish immigrants; all aspects of his origins, however, remain controversial. In 1873 his mother, Catherine, was remarried to William Henry Antrim, whereupon the boy took his stepfather's name and became Henry Antrim. Later, for reasons that are obscure, he adopted the sobriquet William H. Bonney. In adolescence he was called simply Kid, but not until the final few months of his life was he known as Billy the Kid.

The Kid grew up in the mining camp of Silver City, New Mexico, where he was a good student and caused no more trouble than the average male adolescent. After his mother's death in 1874 he had a trivial run-in with the law, which landed him in jail. He escaped and took refuge in Arizona, where he became a petty horse thief. There in 1877, at the age of seventeen, he killed a bully who had been tormenting him and fled back to New Mexico to embark on the life of an outlaw.

Billy the Kid was a notorious gunman until his final confrontation with Sheriff Pat Garrett in Fort Sumner, New Mexico.

The Kid gained experience and notoriety as a gunman in New Mexico's Lincoln County War of 1878. This was a conflict between rival mercantile firms seeking to dominate the county's economy, including federal contracts to supply the military post of Fort Stanton and the Apache Indian agency. The Tunstall-McSween faction sought to displace the entrenched monopoly of the Murphy-Dolan faction. As one of the Regulators, the fighting arm of the Tunstall-McSween faction, the Kid fought in all the skirmishes and battles of the war. With five others, he shared in the ambush slaying of Sheriff William Brady on Lincoln's main street. He also participated prominently in the archetypal western shootout with Buckshot Roberts at Blazer's Mill. The violent climax of the war took place in the town of Lincoln on 15–19 July 1878, when a sheriff's posse attempted to rout the Regulators. The final day featured a siege of the McSween house, in which the Kid and his confederates were barricaded. The appearance of a military force from Fort Stanton, although it supposedly remained neutral, threw the advantage to the posse. In a hail of gunfire, the Kid and three others escaped from the burning McSween house, leaving four of their comrades to be struck down and killed.

After the war the Kid pursued an ambivalent life of petty crime while also trying to free himself of legal entanglements in order to go straight. Based in the village of Fort Sumner, on the Pecos River, he and a handful of friends rustled Texas cattle from the nearby Staked Plains. A bargain with New Mexico governor Lew Wallace to turn state's evidence against other murderers collapsed when the Kid continued to rustle cows and Wallace failed to gain amnesty for him. Captured by a posse under Sheriff Pat Garrett after a gun battle at Stinking Springs in December 1880, the Kid was tried in Mesilla for the murder of Sheriff Brady during the Lincoln County War. He was found guilty and sent back to Lincoln to be hanged. Instead, in April 1881, he broke free from confinement, killing two guards as he went.

Billy the Kid remained free for three months, harbored by Hispanic sheepmen in the Fort Sumner area. On 14 July 1881, however, Sheriff Garrett confronted him in a darkened bedroom at Fort Sumner. Garrett fired first, and Billy died instantly, struck in the heart.

Billy the Kid did not marry. He was, however, extremely popular with young women, especially the Hispanics who idolized him because he spoke their language and did not patronize them. Almost certainly he left an unrecorded progeny. His brother survived him by nearly fifty years and died a Denver derelict.

Even before his death, Billy the Kid had attained legendary stature. Legend credits him with killing twenty-one men, one for each of his twenty-one years. Actually, the number was four for certain plus six encounters in which he participated and may or may not have fired the fatal round. Nor was he the premier outlaw captain the press pictured. He and a few others rustled cows, but there was no organized gang under his leadership.

In history, Billy the Kid rates hardly a footnote. In folklore, he is a towering figure throughout the world. In the public imagination, two Kids have vied with each other since 1881. The first is the merciless outlaw killer; the other is the young Robin Hood whose guns blazed for the poor and downtrodden against the entrenched interests. The latter image, created by Walter Noble Burns's *Saga of Billy the Kid* (1926), was the model for subsequent books, articles, movies, and even an orchestral suite and ballet. For millions, Billy still rides as the ultimate symbol of the violence of the Old West.

R.M.U.

BLACK BART

[FL. 1875–1888]

It would be hard for me not to like Black Bart. As a man who's made a career out of chronicling the fictional exploits of a gentleman burglar, how could I fail to appreciate the archetypal gentleman bandit?

And Bart was the perfect specimen. He never robbed people, only large impersonal institutions. He never shot anybody, and didn't even load his gun. Indeed, the only thing to be held against him is that he took money that didn't belong to him. There are laws against that, and there probably ought to be, but it's hard to work up a great deal of moral indignation over it.

It's interesting that Black Bart left poems behind on a couple of occasions, and even provided the law (and the press) with a nickname. So did Jack the Ripper, among others, and one can but assume both acted out of ego and a desire to achieve recognition while maintaining anonymity (and avoiding capture).

Interesting, too, that the detective on the case managed to develop a good description of Bart, but that it did him no good. One is reminded of today's FBI profilers, determining that the serial killer they're seeking is a white male under forty who wet the bed as a child. That often turns out to be true, but never seems to lead to an arrest.

B lack Bart, stagecoach robber, was born Charles E. Boles, probably in 1832 in either Norfolk, England, or upstate New York. His parents' names are unknown. He had a wife, Mary, and probably three children. He abandoned them all after the Civil War, in which he was wounded while serving as a first sergeant in the 116th Illinois Volunteer Infantry. He probably never saw any of his family again.

Between 1875 and 1883 Boles carried out twenty-nine holdups of stagecoaches, all in northern California. He came to epitomize the highwayman and popularized a new synonym for the latter, "road agent," a term remarked on by Robert Louis Stevenson in his *Silverado Squatters*. Boles

The gentleman bandit left clues behind two holdups signed "Black Bart, P08."

took the name "Black Bart" from a character in a story that he had read. He fixed the nickname by deliberately leaving clues behind after two holdups. These were snippets of "poetry"—actually waggish doggerel—signed "Black Bart, P08."

Bart was the perfect bandit. He always worked alone, wearing a flour sack with eyeholes over his head and a duster over his clothing to hide his identity. He said nothing but "Throw down the [express] box!" so there was no accent or speech pattern to betray him. His victims only knew that his voice was deep and resonant. Bart never traveled on horseback but always afoot, with speed, stamina, and skill. Only once was a mounted sheriff's posse able to track him in the thick chaparral (brush) into which he had disappeared, and the deputies lost the trail in just six miles. James B. Hume, chief of detectives for Wells, Fargo, said Bart was "a person of great endurance, a thorough mountaineer, a remarkable walker; and [he] claims that he cannot be excelled in making quick transits over mountains and grades."

Bart's modus operandi never varied. He would "case" a stage from a temporary sleeping camp to establish its schedule and memorize the terrain. His camps were never too close to a holdup site, he never built a fire at night, and he never slept over after a robbery. He rambled all over, from the Redwood Coast to Sierra Nevada, and only once struck the same place twice. He always stopped a stage as it was forced to slow down on an upgrade, often at a curve that hid him from view until the last moment.

Bart was unique among bad men. He was something of a gentleman bandit and had a sense of humor. He did not smoke, drink, use drugs, or even curse drivers and guards to intimidate them. He does not even seem to have loaded the double-barreled shotgun that he used in robberies. He left the money and jewelry of travelers alone and was gallant toward female passengers. He stole only from Wells, Fargo & Co. and the U.S. Post Office, figuring that both could afford it.

Hume's study of the doggerel rhymes Bart left revealed only that he wrote each line in a different hand. The detective noted that Bart always opened "treasure" boxes with an old ax and slit mail pouches with a distinctive T-shaped cut near the bag's lock. Eventually Hume was able to put together a composite description of a suspect by interviewing people about strangers seen near the sites of stage robberies. The picture of Black Bart that he pieced together proved remarkably accurate but did him no good. The bandit struck, again and again, with impunity. Only once did a guard manage to get off a couple of shots at him.

Fate intervened when Bart, for the first time, made a holdup at the same site as an earlier robbery. In fact, it was the location of his very first robbery eight years earlier. It was on Funk Hill near Copperopolis in the mother lode. The driver, Reason McConnell, had no guard or passengers, so he gave a young deer hunter a lift. Jimmy Rolleri jumped off the stage to look for bucks before rejoining McConnell beyond the hill. Hume had bolted strongboxes inside the coaches, so Bart was still attacking the box with an ax when McConnell returned with Rolleri and the latter's Henry rifle. They took turns firing, and one of Rolleri's bullets nicked Bart in one knuckle. He dropped a bundle as he fled with his loot.

The local sheriff and Hume's assistant found a handkerchief among Bart's abandoned belongings. It bore the laundry mark F. X. O. 7. Hume sent a special investigator, Harry Morse, to trace the owner of the handkerchief, with orders to check all of San Francisco's ninety-one laundries if he had to. Morse soon matched the mark with a middle-aged self-stated mining man who called himself Charles E. Bolton. Hume grilled him for hours and finally elicited a confession to (only) the last robbery.

William Randolph Hearst's *Examiner* protested about a "deal," and it is true that Black Bart received a mitigated sentence promised him by Hume for his cooperation. He drew only seven years in San Quentin and, a model prisoner, actually served only four and a half years, thanks to his good conduct. Still in good spirits while in his cell, he wrote McConnell and Rolleri, praising the former for his driving but adding, "I only regret that I am unable to compliment you on your marksmanship."

A legendary Black Bart grew up in newspapers and dime novels. His exploits and his loot were greatly exaggerated. The real Black Bart probably made far less than the $18,400 in "withdrawals" from Wells, Fargo that some writers estimated.

After his release from prison in 1888, Bart disappeared from public view, but there were stories that he had returned to crime, as new stage robberies were blamed on him. Another rumor had Wells, Fargo putting him on its payroll to *not* rob its express boxes. Bart was reportedly seen in various places, but Hume only stated that he had left California. Hume's assistant, Jonathan Thacker, reported in 1897 that Bart had sailed from Vancouver, British Columbia, on the *Empress of China*, bound for Japan. In any case, he utterly vanished.

R.H.D.

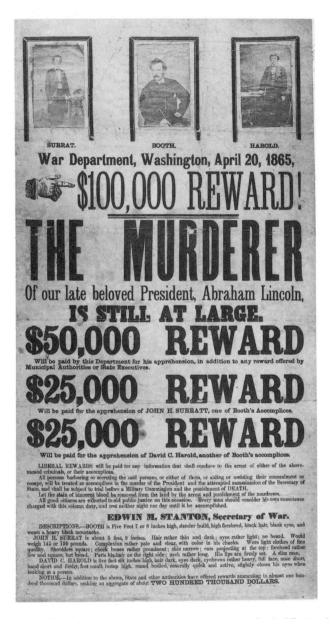

An image of John Wilkes Booth was featured on a wanted poster immediately following the Lincoln assassination.

JOHN WILKES BOOTH

[10 MAY 1838–26 APRIL 1865]

Sometime in the early 1950s, I watched an hour-long television drama on an anthology program called Danger. *Here's the plot: A band of brave men are living under an oppressive dictatorship in an unnamed country. Their own nation has been crushed on the battlefield by a neighboring country, and they've been annexed to this powerful adversary. We're with these guys as they risk everything on a plot to kill the dictator. In fact, we're standing right beside them, cheering all the way, as their leader, a charismatic lad named Johnny, sneaks up on the archfiend and shoots him dead.*

And then Johnny leaps over a rail and down from the balcony, crying out "Sic semper tyrannis!" *and we catch our first glimpse of the slain tyrant, and ohmigod it's Abraham Lincoln.*

It's been fifty years since I saw that show, but I remember it vividly, and recounting it leaves a chill at the bone.

The point, I suppose, is that one man's hero is another man's villain, even as patriotism and treason shift with one's vantage point.

This first presidential assassination was the product of a conspiracy, while the three that followed (plus several attempts) have all been the work of individuals. (The deranged Charles Guiteau, Garfield's murderer, was clearly acting on his own; Leon Czolgosz, who shot McKinley, was a self-styled anarchist, but efforts to link his act to anarchist groups got nowhere. Controversy still clouds Lee Harvey Oswald's assassination of John F. Kennedy.) William Seward and Andrew Johnson were to be murdered the same night as Lincoln; one conspirator lost his nerve, while the other botched the attempt.

John Surratt, whose probably innocent mother was the first woman hanged in the United States, managed to flee the country and led a curiously charmed life abroad until he was arrested in Egypt. A jury failed to convict him, and he lived out his life in Baltimore.

John Wilkes Booth, actor and assassin of President Abraham Lincoln, was born near Bel Air in Harford County, Maryland, the son of Junius Brutus Booth, an actor, and Mary Ann Holmes. His grandfather, Richard Booth, named him after John Wilkes, the British reformer. As a child Booth dabbled in acting, as did some of his brothers and several neighborhood boys, both at the Booth country home, "Tudor Hall," and at their town house in Baltimore. Booth's father actively discouraged his children from entering the theatrical profession, but he toured extensively and died on the road when John was only fourteen. Booth grew up as the darling of his family, somewhat spoiled and temperamental, receiving only intermittent education. One of his four sisters, Asia, recalled his "fitful gaiety" as a youth, tinged with a "taint of melancholy." He followed his father and two older brothers onto the stage, making his professional debut in Baltimore on 14 August 1855 as Richmond in *Richard III*. The seventeen-year-old thespian failed miserably but returned home to study the actor's craft. He next appeared at the Arch Street Theater in Philadelphia, then the theatrical center of America. The handsome young actor charmed his audiences, in spite of his overacting, faulty elocution, and general lack of discipline. He appeared once with his brother Edwin Booth, then performed for a season at Richmond, Virginia. During these and later engagements Booth used various names, apparently trying to protect the family name until he could add some professional luster to it. At the same time he began to develop a reputation as a womanizer and a considerable southern chauvinist. He went so far as to try to join a military group, but he had promised his mother he would not enlist and would continue his acting career.

When Booth returned to Richmond for another season, he learned of John Brown's impending trial at Charles Town. Booth abandoned his job at the Richmond Theatre to attend Brown's execution, later claiming to have helped capture Brown, writing, "I thought that the Abolitionists were the only traitors in the land and . . . deserved the fate of Brown." Goaded by reports of his brother Edwin's success as an actor, he soon sought to make himself into a star, thereby increasing his income and fame substantially. He began to appear as J. Wilkes Booth, often in roles that his father had made famous.

As the Civil War approached and theatricals in the South decreased, Booth began a northern tour, continuing to denounce President Lincoln and the North. In Baltimore he joined a rebel secret society called the Knights of the Golden Circle, wholly convinced that the North was unjustly oppressing his beloved South. He meanwhile continued to expand his professional and personal reputations. On 26 April 1861 one of Booth's jilted lovers, actress Henrietta Irving, tried to kill him but succeeded only in slashing his arm.

By 1863 Booth billed himself as "the Youngest Tragedian in the World." His passion for the Confederate cause intensified; he began to plot the kidnapping of President Lincoln, possibly with the intention of ransoming all Confederate prisoners held by the North. Toward the end of the war, he began to assemble a small band of conspirators in Washington, D.C. Whether or not Booth had any official mandate from the Confederacy remains unclear.

On 25 November 1864 Booth and his brothers Edwin and Junius Jr. appeared together on the stage for the first and only time. The occasion was a benefit production of *Julius Caesar* in New York City to raise funds for a memorial statue of Shakespeare for Central Park. Edwin played Brutus; Junius Jr. impersonated Caesar, and John Wilkes as Antony cried out for vengeance against the assassins. Mary Ann Holmes Booth, the actors' aged mother, proudly attended the performance.

At his greatest popularity as an actor, Booth earned about $20,000 a year. His repertory grew to include *The Lady of Lyons, Money, The Robbers, The Marble Heart, The Apostate, The Stranger,* and *The Corsican Brothers,* as well as the Shakespearean roles of Richard III, Romeo, Hamlet, Macbeth, Othello, Iago, Shylock, and Petruchio. Admirers and critics described him as one of the most charming of men, admired by many men and adored by almost all women. His dark good looks resembled those of Edgar Allan Poe; a friend said he was as handsome as a young god. His acting was described as passionate, explosive, and uneven, lacking the intellectuality of his father or the quiet dignity of Edwin Booth, depending on charisma rather than craft or artistry. Later critics would denigrate his work, but John

Wilkes Booth was definitely an actor with exceptional potential during the Civil War. He appeared on 18 March 1865, for the last time on any stage, as Pescara in *The Apostate*. The performance took place at Ford's Theatre in Washington, D.C.

Booth grew increasingly obsessed with the subjects of slavery and the Confederacy. He recruited two boyhood friends, Michael O'Laughlin and Samuel Arnold, to assist him in kidnapping Lincoln, which they planned for 20 March 1865. Lincoln did not appear as expected; the conspirators panicked and fled. Later Booth added David Herold and George Atzerodt to his band, completing it with Lewis Powell, known also as Lewis Payne. By this time Booth had become acquainted with a young rebel, John Surratt, and his mother, Mary Eugenia Surratt, a rebel sympathizer who operated a boardinghouse in Washington, in which the group would meet from time to time.

The kidnapping plot evaporated when the city of Richmond fell and the war ended. Five days later, on 14 April 1865, Booth learned that President Lincoln planned to attend *Our American Cousin* (starring Laura Keene) at Ford's Theatre. Working quickly, Booth assigned Atzerodt to assassinate Vice President Andrew Johnson and Payne to kill Secretary of State William Seward while Booth himself murdered Lincoln. Atzerodt lost his nerve and made no attempt on Johnson, but Payne, a young giant, wounded Seward severely, as well as several others who tried to defend him.

Booth meanwhile had entered Ford's Theatre at about ten o'clock, moving across the rear of the balcony to the president's box. Waiting for the audience's laughter to cover the report of his derringer, Booth entered the box and fired a single .44-caliber bullet at point-blank range into the back of Lincoln's head. He shouted "*Sic semper tyrannis! The South is avenged!*" according to some, slashing with a dagger at Major Henry Rathbone, who tried to restrain him. Booth then leaped the twelve feet from the presidential box onto the stage, breaking his left leg. He escaped from the theater to a waiting horse and, accompanied by Herold, fled Washington. They stopped at the home of Dr. Samuel A. Mudd in Bryantown, Maryland, to have Booth's leg set, then hid in neighboring woods for six days while federal troops vainly searched for them.

By 23 April Booth and Herold had reached the farm of Richard H. Garrett, three miles south of Port Royal, Virginia, and seventy-eight miles from Washington. Garrett hid the fugitives in one of his tobacco barns. In the early morning of 26 April a band of soldiers arrived and surrounded the outbuilding. Herold surrendered immediately; Booth defied the troops, offering to fight them one by one. Instead the troops set fire to the barn, and they saw Booth inside, using a crutch to stand erect. A bullet felled Booth, but whether he shot himself or was mortally wounded by one of the soldiers, Sergeant Boston Corbett, has never been completely resolved. Booth died at about seven o'clock, his last words being, "Tell Mother I died for my country."

The troops returned the body to Washington for a secret burial at the Arsenal Grounds. A confusing, disorganized trial—a travesty of judicial procedure—ensued. Eventually the government hanged Herold, Payne, Atzerodt, and Mrs. Surratt (who may have known nothing of the plot). Mudd, Arnold, and O'Laughlin received life imprisonment.

Edwin Booth petitioned the government to return John Wilkes Booth's body to his family; on 20 February 1869 the body was buried in an unmarked grave in the Booth lot (Dogwood Number Nine) in Green Mount Cemetery in Baltimore, after identification by several friends and acquaintances. Nevertheless rumors abounded that Booth had escaped, and later a mummified body advertised as Booth's appeared on exhibition around the country. A popular fiction held that Booth committed suicide in 1903 in Enid, Oklahoma, where he was known as David E. George.

Scholars and historians who have examined the evidence carefully agree Booth died at Garrett's farm. Many maintain that by murdering Lincoln, who could have overseen Reconstruction with mercy and justice, Booth struck a staggering blow at his own beloved South. Whatever the case, the first presidential assassination in America forever branded the Booth name with infamy.

S.M.A.

This police mug shot of murder suspect Ted Bundy was taken in 1980, the year he received his third death sentence.

TED BUNDY

[24 NOVEMBER 1946–24 JANUARY 1989]

In one guise or another, he'll be turning up in popular culture for years to come. In films and novels, we can expect to see some Ted Bundy clone serving as the sexual psychopath who does not look the part, the least likely (and thus most dangerous) suspect. Just as Ed Gein served as the prototype for Psycho's *Norman Bates and* The Silence of the Lambs's *Buffalo Bill, along with the wild-eyed villains of countless slasher films, so will the handsome, clean-cut, well-spoken Bundy serve as the real-life model for no end of variations of the Serial Killer Next Door.*

He was driven, I suppose—acting under irresistible compulsion, and yet he looks like nothing so much as a wholly heartless sonofabitch who did what he did because he enjoyed every moment of it. It's hard to imagine him as tortured by his own evil acts, hard to picture him taking up a victim's lipstick and scrawling For God's sake stop me before I kill again *on a mirror. He didn't want to be stopped. He wanted to kill again, and he did, repeatedly.*

By the end, he became less organized, as serial killers typically do, but still he did all he could to stave off the end. In the face of overwhelming evidence, he insisted he was innocent until the last moment, finally trying to blame his whole criminal career on the pornography he claimed to have encountered at an impressionable age.

He is, it must be said, the perfect poster boy for capital punishment. Whatever one's views on the matter, it's hard to deny that the world is a safer place without him in it.

Ted Bundy, serial murderer, was born Theodore Robert Cowell at the Elizabeth Lund Home for Unwed Mothers in Burlington, Vermont, the son of Louise Cowell. (His father's name is unknown.) About two months after Ted's birth, Louise Cowell returned with her son to her parents' house in Philadelphia, Pennsylvania. When Ted was about five, his mother took him to Tacoma, Washington, where she met Johnnie Bundy, a cook at a military hospital. They were married in 1951. For the first few years of Ted's life, he apparently was led to believe that his mother was his sister and that his grandparents were his parents. Despite this somewhat nontraditional upbringing, by most accounts he experienced a happy and normal childhood and adolescence, albeit a frugal one, as the family did not have much money. A good-looking and serious young man, Bundy earned above-average grades and graduated from high school in 1965. That same year he entered the University of Puget Sound, where he felt uncomfortable around the predominantly affluent student body. He transferred to the University of Washington for his sophomore year and finally earned his bachelor's degree in psychology in 1972. During his college years Bundy became involved with Republican party politics, working on the Nelson Rockefeller presidential campaign in 1968. After graduation he was a crisis counselor and worked on Washington governor Dan Evans's successful reelection campaign. As a reward for his diligent service on behalf of Evans, Bundy was appointed to the Seattle Crime Prevention Advisory Committee and later did some contractual work, compiling a criminal justice survey for King County. In 1973 Bundy became assistant to Ross Davis, the chairman of the Washington State Republican Party. Most people who worked with Bundy during this time believed he had a promising political future.

In early 1974, beginning with twenty-one-year-old Lynda Healy, several attractive young women vanished from college campuses and surrounding areas in Washington State and Oregon. In one instance, eighteen-year-old Georgann Hawkins disappeared while walking the 200-foot distance from her boyfriend's fraternity house to her home. In July 1974 two women at a state park outside Seattle told police that a handsome man named Ted had approached them, soliciting their help with his sailboat. Suspicious, they refused, but two other women at the park that day accompanied him to his car and were never seen alive again.

In the fall of 1974 Bundy moved to Salt Lake City, Utah, where he enrolled in law school at the University of Utah. In November Carol DaRonch was lured away from a mall in a Salt Lake City suburb and was attacked by a man dressed as a police officer, but she escaped. That same evening, seventeen-year-old Debbie Kent disappeared from a local school. About this time hikers in the dense forests of Washington found human bones that were later identified as those of the missing women from Washington and Oregon. The murders remained unsolved, and police had few clues to work with.

In August 1975 Bundy, recently baptized into the Mormon church, was stopped by police for driving erratically. A search of his vehicle produced handcuffs, pantyhose cut with eyeholes, and an ice pick, among other suspicious items. Later, DaRonch, whose assailant had tried to handcuff her, identified Bundy as her attacker, and he was subsequently charged with attempted kidnapping. At his trial in February 1976 Bundy, who took the stand in his own defense and waived his right to a jury trial, was found guilty of attempted kidnapping and was sentenced to one to fifteen years in prison.

Meanwhile, police were investigating Bundy's visits to Colorado, which were made, according to charge card receipts, in early 1975, a time when several women had disappeared there. In October 1976 officials presented Bundy, who was serving his time in the Utah penitentiary, with a warrant charging him in the murder of Caryn Campbell, who had been abducted from a ski resort in Aspen and murdered in early 1975. Bundy was soon extradited to Glenwood Springs, Colorado, where the murder trial was to take place. Dissatisfied with his appointed public counsel, he served as his own attorney and began writing a flurry of legal briefs, requesting better prison food, vitamin supplements, and the privilege of appearing in court in street clothes without leg irons, among other demands. In a television interview before the trial, Bundy proclaimed, "More than ever, I am convinced of my innocence." In June 1977, at one of many pretrial hearings, he escaped by leaping from the courthouse window. Though apprehended within a week, Bundy became something of a celebrity around Glenwood Springs, foretelling his future notoriety. On the night of 30 December 1977 Bundy escaped again, this time by crawling through a loose fixture in the ceiling, and by January 1978 he was living in a small apartment in Tallahassee, Florida.

On the early morning of 15 January 1978 Bundy raped, bludgeoned, and strangled to death two women at Florida State University's Chi Omega sorority house. He also assaulted two others, leading authorities to believe that, had he not been surprised and forced to flee by a resident coming home late that night, he would have murdered every woman sleeping in the house. On 9 February Bundy abducted twelve-year-old Kimberly Diane Leach from her school in Lake City, Florida, and brutally murdered her. Six days later Bundy was arrested in Pensacola for driving a stolen vehicle. On 7 April Leach's mutilated body was found in a deserted hog pen near Florida's Suwanee State Park. By this time, compelling clues, including an eyewitness's account that placed Bundy at a disco where the Chi Omegas had gone the night of the murders, made him the prime suspect in the sorority house massacre. In addition, the woman who had startled Bundy on 15 January identified him as the man she saw leaving the house. He was indicted for the Chi Omega killings when, in late April, a mold of his teeth matched bite marks found on the body of one of the victims. In July testimony and evidence connecting Bundy to Lake City and the disappearance of Leach led a grand jury to indict him for her murder also.

After brazenly turning down a plea bargain whereby he would plead guilty to all three Florida killings in exchange for three twenty-five-year sentences, Bundy went on trial in June 1979 for the murders of the two sorority women. In the nationally televised trial, in which he occasionally acted as his own attorney, Bundy was convicted of both murders and was sentenced to die in the electric chair.

In early 1980 Bundy was given his third sentence of death after being found guilty in Leach's slaying. During his sentencing hearing a couple of days after his conviction, Bundy surprised court onlookers when he married Carole Boone, whom he had called to the stand as a character witness. They had been close since his time in Utah, and she was convinced of his innocence. He spent the last nine years of his life uncharacteristically avoiding interviews, filing appeals, and dodging three signed death warrants. His appeals finally ran out in January 1989, and Bundy, his usual cocky demeanor more subdued, was electrocuted at the Florida state prison in Starke, while a carnival-like atmosphere prevailed outside. A few days before his death Bundy, who until that time professed his innocence, told details of murders of more than fifty other women, citing his obsession with, and early exposure to, pornography as a primary motive. While some speculate the figure could be as high as 100, the true number of his victims will never be known.

Bundy has the dubious distinction of making the term "serial killer" a household word. What caused the handsome, intelligent Bundy to begin the grisly killing spree that made him one of the most notorious mass murderers in American history remains unknown. Using his charm and good looks, he lured trusting strangers to certain death and, once caught for his crimes, mocked the legal system, filing appeal after appeal, costing the state of Florida at least $5 million to execute him. In addition to the sheer number of his victims and the frighteningly random nature of his crimes, Bundy became so infamous because his seemingly "normal" exterior masked evil within, compelling people to question the intentions of those around them and causing them not to take polite, handsome strangers at face value. In 1986 Bundy told the *New York Times*, "If anyone considers me a monster, that's just something they'll have to confront in themselves.... To dehumanize someone like me is . . . a[n] understandable way of dealing with a fear and a threat that is incomprehensible."

S.H.

The media called him "Scarface," but Al Capone hid his scar with makeup.

AL CAPONE
[17 JANUARY 1899–25 JANUARY 1947]

"Scarface," the press called him.

There's a wonderful story about the scar. In a Brooklyn saloon, he said some-thing uncomplimentary about a woman at the bar. Her brother, a hoodlum named Frank Gallucio, took exception to Capone's remark and whipped out a stiletto, leaving an ugly triple scar on the left side of Capone's face.

Capone hated the scar, and spent the rest of his life trying to hide it with makeup. He was known to claim it resulted from shrapnel while he fought with the famed Lost Battalion in France. Interestingly, he never avenged himself on Gallucio, but actually hired the man later as a bodyguard.

It's hard to say what has made Capone endure as the epitome of the Prohibition-era gangster. Until the government managed to jail him, he did bestride Chicago like a colossus, after achieving that preeminence in wars that cost perhaps a thousand lives. And he did things that caught the imagina-tion. Once, at a large private dinner party, he beat three men to death with a baseball bat. Later, of course, his men dressed as police to murder most of the leadership of Bugs Moran's mob. ("Only Capone kills like that," was Moran's reaction and, fortuitously enough, the incident occurred on February 14; a day earlier or later and we wouldn't know it as the St. Valentine's Day Massacre.)

There were a few lines of Capone's that resonate nicely. In an apologia for his enterprise: "If people did not want beer and wouldn't drink it, a fellow would be crazy for going around trying to sell it. I've seen gambling houses, too, in my travels, and I never saw anyone point a gun at a man and make him go inside."

"I want peace," he said on another occasion, "and I will live and let live." Yeah, right. But my favorite is this: "You can go further in this world with a kind word and a gun than you can with a kind word alone."

A l Capone, Chicago bootlegger and symbolic crime figure, was born Alphonse Capone in Brooklyn, New York, the son of Gabriel Capone, a barber, and Teresa Raiola, both immigrants from the Naples region of Italy. At age fourteen, Capone dropped out of school, joined the gang life of the streets, and soon worked as a bartender and bouncer at Coney Island. In 1917, in a brawl with a customer, he received the knife wound that earned him the media nickname "Scarface" (although his friends called him "Snorky"). In December 1918 he married Mary "Mae" Coughlin, the daughter of a laborer.

There is disagreement concerning when Capone arrived in Chicago to work in the rackets run by John Torrio, another transplanted New Yorker. Torrio was a partner of James "Big Jim" Colosimo, a famous Chicago restaurateur and entrepreneur in Chicago's notorious South Side red-light district. In May 1920, shortly after the beginning of Prohibition, Colosimo was assassinated, and Torrio thereafter oversaw the red-light activities while expanding rapidly into bootlegging. By most accounts, Capone was in Chicago in time to assist Torrio in planning Colosimo's assassination, and he certainly worked with Torrio afterward in managing red-light activities in Chicago and the suburbs and in developing the illegal liquor business. As the bootlegging expanded, Capone brought his brothers, Ralph and Salvatore (Frank), to Chicago to assist in the operations. Emphasizing wholesaling, the Torrio operation supplied liquor to speakeasies in the downtown Loop and in several suburbs west and south of the city while also selling liquor to bootleggers in other parts of the city. By 1923 Torrio had patched together a loose territorial agreement with other bootleggers.

In April 1924 Capone began to capture the headlines that would make him America's most famous criminal. He organized gunmen to control an election in Cicero, a town west of Chicago. Although his brother Frank was killed in a shootout with the police, his candidates won, and Capone and his associates expanded their participation in Cicero gambling houses. Soon afterward the truce among Chicago bootleggers collapsed. In January 1925 Torrio pleaded guilty to an earlier bootlegging charge and a week later was shot and seriously wounded in front of his home. On release from the hospital in February, he began a nine-month sentence and made plans to return to New York. In late 1925 Capone became the most famous member of the coalition that took over Torrio's Chicago operations.

To coordinate their varied enterprises, Capone and his associates worked out a set of partnerships within an essentially decentralized system. There were four senior partners—Al Capone, his older brother Ralph, their cousin Frank Nitti, and Jack Guzik—who split their profits more or less evenly. These four supported an entourage that hung out at their headquarters in Chicago's Metropole Hotel beginning in 1925 and the Lexington Hotel in 1928. To operate their enterprises, the senior partners gave a share of the profits to those who provided day-to-day oversight of a gambling house, bootlegging operation, parlor house, or other activity. Among the senior partners, Capone often exercised leadership because of his dominating personality, his occasionally volcanic temper, and his willingness to take decisive action. Because he was frequently absent from the city, however, the other partners assumed much of the oversight.

Capone achieved notoriety in part because Chicago's bootlegging wars were more violent and persistent than those in other cities. Among the high points of the beer wars were the 10 November 1924 shooting of North Side bootlegger Dion O'Banion in his flower shop; the April 1926 assassination of Assistant State Attorney William H. McSwiggin; the widely reported October 1926 peace treaty of two months' duration, negotiated by leading Chicago bootleggers in a hotel room; the April 1928 "Pineapple Primary" bombings to aid the candidates backed by Capone ally Mayor William Hale "Big Bill" Thompson; and finally the notorious St. Valentine's Day massacre of 1929, which eliminated the North Side gang as a serious rival. Through it all, Capone was available to the press, acknowledged the cheers of the crowds at sporting events, drove down Michigan Avenue in his armored car, threw large tips to waiters and newsboys, and gloried in the attention he received.

Through it all, too, Capone and his growing network of associates expanded their business activities and political influence. As their wholesale activities grew, they developed contacts to obtain imported liquor from

Detroit, New York, and Miami; diverted industrial alcohol from Philadelphia; and purchased beer from towns in Wisconsin and downstate Illinois. After the St. Valentine's Day massacre, Capone's associates expanded the wholesaling of liquor to the growing nightclub district on the Near North Side, and some became owners of nightclubs. In 1927, in addition, the senior partners joined Edward J. O'Hare to establish the Hawthorn Kennel Club in Cicero for dog racing. Extending their influence, members of Capone's group provided protection for labor racketeers or became labor racketeers themselves.

Capone's notoriety, however, placed him under pressure and removed him from daily oversight of operations. In autumn 1927 Mayor Thompson, pursuing unrealistic presidential ambitions, ordered his police chief to harass Capone out of Chicago. That winter Capone moved to Florida and, in March 1928, purchased a mansion on Palm Island in Miami Beach. Although he periodically returned to Chicago, he mostly lived in informal exile, and his influence waned. In May 1929, after attending a conference of leading bootleggers in Atlantic City, Capone was arrested while changing trains in Philadelphia and received a year's sentence for carrying a concealed weapon.

When Capone left the Philadelphia jail on 17 March 1930, his partners were in trouble for tax evasion, and federal authorities were under instructions from President Herbert Hoover to put Capone in prison. The Internal Revenue Service probed his Chicago and Florida finances while the Prohibition bureau investigated his bootlegging. In March and June 1931 Capone was indicted for income tax fraud. At first he agreed to plead guilty in return for a short sentence, but when the judge refused to be bound by the agreement, Capone withdrew his plea. In October a federal jury found him guilty on five of twenty-three counts. The judge sentenced him to eleven years in prison plus fines and court costs.

When the U.S. Supreme Court refused to hear his appeal on 2 May 1932, Capone was transferred from the Cook County jail to the federal penitentiary in Atlanta, Georgia. In August 1934, when a maximum-security prison was opened at Alcatraz in San Francisco Bay, Capone was among its first occupants. In early February 1938, doctors confirmed a diagnosis of syphilis of the brain. Released on 16 November 1939 (with reduced time for good behavior), he sought treatment in a Baltimore hospital and then retired to his Palm Island estate with his wife and only son. Before dying from a stroke in Miami, he alternated between periods of recovery and periods of increasing mental and physical deterioration.

Capone was a major underworld leader from late 1925 until late 1927, when his absence from Chicago reduced his involvement. At age thirty-two, Capone's influence ended completely with his last tax-fraud conviction, but his myth, exaggerating his brief career, had barely begun. Through media coverage, numerous exciting biographies, several movies, and a popular television series (*The Untouchables*), he came to represent the violence of Chicago in the 1920s and the place of crime in American society during and after Prohibition.

M.H.H.

Frankie Carbo parries newsmen's questions while in the state police barracks in Berlin, New Jersey, after his capture 30 May 1959.

FRANKIE CARBO

[10 AUGUST 1904–10 NOVEMBER 1976]

Boxing has long struck me as the most basic sport. Two men get in a square ring sixteen to twenty feet square, unequipped save for the gloves they wear to protect their hands. While they may have a whole retinue of trainers and managers and cut men and sparring partners, everybody else is out of the ring when the bell sounds. They face each other and try to hit each other accord-

ing to the rules of the sport. Generally one wins and the other loses, and the outcome is determined by a combination of factors—natural skill, training, strategy, and the essential intangible we know as heart.

It's a shame such a pure sport is so profoundly rotten. Throughout its history, boxing has been corrupted on all levels, and the occasional fixed fight (and there are fewer of those than you probably think) is the least of it. Corruption keeps deserving fighters from getting title shots, bleeds boxers of their earnings, and siphons off vast amounts of the revenue it generates to the sort of men who give crime a bad name.

Frankie Carbo ran boxing in his day, and made of it a criminal enterprise not unlike gambling and bootlegging. The sport ceased to belong to the mob with his exit from it, but things haven't changed that much; other ex-cons play as dominant a role today as Carbo once did, and with much the same effect on the sport.

But when you've got the right matchup in the ring—think Robinson–LaMotta in Carbo's day, or Ward–Gatti in ours—then you understand why A. J. Liebling called it the sweet science, and it no longer seems to matter who's pulling the strings.

F rankie Carbo, Italian-American gangster and "underworld czar of boxing," was born Paul John Carbo and reared on New York's Lower East Side. His parents' names and occupations are unknown. Carbo was first arrested at age eleven and spent much of the next four years at the Juvenile Catholic Protectory. Arrested again in his late teens for felonious assault and grand larceny, he then became an enforcer for a Bronx taxicab protection racket. In 1924 he murdered a cab driver who resisted a shakedown, and he served twenty months in Sing Sing for the crime. Thereafter, he was involved in beer-running and bookmaking and was indicted four more times for murder, but he was never convicted.

In 1939 Carbo, Bugsy Siegel, and Champ Segal were indicted for the gangland execution of Harry "Big Greenie" Greenberg, allegedly at the behest of Louis Lepke Buchalter, head of Murder Inc. The first trial, despite eyewitness testimony by getaway driver Allie Tannenbaum and corroboration by Abe Reles, a close associate of Buchalter, ended in a hung jury. A second trial resulted in no decision, largely because Reles, despite twenty-four-hour police protection, fell from a sixth-story window of a Coney Island hotel before he could testify.

Carbo's principal source of income by the mid-1930s was boxing. He had a highly regarded ability to identify talent and took advantage of underworld connections, a power vacuum among managers and matchmakers in the middle and lower weight classifications, and the absence of an effective independent regulatory commission to become a major figure in prizefighting from the mid-1930s through 1960. Because, as an ex-felon, he could not get a managerial license, he had to secretly gain control of several champions and most of the leading contenders. In so doing he dominated the middleweight division. He subsequently expanded his influence into all weight classes and, by the late 1940s, he wielded unrivaled power. While considered soft-spoken and retiring, he had no qualms about using violence or threats to get his way.

Carbo was known in boxing circles as "Mr. Gray," a name often mentioned in government wiretaps of organized crime figures. His front men included underworld characters and "respectable" businessmen. His right-hand man was Gabe Genovese, first cousin of Vito Genovese, head of the most powerful New York crime family; Gabe Genovese acted as an unlicensed manager who operated through front men. Carbo's other principal aide was Philadelphia gambling kingpin Frank "Blinky" Palermo, whose champions included Ike Williams, Johnny Saxton, and Sonny Liston. Williams was an outstanding lightweight who was blacklisted by Carbo in 1946 until he agreed to work for Palermo. Palermo helped him become champion by arranging key fights, but he cheated Williams financially. Other managers who fronted for Carbo included such ostensibly legitimate businessmen as Herman "Mink" Wallman, a New York furrier, and *Ring* magazine's 1957 Manager of the Year Bernard Glickman, a Chicago awnings dealer.

Carbo's clout got his fighters good bouts—particularly prestigious television matches—to advance their careers; he also arranged for the assignment of cooperative referees and judges. However, recalcitrant fighters were dealt with sternly. In 1951 welterweight contender Billy Graham rejected Carbo's offer of the championship for 20 percent of his earnings. In response, the mob ordered a judge in the Graham–Kid Gavilan title fight to vote for Gavilan, who won a split decision. Carbo was Gavilan's secret manager, and in 1954, after Gavilan opted for a dancing tour instead of training, Carbo punished him by arranging to have his title taken away in his next defense against Johnny Saxton, a surprising winner in a controversial decision.

Carbo prearranged other bouts, including the Jake LaMotta–Billy Fox match in 1947, aimed at setting up Fox for a light heavyweight championship fight. For years LaMotta was the number one middleweight contender, but he never got a title bout because of his independence. However, this time he accepted Carbo's offer of $100,000 and a title match if he would take a dive. The referee stopped the fight in the fourth round after LaMotta made no effort to defend himself. The outcome was so suspicious that LaMotta had to wait two years before the New York State Boxing Commission would approve a championship fight.

Carbo's control over top fighters and his influence in the hiring of prominent match-makers like Billy Brown of Madison Square Garden gave him enormous influence with the men who planned bouts, and they consulted with him on a regular basis. His power was primarily in New York and Chicago, the major centers of prizefighting, but it extended to the West Coast through Babe McCoy, the leading Los Angeles matchmaker, who in 1941 had managed a Carbo fighter.

Carbo developed close ties to all the top promoters because of his influence with the leading managers, fighters, and matchmakers. Virtually every notable bout required his approval and financial involvement. Carbo even had clout with Mike Jacobs, the principal boxing promoter in the United States from the mid-1930s until 1946. In 1949 James Norris Jr. and Arthur Wirtz established the International Boxing Club (IBC) to replace Jacobs, who had suffered an incapacitating stroke. The IBC dominated world championship fights between 1949 and 1953, promoting four-fifths of those staged in the United States and nearly monopolizing the booming television market. Norris worked closely with Carbo, who had an office at IBC headquarters in Madison Square Garden. The IBC paid Carbo's future wife, Viola Masters, $45,000 from 1954 to 1957 for no apparent duties. Carbo's role in the IBC escalated after 1954, and one year later he took it over. In 1956 he married Masters; they had no children.

Carbo's downfall began in July 1958 when he was indicted in New York as an unlicensed boxing manager. He went underground to avoid prosecution, and in August the Internal Revenue Service sued him for tax evasion. Carbo was arrested in Haddon Township, New Jersey, in May 1959. Shortly thereafter, Gabe Genovese became the first person convicted as an unlicensed manager, and Carbo subsequently pleaded guilty and received a two-year prison sentence.

In mid-1960 Carbo was at the center of a major U.S. Senate investigation of boxing, during which he took the Fifth Amendment twenty-five times. While in prison, he and four coconspirators were charged in a federal indictment with extortion for using intimidation to seek control of welterweight champion Don Jordan. In 1962, based on wiretap evidence, Carbo received a twenty-five-year sentence to the federal prison on McNeil Island, Washington. He was also convicted of tax evasion for the years 1944–1946 and 1949–1952. The mob's control of boxing ended with Carbo's conviction, although other nefarious characters later took over his place. Shortly after Carbo was pardoned from prison for ill health, he died in Miami Beach, Florida.

S.A.R.

Outlaws Harry Longabaugh (the Sundance Kid), William Carver, Ben Kilpatrick, Harvey Logan, and Butch Cassidy (far right) posed for their famous photograph in Fort Worth, Texas, 1900.

BUTCH CASSIDY

[13 APRIL 1866–1908? 1937?]

"Not that it matters," William Goldman wrote at the beginning of his screen-play for Butch Cassidy and the Sundance Kid, *"but most of what follows is true."*

And the movie does seem remarkably authentic. If Butch and Sundance were not as handsome as Paul Newman and Robert Redford, still they were good-looking men, and the formal group photo of the Wild Bunch, showing the pair with William Carver, Ben Kilpatrick, and Harvey Logan, shows them as such, and hints at their playful nature. If the film's one of the all-time great buddy movies, that too is authentic; Butch and Sundance seem to have been genuine buddies, fond enough of each other's company to keep the act going clear to Patagonia.

The movie also gets across the way these two and the rest of the Wild Bunch were around for the end of an era—Wild West outlaws at a time when the West was beginning to outgrow its wildness. Once, when things got too hot for a man, he could ride a hundred miles and start over. Butch and Sundance had to go clear to South America, and starting over didn't work too well there, either.

Like so many mythic outlaws, rumors of Cassidy's survival persisted—understandably, in his case, because of the lack of clear evidence of his death. It's quite possible that he was killed in Bolivia in 1908, and just as plausible that he returned to the States and survived another thirty years.

B utch Cassidy, outlaw and rancher, was born Robert LeRoy Parker in Beaver, Utah, the oldest of thirteen children of Maximillian Parker and Ann Gillies, small ranchers. His British-born parents were Mormons who pulled handcarts across the Great Plains to Utah in 1856. As a teenager growing up near Circleville, Utah, Parker was influenced by cowhand Mike Cassidy, who taught him to ride, shoot, rope, brand, and rustle cattle and horses. Under suspicion by local authorities, Parker and Cassidy left Utah in 1884. Parker went to Telluride, Colorado, where he found employment with a mining company. There he met Tom McCarty, a bank robber, and soon joined the McCarty Gang. On 24 June 1889, he participated in a bank robbery at Telluride, after which he drifted into Wyoming. Because he was now wanted by the law, Parker took the surname of his boyhood idol, calling himself George Cassidy. While working in a butcher's shop in Rock Springs, Wyoming, he became Butch Cassidy.

During this period he met several of the men who later joined him to form a band of horseback outlaws widely known as the Wild Bunch. At the time of the 1892 war between cattlemen and homesteaders in Johnson

County, Wyoming, Butch Cassidy and the Wild Bunch found themselves in the midst of the conflict, their sympathies with those who rustled cattle from the big ranchers. The outlaws and the fugitive homesteaders both took refuge in a hideout behind a high ridge that could be entered only through an easily defended defile known as the Hole-in-the-Wall. For years afterward, the Wild Bunch was also known as the Hole-in-the-Wall Gang.

In 1892 Cassidy was arrested for stealing a horse valued at five dollars. His defense was that he had unknowingly bought the animal from a rustler. He was convicted, but because of legal delays he was not sentenced to the Wyoming Penitentiary until 1894. According to some of his friends, this confinement, which he considered unfair, helped to deepen his contempt for the law.

After Cassidy's release in 1896, bank and train robberies charged to the Wild Bunch increased in number. Scores of Pinkerton detectives joined sheriffs' posses in futile pursuit of the gang throughout the West, from Montana to New Mexico. After a daring robbery of a Winnemucca, Nevada, bank in September 1900, several members of the band rendezvoused at Fort Worth, Texas. Cassidy and four companions posed there for a studio photograph and then sent a print of it to the Pinkerton Detective Agency. Weary of being continually harassed, however, Cassidy and another member of the gang, Harry Longabaugh (the Sundance Kid), decided to go to South America.

At this point in Cassidy's career, the Pinkerton Agency's profile described him as being flaxen-haired, blue-eyed and of light complexion, 5' 7" tall, weighing 165 pounds, with a "sandy beard, if any." By all accounts he was a handsome and affable man. Evidence exists that he courted women, but apparently he never married.

Cassidy, Longabaugh, and the latter's mistress, Etta Place, sailed to South America from New York City in 1901. In a letter from Cholila, Argentina, to a friend in Utah, dated 10 August 1902, Cassidy described a well-stocked ranch they had purchased in the Patagonian grasslands.

Evidently the ranch proved unprofitable. At any rate, Cassidy and Longabaugh turned to robbing banks again. In December 1907, they sold the ranch and vanished from the Cholila area. A year later they were reported to be working for a tin mine in Bolivia. From there, the trail of Butch Cassidy becomes lost in undocumented and controversial legends. Possibly he and the Sundance Kid robbed again and were tracked down at San Vicente by Bolivian cavalry and killed. But even accounts that agree in citing this as their fate vary, dating their deaths anywhere from 1908 to 1911.

In the years that followed, "sightings" of Cassidy were occasionally reported by people who had known him. William T. Phillips, an engineer in Spokane, Washington, claimed to be Cassidy and wrote an account of his life. He died on 20 July 1937. Cassidy's sister, Lula Parker Betenson, who published an account of her brother's life, told an interviewer in 1970 that Cassidy had visited her in 1925. She said he had lived under an assumed name in the Northwest and that he had died in 1937, but that William Phillips was not her brother.

Like other romantic outlaws, including Jesse James, whose ends appear to be controlled by an inexorable destiny, Butch Cassidy has achieved a place in American mythology.

D.B.

Mickey Cohen associated with newspaper editors and reporters to keep himself in the public eye.

MICKEY COHEN
[4 SEPTEMBER 1913–29 JULY 1976]

Mickey Cohen was as fond of Hollywood society as the more charismatic Ben "Bugsy" Siegel, and even fonder of the limelight. He made himself readily accessible to journalists, and was always ready with a quotable quip.

Over and above his instinct for self-promotion, Cohen stood out from his fellows in a couple of respects. He was a tireless and effective fund-raiser for the new state of Israel, and told in his autobiography of one event he ran at Slapsie Maxie's, where mobsters and Hollywood celebrities alike contributed to the Irgun, a Jewish underground military group. Cohen arranged similar fund-raisers around the country, including one in Las Vegas that raised half a million dollars, and used his dockside connections in New York and New Jersey to smuggle arms to the Irgun. The first two P-51 Mustangs in the Israeli Air Force were allegedly purchased from airfields in France and Belgium with funds furnished by Cohen.

Sometime in the 1940s, Cohen became friendly enough with William Randolph Hearst to prompt the newspaper owner to order his editors to cease referring to Cohen as a hoodlum and call him a gambler instead. Years later, when Patty Hearst was kidnapped by the Symbionese Liberation Army, representatives of the Hearsts sought Cohen's aid because of his connections in the black underworld, which derived from his involvement in the numbers racket and allied gambling activities. Cohen ran down various leads, visited one contact in Soledad Prison, and ultimately reached three SLA associates. "It became a real cloak and dagger operation," Cohen wrote. "We met at night in different places, changing cars all the time."

His investigations led him to suspect the heiress was in Cleveland, which ultimately turned out to be the case. At the request of the Hearsts, who were concerned that Patty's recovery might lead to her imprisonment—justifiably, as it turned out—he suspended his efforts.

Mickey Cohen, criminal and celebrity, was born Meyer Harris Cohen in Brooklyn, New York, the son of Max Cohen, whom Cohen remembered as having been in the "import business with Jewish fishes," and Fanny (maiden name unknown). Both parents were Jewish immigrants. His father died shortly after Cohen's birth, and Cohen's mother moved the family to the Boyle Heights Jewish district of Los Angeles, where she opened a grocery store. According to his own account, he attended school rarely, if at all, rejected religious education, and was incorrigible from his earliest days selling newspapers, using his natural pugnacity to secure the best locations. He committed minor crimes and took up amateur boxing. Cohen ran away from Los Angeles around age fifteen to avoid having to attend school further.

The next several years Cohen spent as a professional prizefighter, chiefly in Cleveland and Chicago. He insisted he had been encouraged by some of the outstanding boxers of that era and later told a Senate committee that he had appeared in thirty-two main events in which he was chiefly victorious. His career was probably less than what he liked to recall, and he was described by a reporter as "a second-rater with a glass chin" who was "knocked out in most of his fights."

His boxing career over, Cohen drifted into petty crime. Later, he liked to boast himself an acquaintance of mob leader Al Capone. It is more likely he made a connection to Capone's accountant, Jack "Greasy Thumb" Guzik, for whom he conducted bookmaking and an occasional pistol-whipping. It was after one such event in 1939 that he left Chicago and returned home to Los Angeles.

In Los Angeles Cohen operated a portable craps table, which he trucked to wherever he could get a game. He later was associated with Benjamin "Bugsy" Siegel, a more formidable gangster, who operated gambling and bookmaking on the West Coast. Cohen asserted that in 1945 he had been put in charge of local southern California gambling operations when Siegel turned his interest to Las Vegas. Others insisted Cohen was never more than an errand boy.

Los Angeles in the post–World War II era underwent rapid growth, and disorganization and disruption rippled through political life and law enforcement. Cohen, loving notoriety and enamored of Hollywood's café society, thrived in the unsettled postwar city. He associated with newspaper editors and reporters, the most famous of whom was the *Los Angeles Herald*'s James Richardson, who had a reputation for recasting mundane events in headline-sized stories. In exchange for headlines, Cohen passed along information and offered his opinions, and in general whenever some outrage to public order occurred, "the Mick" seemed inevitably somewhere in the vicinity.

Cohen was the perfect front-page gangster. He spent lavishly in the city's nightclubs and was always accompanied by well-endowed striptease artists and Hollywood celebrities—Cohen seemed to know them all. At the drop of a hat he would show visitors closets stocked with five hundred pairs of socks and sixty pairs of shoes. In his heyday he refused to wear his custom-made suits after they had been dry-cleaned. At one time Cohen opened a haberdashery, Michael's, but it was not successful.

In 1945 Cohen shot and killed gambler Maxie Shaman but was cleared on grounds of self-defense. On several occasions there were attempts on Cohen's life. In 1948 gunmen entered Cohen's place of business and opened fire. Cohen evaded death, having moments before gone to the bathroom, but one of his bodyguards was killed. A year later, outside a Sunset Strip nightclub, Cohen was again the target of gunshots, which missed him but killed another of his attendants. That same year a bomb exploded outside Cohen's fashionable West Los Angeles home; Cohen was not injured, but his neighbors complained.

Cohen was married in 1940 to LaVonne (maiden name unknown). They were divorced in 1956. There is no record of his having had children. He was linked romantically to a number of members of the gangster demimonde, including strippers Liz Renay and Candy Barr.

In the early 1950s the federal government took an interest in Cohen's finances. In 1952 he was convicted of tax evasion and spent three and one-half years at McNeil Island Federal Prison. When released, he returned to Los Angeles and his "wise guy" role. Cohen's fame was boosted by unseemly incidents, such as when one of his henchmen, Johnny Stompanato, became romantically involved with movie star Lana Turner and was stabbed to death by Turner's daughter.

In 1962 Cohen was again convicted of tax evasion and was sent to the federal prison at Atlanta. He was clubbed by a fellow prisoner for unknown reasons and suffered brain damage and paralysis as a result of the attack. Cohen sued the federal government and eventually won a judgment of $110,000, which was promptly seized by the Internal Revenue Service. Cohen was released in January 1972. He lived the balance of his years in

West Los Angeles, never reluctant to give an interview or inject himself into the criminal events of the day. Near the end of his life he offered to use his underworld connections to locate kidnapped heiress Patty Hearst. At the time of his death in Los Angeles, the *Los Angeles Times* noted that Cohen "seemed to be striving for the title of 'Public Enemy no. 1'" but that local lawmen rated him "no higher than the leading public nuisance."

B.H.

Organized crime boss Joseph Anthony Colombo Sr., shown here in 1971, was an outspoken advocate for Italian-American rights.

JOSEPH ANTHONY COLOMBO SR.

[16 JUNE 1923–22 MAY 1978]

While Joe Colombo achieved success and a measure of prominence as a boss of one of New York's five crime families, it was his crusade to improve the image of Italian-Americans that provided him with a measure of immortality, even as it brought on his mortality.

The Italian-American Civil Rights League, Colombo's personal creation, managed to be at once a political force and a joke. On the one hand, it mobilized understandable resentment of the way the popular media tarred a huge and influential ethnic group with the brush of organized crime; at the same time, the irony of a notorious criminal protesting such a characterization was not lost on much of the public. As one comedian paraphrased the IACRL's message, "Stop calling us hoodlums, or we'll break your legs."

It's hard to know how much all of this really meant to Colombo. He seems to have gloried in the role of champion of his people, and it was clear at the time that he delighted in the media attention. It's not impossible, however, that he saw this organization of his as a potential profit center, and was looking to make a buck from it.

Whatever his motives, he managed to alienate the man who'd put him in power in the first place, Carlo Gambino, with predictable results. The shooting that left him disabled for life was not the quiet hit in which Gambino ordinarily specialized, but one specifically designed to capture as much media attention as possible, and right in the middle of his Columbus Circle rally. Remarkably, Colombo survived, and had the next seven years to think about it.

Joseph Anthony Colombo Sr., organized crime boss, was born in Brooklyn, New York, the son of Anthony Colombo, who was also connected with organized crime and was garroted while Joseph was still a teenager. His mother's name is unknown. When asked if he ever sought vengeance for his father's murder, Joseph Colombo replied, "Don't they pay policemen for that?" After attending New Utrecht High School, he entered the Coast Guard, from which he was given a medical discharge in 1945 (he allegedly suffered from some sort of "psychoneurosis"). Colombo thereafter balanced a life of crime with legitimate jobs. He began working as a longshoreman soon after leaving the service, while also gaining experience as a small-time criminal, principally involving himself in modest gambling operations. For six years he was a salesman for a Mafia-controlled meat company. Then Colombo became a real estate agent in Bensonhurst, where he continued to work for a $20,000 annual salary throughout his career as an organized crime boss.

After working as a hired killer for Joe Profaci and serving as underboss to Joe Magliocco, Colombo became one of the youngest organized crime bosses in the United States in 1964, when he was given leadership of a Brooklyn "family" that, under his control, eventually comprised 200 members and associates. He had ascended to power by advising puissant Mafia boss Carlo Gambino of a scheme to assassinate Gambino and other highly placed leaders by Joseph Bonanno, who longed to become "boss of all bosses." His plan exposed, Bonanno relinquished his power, and Colombo was rewarded with control of Magliocco's family after the latter died. Colombo also became a member of the powerful Mafia national commission.

Colombo's seven-year reign as an active crime boss was relatively uneventful, as he led his family in such moneymaking activities as loan-sharking, gambling, hijacking, and fencing stolen goods. He also involved himself in licit pursuits, at one time holding interest in at least twenty legitimate businesses in New York City. Preoccupied with his family's image, Colombo angered many men under his command by requiring all to hold down a "real" job.

Colombo became well known outside the underworld for his work in promoting the civil rights of Italian Americans. In the spring of 1970, angered by what he saw as harassment of his son by the Federal Bureau of Investigation, who had arrested the younger Colombo for conspiracy, Joseph Colombo began picketing the FBI offices in Manhattan. He criticized the media and the FBI for using terms such as "Mafia" and "Cosa Nostra," accusing the authorities of blaming unsolved crimes on this created entity to take pressure off themselves. He laughed at his image as an organized crime heavyweight, questioning, "Mafia, what's the Mafia? There is not a Mafia. Am I head of a family? Yes, my wife and four sons and a daughter. That's my family."

Believing in the existence of a "conspiracy in this country against all Italian people," in 1970 Colombo, in alliance with union organizer Natale Marcone and Colombo's son Anthony, founded the Italian-American Civil Rights League. The league, whose membership reached 45,000 under Colombo's rule (even New York governor Nelson Rockefeller took honorary membership), had more than twenty chapters in the New York City area and many more across the country. Concerned with the public's perception of organized crime in particular and Italian Americans in general, Colombo and the league successfully lobbied the producers of *The Godfather* (1972) to delete all references to a "Mafia" from the film. The TV show *The F.B.I.* followed suit. Alka-Seltzer even withdrew its commercial that proclaimed, "Mamma mia, thatsa some spicy meatball."

Despite his activist public image, Colombo did not totally forgo his duties in the Mafia underworld. At the time of the second annual Columbus Circle Italian-American Civil Rights League rally in June 1971, he had been accused of several misdeeds, including income tax evasion. He also stood accused of perjury for not revealing his criminal record (thirteen arrests and three convictions) when applying for his real estate license. He was under indictment for numerous other crimes, the most serious of which involved allegations that he managed a $10 million-a-year gambling organization in three New York counties.

On 28 June 1971, about an hour before the Columbus Circle rally's scheduled start time, Colombo was shot in the head, neck, and jaw. His assailant, Jerome Johnson, a young black man posing as a photographer and holding a rally-issued press pass, was killed almost immediately in the ensuing pandemonium. New York City police denied shooting Johnson, and no one ever claimed responsibility for Johnson's murder. Colombo, critically wounded, was rushed to the hospital for emergency surgery, while the rally continued as scheduled.

Organized crime figures Joseph Gallo and Albert Gallo, who operated under Colombo's leadership, were questioned in connection with the attempt on Colombo's life but were released. Long-standing hostility between the Gallo brothers and Colombo had been revived when the Gallos ordered shops in the area to remain open during the rally in spite of Colombo's mandate to close them. In fact, many Mafia leaders, especially Gambino, who had warned Colombo weeks before the shooting to discontinue his attention-getting activities (supposedly Colombo spat in Gambino's face in response to this admonition), were uneasy about Colombo's ever-expanding ego, his thirst for recognition, and his very public identification with Italian-American rights, not to mention the unwanted notice his picketing of the FBI offices got from law-enforcement agencies. Joseph Gallo's 1972 murder in Little Italy was judged by some a revenge killing, and many believe that Gambino probably hired the Gallos to kill Colombo.

Colombo was left almost totally disabled by the attempt on his life, and he spent his last seven years at the fortress in Blooming Grove, New York, that had formerly been his vacation home. He died of a heart attack at St. Luke's Hospital in Newburgh, New York. After his incapacitation, the Colombo crime family continued under new administration, as did the Italian-American Civil Rights League.

Colombo represents a deviant, perhaps a modern, type of mobster. Eschewing the back-room secrecy of those who preceded him, he was a firebrand when it came to Italian-American rights, a cause in which he no doubt passionately believed. He was unafraid of public scrutiny and brash in his pursuit of attention, in the process angering both the federal authorities and the "family." His rabble-rousing did not blend well with the traditional powers in organized crime, and Colombo became an incendiary that had to be extinguished.

S.H.

FRANK COSTELLO

[26 JANUARY 1891–18 FEBRUARY 1973]

Frank Costello did a better job than most at establishing himself in legitimate business. He was also unparalleled at cultivating influential persons outside the field of organized crime.

One of these relationships was with FBI chief J. Edgar Hoover, who had a disconcerting number of social acquaintances of Costello's sort. There's a story told of a visit to a racetrack in which Hoover and Costello wagered what Hoover assumed was fifty dollars on some proposition or other. When Hoover won the bet, Costello paid him fifty thousand dollars.

Hoover protested that the bet was only fifty bucks. "I said 'fifty,'" Costello told him. "When I say that, I mean fifty grand. If I'd meant fifty dollars, I'd have said 'five-oh.'" But, Hoover wondered, suppose Costello had won. Then, said Costello, he'd have collected fifty dollars, since that was Hoover's understanding of the wager. But in fact Hoover had won, and thus Costello insisted upon paying him the full fifty thousand.

I can't swear that his ever happened, but as I understand it, Hoover liked to tell the story, and evidently did so without it even occurring to him that the payment was a subtle bribe.

Vito Genovese's attempt on Costello's life, which sent the intended victim into retirement, was carried out by Vincent "Chin" Gigante, who called out, "This is for you, Frank," fired off a single shot, and ran off without waiting to assess its effect. Chin's in prison at this writing, but he spent years shuffling around Greenwich Village and mumbling to himself while his lawyers worked to convince judges that he was too far gone mentally to stand trial for various offenses. In the neighborhood, the consensus is that Chin's crazy like a fox.

Costello's voice, made famous during the Kefauver hearings, may well have inspired Marlon Brando's characterization of Don Corleone in The Godfather.

Frank Costello kept a low profile and profited from partnerships with Italian, Jewish, and Irish racketeers.

Frank Costello, criminal entrepreneur, was born Francesco Castiglia in Lauropoli, near Cosenza in Calabria, southern Italy, the son of Luigi Castiglia and Maria (maiden name unknown), farmers. At age four Costello moved to New York City with his father; his mother and the rest of his immediate family followed two years later.

The Castiglias settled in Manhattan's East Harlem Italian district, where they eked out a subsistence living running a small grocery shop. Despite being considered one of the neighborhood's brightest boys, Costello turned to crime after finishing elementary school. Americanizing his name with a useful touch of Irish, Costello became the leader of the Italian 104th Street gang and gained a reputation as one of the toughest young hoodlums in the area.

By 1911 Costello had been arrested twice and freed twice on charges of assault and robbery. After an attempted robbery at age twenty-four, he was convicted of carrying a gun and sentenced to a year in prison. Despite his reputation he was released after ten months for good behavior. In 1914 he married a Jewish woman named Loretta Geigerman. His experience in prison convinced him of the need to operate beyond public scrutiny, and he started to develop legitimate business fronts and cultivate New York politicians while pursuing bootlegging and gambling ventures. In August 1919, with Harry Horowitz, Costello formed the Harry Horowitz Novelty Company and cashed in on the punchboard craze that was sweeping the country.

Throughout his career Costello ignored traditional ethnic divisions within the underworld, entering lucrative partnerships with Italian, Jewish, and Irish racketeers alike; these included Charles "Lucky" Luciano, Arnold Rothstein, Meyer Lansky, and "Big Bill" Dwyer. During the 1920s Costello and Dwyer exploited the profitable opportunities created by Prohibition. Their activities soon made them millionaires, although the partnership ended in 1925 when they were indicted for bribery and rum-running. Costello survived the indictments and prospered, teaming up in brewing and bootlegging with Owney "The Killer" Madden. Wealth from bootlegging enhanced Costello's hold over New York politics, particularly in the city's Midtown area. Yet while other criminals maintained a high public profile, Costello remained quiet and dignified. He shunned unnecessary violence and acted as a go-between for the underworld and Tammany Hall politicians.

During the late 1920s and early 1930s Costello forged a partnership with former Rothstein Wall Street operator "Dandy Phil" Kastel, increasing his stake in gambling and the legal liquor business. In 1931 Costello and Kastel obtained the New York territory from the Mills Novelty Company of Chicago, the largest makers of slot machines in the country. During its first year, Triangle Mint Company, the company they set up to handle their slot machine business, placed 5,186 slots around the city and made profits estimated between $18 million and $36 million. In 1934 Costello's business became the target of reform mayor Fiorello La Guardia, who began a campaign against slot machines in New York. La Guardia's attention encouraged Costello to move the operation to New Orleans, where its safety was guaranteed by Senator Huey P. Long.

Despite the end of Prohibition Costello continued to profit from distributing alcohol. He and Kastel became agents for Alliance Distributors Inc., a New York corporation formed at the time of repeal in December 1933. In 1938 Costello provided financial backing for Kastel to purchase all the stock of J. G. Turney and Sons Ltd. of London. Costello was appointed the personal agent for Turney and Sons in the United States and given a $25,000-a-year salary. Costello also increased his gambling interests in 1947 by investing in the Flamingo Hotel casino in Nevada. During the late 1940s increasingly exaggerated claims were being made concerning the extent of Costello's grip over organized crime in America.

Despite his efforts to keep a low public profile, by 1949 he had become a national celebrity, appearing on the cover of *Time* (17 Oct.) and *Newsweek* (21 Nov.). Costello was seen as a master criminal who ruled a vast mysterious empire and was duly nicknamed the Prime Minister of the Underworld. Nevertheless, the news magazines could find little evidence to confirm such popular suspicion. Costello had substantial legally declared real estate investments and earnings from liquor distributorships. These may have been legacies of bootlegging, but they were nonetheless legitimate.

In March 1951 Costello endured a grueling interrogation before the Senate Crime Investigating Committee, chaired by Senator Estes Kefauver. The committee adopted the popular contemporary perception of Costello as the most influential underworld leader in America. In an attempt to preserve what was left of his anonymity, Costello refused to show his face at the televised hearings. Instead he permitted only his hands to be filmed. On many occasions he invoked the Fifth Amendment, answering other questions in the gruff whisper that had characterized his voice since he had undergone a botched throat operation as a child. The impression created by Costello's nervous hand movements, combined with the voice one commentator described as the death rattle of a seagull, seemed to add weight to his status as the underworld's kingpin. Costello was convicted for contempt and started to serve an eighteen-month sentence on 22 August 1952. In April 1954 Costello was convicted of income tax evasion and in May 1956 began serving an eleven-month prison sentence.

In 1957 Costello survived a gang assassination attempt inspired by Vito Genovese. He then decided to retire, but evidence found at the scene linking him to the Tropicana Casino in Nevada resulted in another prison sentence. In June 1961, after serving forty-two months of a five-year term, Costello was released. His years of retirement were spent fighting the attempts of the Immigration and Naturalization Service to deport him to Italy. In his old age Costello maintained some links with the underworld and enjoyed providing advice to those who asked for the benefit of his great experience. Costello died in New York City.

Costello was an extremely successful mobster whose approach to racketeering brought some order to the business of crime. However, his overstated image as the leader of the underworld merely provided the media and law enforcement authorities with a convenient scapegoat for the problem of organized crime in America.

D.R.B.

DEPARTMENT OF POLICE, Buffalo, N. Y.   BUREAU OF IDENTIFICATION.

Leon Czolgosz's police record describes the crime: "While Wm. McKinley the President of the United States was holding a public reception in the Temple of Music at the Pan-Amer. Exposition, he was shot in the abdomen twice with a .38 cal. revolver."

LEON CZOLGOSZ

[1873–29 OCTOBER 1901]

It's just over a century since Leon Czolgosz (pronounced chol-gosh, you'll be relieved to know) became the third person to assassinate an American president. Looking at the act and its aftermath, one can reflect on some of the ways things have changed in the past hundred years, and the ways they've remained the same.

The idea of a man with a gun in his hand (albeit cloaked by a handker-chief) being able to get within handshaking distance of the president seems inconceivable nowadays. (And yet, and yet. Sirhan Sirhan got about that close to a presidential candidate, and Jack Ruby to a presidential assassin.) Far more astonishing, I would contend, is the fact that Czolgosz went to the electric chair just fifty-four days after he fired the fatal shots, and less than seven weeks after McKinley's death. The entire process took less time than we would nowadays expect to spend picking a jury.

Because justice worked so swiftly, it's hard to know whether Czolgosz was a committed anarchist or just a nut job. He seems to have acted alone, with-out encouragement from others, but it's a fact that one school of thought in the day's anarchist movements did endorse assassination as a legitimate tac-tic to achieve political ends. "If enough kings are killed," it was said, "no one will want to be king." The argument, while simplistic, has nevertheless a numb-ing logic to it.

Leon F. Czolgosz, assassin of President William McKinley, was born in Detroit, Michigan, the son of Paul Czolgosz, a menial laborer. His mother's name is unknown. His parents emigrated from southern Poland to the United States just prior to Leon's birth. As a boy Czolgosz shined shoes and sold newspapers. In 1880 the family moved to Rogers City in northern Michigan, but after five months they settled in the Polish com-munity in Posen. Czolgosz intermittently attended public and Catholic parochial schools and developed a lifelong interest in reading, chiefly Polish magazines. In 1885 his mother died in childbirth. That year the family moved to Alpena, near Detroit, and in 1889 to Natrona, a predominantly Polish community near Pittsburgh. There Leon worked in the searing heat of a glass factory, earning seventy-five cents a day. In 1892 the family moved to Cleveland, where he found a job tending machinery at the Newberg Wire Mills. He was a steady and quiet worker who managed to save $400, which he contributed to a family fund to buy a farm. On one occasion the wire spool snapped, slashing and scarring his face.

The depression of 1893 forced many firms to cut wages, including the Newberg Wire Mills, and its workers went on strike. Czolgosz joined them and was fired, but the following year he successfully applied for a job at the plant using the alias Fred C. Nieman. The strike and its aftermath affected him profoundly. Formerly a devout Catholic who read the Bible regularly, Czolgosz abandoned religion and was increasingly drawn to radical groups, first to a Polish socialist club that met in a room above the small saloon his father bought in 1895. Czolgosz joined the organization though he seldom took part in its discussions.

In early 1898 Czolgosz experienced some sort of health-related or emotional crisis. He seemed tired and depressed and complained of stomach and lung problems. In August he quit the wire mill and moved to the family farm near Cleveland. Mostly he lounged in his room and read newspapers, especially the anarchist *Free Society*. He was especially fascinated by an account of Gaetano Bresci, an anarchist from Paterson, New Jersey, who in 1900 shot and killed King Humbert I of Italy. Czolgosz kept the article by his bed.

In the spring of 1901 Czolgosz asked his family to return the money he had put up for the farm so that he could seek work in the West. They initially balked but eventually advanced him seventy dollars, which financed his subsequent travels. On 5 May he went to Cleveland and was moved by a speech by the anarchist Emma Goldman. Introducing himself as Fred Nieman, Czolgosz also approached Emil Schilling, treasurer of the Liberty Club, the anarchist group that published *Free Society*. Schilling and other anarchist officials were put off by Czolgosz's ignorance of anarchist doctrine and his incautious queries, such as when he asked whether the group was "plotting something like Bresci." In late July Czolgosz took advantage of low excursion rates to travel to Buffalo, site of the Pan-American Exposition. He took a room in a boardinghouse in West Seneca, outside Buffalo, probably in the hope of finding work. McKinley's decision to visit the exposition was not made public until August.

About this time, too, the officers of the Liberty Club learned that Czolgosz had not given them his real name, and they assumed the worst. The

1 September issue of *Free Society* warned readers that a probable government spy, "well dressed, of medium height, rather narrow shouldered, blond, and about twenty-five years of age," had recently attempted to infiltrate the organization. The article may have driven Czolgosz to take desperate action to prove his loyalty. Early in September he bought a .32-caliber Iver Johnson revolver.

On 5 September Czolgosz attended the exposition. It was "President's Day," and Czolgosz was infuriated: "I thought it wasn't right for any one man to get so much ceremony," he said later. The next day Czolgosz returned to the exposition, concealed his revolver in a handkerchief, and took a place in line at the Temple of Music. When his turn came to shake hands with the president, Czolgosz pushed McKinley's arm away, thrust the revolver forward, and fired two shots through the handkerchief. McKinley stiffened and then slumped into the arms of his aides. Soldiers and Secret Service men knocked Czolgosz down and beat him. "Be easy with him, boys!" McKinley called out. Lengthy surgery proved ineffective; the president died eight days later.

Before the end of the month, Czolgosz was put on trial for murder. When medical experts sought to determine his sanity, he flatly admitted his culpability: "I fully understood what I was doing when I shot the President." He took no part in the trial other than to utter the word "guilty," a plea the judge could not accept. Czolgosz's court-appointed lawyers called no witnesses, and the trial lasted only eight hours. The jury deliberated thirty-four minutes before pronouncing him guilty. He was sentenced to death by electrocution. There was no appeal. On the morning of 29 October, as he was being strapped into the electric chair, Czolgosz's explanation of his actions was terse: "I killed the President because he was the enemy of the good people—the good working people. I am not sorry for my crime." He died in the Auburn penitentiary.

Czolgosz's act provoked a crackdown by federal and state law enforcement agencies on anarchists and socialists; prompted Congress to amend immigration laws to exclude anarchists and other radicals; and forced the Secret Service to tighten security for the president and other key federal officials. Although most radicals distanced themselves from Czolgosz, Emma Goldman called him an idealist who hoped for a better world.

In 1902 psychiatrist Walter Channing argued that Czolgosz had been insane. He cited Czolgosz's shyness, his preference for solitary pursuits such as reading, and his avoidance of women. Nineteen years later L. Vernon Briggs expanded on Channing's analysis and claimed that Czolgosz suffered from "dementia praecox," or paranoid schizophrenia. But Czolgosz's act, though unreasonable, was not wholly irrational. McKinley's administration was in fact beholden to powerful business interests whose excesses came at the expense of poor people. Assassination, moreover, was consistent with the violent political doctrines of the Russian anarchist Mikhail Bakunin. Yet it is difficult to discern a rational purpose in Czolgosz's action if only because his political beliefs were confused. Though he endorsed violence and anarchy, his favorite book was a Polish translation of Edward Bellamy's *Looking Backward* (1888), which evoked a genteel socialist utopia, and Czolgosz had joined and sympathized with many socialist organizations, whose goals were antithetical to those of the anarchists.

Neither pathological nor exclusively political, Czolgosz's act was essentially that of an awkward and dull-witted young man who rarely attracted much notice, except for one day when, energized in some complex way by radical rhetoric, he set forth on a path that fatefully intersected with that of the president.

M.C.C.

BOB DALTON

[13 MAY 1869–5 OCTOBER 1892]

One day in the late 1980s, my wife and I visited two small Kansas museums devoted to the Dalton brothers. One, in the western part of the state, consisted of a house where the brothers had lived, with an escape tunnel purportedly running to the barn. The tunnel was closed off, conveniently enough, and one had to wonder if it had ever existed. Who'd dig a hundred-yard tunnel on the off chance that such an escape route might come in handy sometime? Anyone that painstaking would probably choose a safer and more deliberate career than bank robbery.

The second museum was in Coffeyville, housed in one of the two banks the Daltons set out to rob, with the disastrous results recounted below. Emmett Dalton survived the debacle, though just barely; they dug more than twenty bullets out of him before sending him to prison. But it was his later life we found especially fascinating. Pardoned in 1907, he relocated in Los Angeles, where he led an exemplary life for the next thirty years, writing screenplays and dealing in real estate.

Some of us who've had our dealings with Hollywood would contend that he'd had the best possible training for both of those careers.

Bob Dalton, outlaw, was born Robert Rennick Dalton in Missouri (probably Cass County), the son of James Lewis Dalton, a farmer, horse breeder, and trader, and Adeline Lee Younger. His mother was a half-sister of Henry Younger, the father of the Younger brothers of James-Younger gang notoriety, and thus the Younger brothers and the Dalton boys shared the same grandfather, Charles Lee Younger. Four of the fifteen children born to Lewis and Adeline Dalton died violent deaths. The family lived in Cass, Bates, and Clay counties in western Missouri, an area plagued before, during, and after the Civil War by border conflicts and rampant outlawry. About 1882 the family moved to Coffeyville, Kansas, and shortly thereafter

Bob Dalton posed for this picture in 1889 with his sweetheart Eugenia Moore.

into Indian Territory near present-day Vinita, Oklahoma. While still an adolescent, Dalton followed his older brothers Frank and Gratton into law enforcement; all three brothers served as deputy U.S. marshals in Indian Territory. On 27 November 1887 Frank was killed while making an arrest. In August 1888, in Indian Territory near Coffeyville, Dalton, acting as a posseman under his brother Grat, shot and killed a suspected horse thief named Charles Montgomery. He was only nineteen years old when he was sworn in as a deputy U.S. marshal in January 1889. He was also employed as a detective for the Osage Indian Agency during this period. The first recorded incident of lawbreaking by any of the Dalton boys occurred on Christmas Day 1889, when Dalton and another brother, Emmett, allegedly "introduced whiskey into Indian Territory." Charges against Emmett were later dropped but Dalton was bound over for trial. He did not appear, his bonds were forfeited, and he never stood trial. In August 1890 Dalton, Emmett, and Grat were charged with horse stealing. Grat was jailed for a time, but eventually the charges were dropped. In a dispute over fees unpaid by the government, Dalton and Grat left the marshal's service about this time. Late in 1890 Dalton, Grat, and Emmett went to California to visit their brother Bill. When a Southern Pacific train was held up and robbed at Alila, California, on 6 February 1891, detectives focused their investigation on the Dalton brothers. Recognized as the leader of what officers were now calling the "Dalton gang," Dalton was described on a Southern Pacific Railroad reward poster as "about twenty-three . . . ; height, 6 ft. 1 inches; well built and straight; light complexion, but florid and healthy looking; boyish beard and mustache; light hair and eyes; weight 180 to 190 lbs.; large, bony, long-fingered hands, showing no acquaintance with work; large nose and ears; white teeth; long sunburned neck, square features. . . . Is a good poker and card player; drinks whisky in moderation, but does not chew tobacco; smokes brown paper cigarettes occasionally." Dalton and his brothers Emmett, Grat, and Bill were indicted on 17 March 1891 and charged with train robbery and assault with intent to murder the express car messenger. Dalton and Emmett eluded the officers and escaped back to Indian Territory, but Grat and Bill were arrested.

In separate trials at Visalia, Tulare County, Bill was acquitted but Grat was convicted of train robbery. At Grat's trial, eyewitnesses to the holdup were shown photographs of Dalton and identified him as one of the robbers.

Back in their familiar haunts, which had become Oklahoma Territory, Dalton and Emmett enlisted other desperadoes and began a campaign of outlawry that would make the Dalton gang as well known as the earlier James-Younger gang. Although various outlaws drifted in and out of the gang, Dalton remained the acknowledged leader. Emmett was at his side, as was Grat, who later broke jail in California and joined his brothers in Oklahoma. In May 1891 the gang held up a Santa Fe train at Wharton Station, Indian Territory; in September they struck a Missouri, Kansas & Texas (MK&T) train at Lillietta Station, Indian Territory. In June 1892 they held up a Santa Fe train at Red Rock in the Cherokee Strip and the following month an MK&T express at Adair in Indian Territory.

Emboldened by these successful train holdups and the national publicity they had engendered, Dalton planned a double bank robbery that would top the exploits of the storied James-Younger gang. His targets were the C. M. Condon & Co. Bank and the First National Bank of Coffeyville, Kansas, a town in which the Daltons had lived and with which they were familiar. On the morning of 5 October 1892, the three Dalton brothers and two other outlaws rode into Coffeyville and simultaneously held up the employees of both banks. When an alarm was sounded by a passerby, a furious gun battle erupted. All five outlaws were struck by multiple bullets. Dalton, Grat, Bill Power, and Dick Broadwell were killed outright, and Emmett was seriously wounded. Four Coffeyville citizens, including the town marshal, were killed and three others wounded. Emmett survived and at a March 1893 trial was convicted of murder and sentenced to life in prison. He was later paroled and wrote two books recounting the experiences of the Daltons. Dalton and Grat were buried together in a Coffeyville cemetery not far from the gravesite of Frank, their slain lawman brother, as was their companion, Bill Power.

A well-built, handsome young man, Dalton undoubtedly possessed admirable qualities. He was temperate in his habits, staunchly loyal to his family, and fearless and bold to the point of recklessness. He started adult life as a peace officer and might have become one of the best had he been more fairly treated by the government that employed him. Although his great double bank robbery attempt at Coffeyville ended in disaster and resulted in the deaths of himself and seven others, it did ensure his place in the national memory as one of the most daring outlaws of the West.

R.K.D.

Prickly and contentious, John Deitz defended the Cameron Dam at gunpoint.

JOHN F. DEITZ

[3 APRIL 1861–8 MAY 1924]

The rugged individualist, the little man doggedly asserting his rights, is very much an American archetype. To this day, such mavericks can find themselves in armed standoffs with the forces of law and order. For all that the American frontier has vanished, incidents in recent years at Waco and Ruby Ridge make it clear that the mindset of the frontier endures.

Then, as now, politics largely determined whether one saw the besieged as heroes or villains. Here's posse member Mont Wiley's version of the capture of John F. Deitz, from a 1957 booklet called "White Pines and White Tails," edited by Leighton Morris:

> On October 7, 1910, a cold foggy morning, the posse was ready for action. Two of the deputies, Oscar Harp and Mont Wiley, were together. Harp said, "Come on, Mont, let's move up closer. Deitz can't get us." So they crawled over a knoll and moved up closer to the house. Deitz shot at Harp, the bullet hitting him in the mouth, killing him instantly. Another shot was fired at Wiley, but missed, as Wiley dodged just in time. The rest of the posse were informed, then the firing and exchange of shots really took place. About a half hour later, Deitz's little daughter, Helen, ran out of the house waving a white handkerchief. She sought the sheriff and told him that the family would surrender if they promised not to kill her daddy who had been wounded. Upon her return to the house, Deitz came out with two luggers strapped to his side and a rifle under his arm. The posse covered him with guns, handcuffed him and his son, Leslie, then brought them to Hayward. The whole family was jailed.

John F. Deitz, farmer and outlaw, was born in Winneconne, Wisconsin, the son of John Deitz (also spelled Dietz) Sr., a New York farmer who moved to Wisconsin before the Civil War. His mother's name and occupation are unknown. A few years after the war, the Deitz family moved north and west, seeking cheap farmland in the logged-over region of Wisconsin known as the Cutover. John Jr. grew up in a log cabin, attended common school, and as a young man dabbled in real estate, ran for minor local offices, and eked out a marginal existence from a small farm. Like many another backwoods farmer, he also hunted, trapped, did odd jobs, and seasonally worked for the logging companies. In 1882 he married Hattie Young, a part-time schoolteacher, with whom he had six children.

In 1900 Deitz and his wife purchased a 160-acre farmstead abutting the Thornapple River in southeastern Sawyer County, in the heart of the Wisconsin pinery. On a corner of their property stood part of the Cameron Dam, one of many small wooden dams erected by logging companies on this important tributary of the Chippewa River. The dam itself was the property of the Chippewa Lumber & Boom Co., an affiliate of the vast Weyerhaeuser syndicate for whom Deitz had previously worked as a dam tender.

Throughout his life Deitz was a prickly and contentious man with a flair for promoting himself and for publicizing the wrongs he had suffered at the hands of "the corporations." He now claimed that the lumber company owed him back wages, and he demanded a toll on all logs sluiced downriver through the dam in recompense. Rifle in hand, he drove off representatives of the company and a series of sheriffs' deputies sent to serve warrants on him. For almost ten years he refused to permit any logs to be driven through "his" dam, defending it at gunpoint and foiling all attempts by local authorities to arrest him.

In 1904 a deputy sheriff and one of Deitz's sons were wounded in a gun battle on the farmstead, and the "Defender of Cameron Dam" attained national prominence as an outlaw-hero who stood up to the "lumber trust." Although his claims had no legal merit, Deitz was widely supported and admired by reformers, socialists, and ordinary people throughout the Midwest—somewhat to the embarrassment of Governor Robert M. La Follette and other Progressives whose rhetoric posed "the people" versus "the interests." Because Deitz was lionized by the press, La Follette was reluctant to marshal the full powers of the state against this outspoken backcountry anarchist.

In 1910, on one of Deitz's rare trips to the nearby town of Winter, he shot and wounded a local man in a street fracas. Shortly thereafter, two of Deitz's children were wounded by sheriff's deputies in an ambush gone badly awry. State authorities attempted unsuccessfully to negotiate a settlement, but Deitz refused all entreaties. Thereupon a large posse of deputies surrounded his farm. In the ensuing battle, a deputy died and Deitz was wounded and captured. In the trial at the county seat of Hayward, he defended himself against a charge of murder, contending that the state could not prove whose gun had fired the fatal bullet. But he was found guilty and received a life sentence. During and after his trial, a stage play and a movie portraying Deitz as a hero played to packed houses in Wisconsin and Minnesota.

Deitz served ten years in the state penitentiary, but continuing public pressure eventually persuaded Governor John J. Blaine to grant him a pardon in 1921. A cranky but charismatic figure of the Progressive Era, Deitz died in Milwaukee, estranged from family and friends but still protesting the righteousness of his cause.

P.H.H.

Questions surround the circumstances of John Dillinger's death.

JOHN DILLINGER

[22 JUNE 1903–22 JULY 1934]

He'd be a hundred years old now, if he were alive. And it's hard to say with certainty that he's not.

Dillinger, of course, was the sort of criminal likely to inspire myth. His robberies were carried out with brio, his escapes were legendary, and he was a better fit than many for the Robin Hood aura that surrounded so many midwestern outlaws. Robbing banks during the Great Depression struck a fair number of people as perfectly reasonable, and Dillinger only took money from the bank, not from the farmers waiting on line to make deposits. Finally, Dillinger was rumored to possess masculine endowment of extraordinary—one might say equine—dimension.

Folk heroes have been made out of less, and men whose deaths have been far more convincingly documented have been rumored to live on. Jesse James, for example, was very definitely shot dead by Robert Ford, but self-proclaimed Jesses kept popping up for years, the last one as old as Dillinger would be today.

In Dillinger's case, there's some fairly persuasive evidence that the man betrayed by the woman in red and gunned down in front of the Biograph Theater was someone other than John Herbert Dillinger, Public Enemy Number One. An autopsy, which went conveniently missing for thirty years, points up some stunning discrepancies. The dead man's eyes were brown, while Dillinger's were blue. The dead man had had rheumatic heart disease since childhood; Dillinger had not. The dead man was both shorter and heavier than Dillinger, and did not have any of Dillinger's well-documented scars and birthmarks. Nor did he show any evidence of having had plastic surgery, which was the FBI's explanation for the fact that his face didn't look much like Dillinger's. Finally, the dead man had apparently lived in the neighborhood for two years, during much of which time John Dillinger was housed in prison in Michigan City, Indiana.

Well, I can't say I think there's much chance he's still alive. But I have a feeling he was still going strong when Martin Zarcovich and Melvin Purvis were busy taking credit for killing him.

The film Dillinger, *incidentally, is reasonably accurate, although it never questions the FBI version of Dillinger's death. Warren Oates bore a strong resemblance to Dillinger, and may well have looked more like him than the man they wound up shooting.*

John Dillinger, criminal, was born John Herbert Dillinger in Indianapolis, Indiana, the son of John Wilson Dillinger, a grocer, and Mary Ellen Lancaster. When he was three, his mother died, and his seventeen-year-old sister took over his care. He attended public schools in Indianapolis, disliked arithmetic, enjoyed reading, and excelled in schoolyard fights. In 1920 his father, by then remarried, moved to nearby Mooresville with his family, including two stepsons, and Dillinger quit school and began to work in a machine shop and furniture factory. In 1923 he joined the navy, was punished for being absent without leave, deserted, and was dishonorably discharged. He married Beryl Hovious in 1924; they had no children. Dillinger worked as an upholsterer in Mooresville, but he got drunk with a friend and was caught trying to rob a grocer. He served time in the Indiana reformatory at Pendleton and then the state prison at Michigan City. He attempted to escape, was ordered to serve more time, and was punished for gambling and disorderly conduct. His wife divorced him in 1929 and remarried. Though sentenced to ten to twenty years, he was paroled in May 1933 and promptly went on a crime spree, usually with accomplices who were often less lucky than he.

In a botched robbery in Monticello, Indiana, Dillinger shot and wounded a mill manager. He was involved in at least five bank robberies, in Indiana (Daleville, Indianapolis, and Montpelier) and Ohio (Bluffton and New Carlisle), netting more than $50,000, and in one tavern robbery. He was also suspected in three other bank robberies before being arrested in September in Dayton, Ohio. He was charged with multiple bank robberies and jailed in Lima, Ohio. Four days later ten of Dillinger's friends broke out of the Indiana State Prison with guns he had smuggled to them earlier. On 12 October four of these men—Russell Clark, John Hamilton,

Charles Makley, and Harry Pierpont—and a friend named Harry Copeland killed the Lima sheriff and freed Dillinger. Between capers that summer, Dillinger and a pair of girlfriends attended the World's Fair in Chicago, and he amused himself by photographing a policeman. Later in October Dillinger, Pierpont, and a friend raided two police stations in Indiana (Auburn and Peru) for guns and bulletproof vests; then Dillinger, Clark, Copeland, Makley, and Pierpont took $75,000 from a bank in Greencastle, Indiana, after which Dillinger returned to Chicago.

November was crime filled. Authorities set a trap for Dillinger outside a Chicago dermatologist's office, but he and Evelyn Frechette, a new girlfriend, shot their way out. Copeland was arrested in Chicago and later sentenced to twenty-five years for the Greencastle robbery. Dillinger, with Clark, Hamilton, Makley, Pierpont, and a friend named Leslie Homer, robbed a bank in Racine, Wisconsin, wounded two men, kidnapped two others and one woman, and escaped; Homer was arrested in Chicago and later sentenced to twenty-eight years for the Racine robbery. In December Chicago authorities placed Dillinger and eight conferderates, including two women—Pearl Elliott and Mary Kinder—on their list of public enemies and organized a forty-man "Dillinger Squad." Dillinger was a suspect in several other robberies. While he and his gang were spending the Christmas season in Florida, police raided an apartment in Chicago and killed three criminals mistakenly thought to be members of his gang.

In January 1934 Dillinger, Hamilton, and others never identified robbed a bank in East Chicago, Indiana, of $20,000, during which a policeman named William Patrick O'Malley was killed, and Hamilton was wounded. Ten days later Dillinger, Clark, Frechette, Kinder, Makley, and Pierpont were captured in a hotel in Tucson, Arizona. Extradited to Indiana for the O'Malley murder, Dillinger, while in jail in Crown Point, whittled a toy gun out of wood and blackened it with shoe polish. In March he threatened guards with the toy and escaped, with an inmate named Herbert Youngblood and two hostages, in the sheriff's car. For crossing state lines in a stolen vehicle, he was placed on a federal complaint. J. Edgar Hoover, director of the Federal Bureau of Investigation, named agent Melvin Purvis to head a team to capture Dillinger. Forming a new gang including Eddie Green and Lester "Baby Face Nelson" Gillis, Dillinger robbed a bank in Sioux Falls, South Dakota, of $49,500. While robbing a bank in Mason City, Iowa, of $52,000, Dillinger and Hamilton were wounded. Youngblood was killed by police in Port Huron, Michigan. Pierpont and Makley were sentenced to death in Lima, Ohio; Clark was given a life sentence. Dillinger, Frechette, and longtime friend Homer Van Meter shot their way out of an FBI trap in St. Paul, Minnesota. While dying of wounds and delirious in St. Paul in April, Green revealed information of much value to the FBI. Frechette was captured by Purvis in a Chicago tavern, but Dillinger escaped unseen. He and Van Meter stole guns and vests in Warsaw, Indiana. Dillinger, Hamilton, and Nelson shot their way out of a botched FBI trap at the Little Bohemia Lodge near Rhinelander, Wisconsin; Nelson killed one agent, and agents killed one civilian and mortally wounded Hamilton, whom Dillinger helped bury outside Oswego, Illinois.

In May, in the wake of new federal laws, Dillinger, Nelson, and Van Meter were indicted in Madison, Wisconsin, for conspiracy. Substantial rewards were posted for Dillinger's capture. Plastic surgeons in Chicago altered his face and that of Van Meter. In June grand juries indicted Dillinger on sundry charges. In Chicago he met Polly Hamilton, celebrated his thirty-first birthday with her in a nightclub, and through her met Anna Sage, a prostitute and madam from Romania. Dillinger, Nelson, Van Meter, and others robbed a bank in South Bend, Indiana, of $30,000, killing a policeman in the process. Dillinger returned to Chicago. Sage, seeking to avoid being deported, informed Purvis that on 22 July Dillinger would take her, along with Polly, to a movie at the Biograph Theater on Lincoln Avenue. Purvis assembled a large team of federal agents and Chicago policemen, including Martin Zarkovich, to surround the place. When Dillinger emerged, he was shot in the head and left side and died within five minutes.

Questions immediately arose. Who actually shot Dillinger? Did he ever draw a weapon, or was he simply executed? What was the background of Sage, the "Woman in Red"? Did Zarkovich, who was her lover, take money from the dead man's pockets? Why did Purvis resign from the FBI in

1935? Why was Sage deported in 1936? Was Dillinger ever killed, or was a petty criminal set up by the authorities in his place? The metamorphosis of the Dillinger legend follows a classic pattern. The hero, who had a deprived childhood, never robbed from the poor; he managed fabulous escapes and acclaimed reappearances; his associates gained fame; he was betrayed by a woman; his fall paradoxically proved that crime does not pay; the victors argued over who deserved the most credit; memorabilia, including his alleged weapons and even traces of his blood, were treasured; rumors of his grand sexuality circulated; and he may have survived after all.

R.L.G.

Guthrie, Oklahoma Territory, is pictured here in 1895, the year before William Doolin broke out of the town's federal jail. Doolin was buried in Guthrie after his death in an ambush led by Deputy Federal Marshal Heck Thomas.

WILLIAM DOOLIN

[1858–25 AUGUST 1896]

Bill Doolin missed the Dalton Gang's raid on two banks in Coffeyville, Kansas, presumably because his horse pulled up lame en route. When the Daltons were promptly gunned down by the local citizenry, a lesser man than Doolin might have thought seriously about a career change. Instead, he rode off to Oklahoma and lost no time in putting another gang together.

After the Battle of Ingalls, a posse headed by Bill Tilghman and Heck Thomas, and financed by the banks and railroads Doolin had victimized, hunted the gang relentlessly. At times they got very close to their quarry, occasionally with amusing results.

Once, Doolin and his fellows were staying at an isolated farmhouse, posing as members of a posse themselves. At breakfast one morning they learned from an informer that the Tilghman-Thomas posse was a few miles distant and headed their way. Doolin told his host that "the rest of the posse" would be coming along shortly, and that they'd be hungry, so he ought to have a big breakfast waiting for them. And, he added, they'd cover the whole tab. And off he went, leaving Tilghman and Thomas to pay for his breakfast.

William Doolin, cowboy and bank and train robber, was born in Johnson County, Arkansas, the son of Michael Doolin and Artemina Beller, farmers. Bill Doolin had a normal childhood and remained on the family farm until 1881. He was a tall, slender man, lacking a formal education and barely literate but generally regarded as intelligent and personable. At twenty-three, Doolin left home to seek his fortune on the closing frontier. He quickly became a proficient cowboy for Oscar Halsell and other ranchers operating near the Cimarron and Arkansas rivers of the Oklahoma Territory. For several years Doolin worked his way across the western ranges of Wyoming, Montana, California, Arizona, and New Mexico, earning the reputation of a reliable, capable, and good-natured hand. He was considered to be a fine rider, an excellent shot, and a natural leader when he returned to the cattle ranches of Oklahoma.

Doolin and several other cowboys visited nearby Coffeyville, Kansas, for the Fourth of July celebration in 1891 and perhaps inadvertently launched a prominent career in crime. When local constables attempted to confiscate the visitors' illegal beer, a gunfight erupted, and the lawmen were shot. Probably already bored with ranch life, Doolin joined the notorious Dalton gang of train robbers. For thirty-three years the former cowboy had lived an ordinary life, giving no indication of a proclivity for criminal behavior, but within months Doolin would be widely known as a desperate, dangerous fugitive, and "King of the Oklahoma Outlaws."

Doolin soon participated in several Dalton depredations in the Indian Territory, but although he was credited with at least six killings, he remained only a peripheral member of the outlaw band. On 5 October 1892 the Daltons attempted to rob two banks simultaneously in Coffeyville, Kansas. The raid proved disastrous, with four members of the gang killed by townsmen. Doolin either escaped or was not involved in the fighting. Instead, he quickly emerged as the new leader of a reorganized and even more formidable outlaw organization. Doolin's gang struck repeatedly at trains and banks in Kansas, Missouri, and the Oklahoma Territory. About twenty individuals participated in these offenses, but typically only three to five members were involved in any specific act. The robberies were marked by careful planning, rapid execution, violence when necessary, and skillful escape.

The leader of these versatile and active criminals found time for a family. In 1893 Doolin married nineteen-year-old Edith Ellsworth, daughter of a Methodist minister. The couple had one son, Jay. Doolin and his criminal colleagues enjoyed good relations with many settlers, furnishing them with provisions and money in return for information and warnings of any efforts at apprehension. Helpful spies for the gang included two young women, Annie McDoulet and Jennie Stevens, popularly known as "Cattle Annie" and "Little Breeches."

Doolin's robbers usually operated from Ingalls, a small community in the Oklahoma Territory about ten miles east of Stillwater. Deputy federal marshals learned of this center for crime, realized the futility of direct attack, and decided to infiltrate the settlement by masquerading as homesteaders hiding in covered wagons. On 1 September 1893 the plan reached its climax with the "Battle of Ingalls," one of the bloodiest confrontations between outlaws and lawmen on the frontier. Doolin and most of the gang escaped, leaving four members of the posse and one innocent citizen killed or fatally wounded in the five-hour gunfight. The raid on Ingalls was a disastrous effort to apprehend the outlaws, but it led to the gradual disintegration of their organization.

A massive manhunt involving federal marshals, private detectives, and local peace officers began. The reward offered for Bill Doolin reached $5,000 "dead or alive," despite which he continued to direct robberies for two years.

Public support for the outlaws eroded, however, and such members of the gang as "Arkansas Tom" (Ray Daugherty), Bill Dalton, "Tulsa Jack" Blake, Charley Pierce, and George "Bitter Creek" Newcomb were killed. By 1895 the surviving outlaws had scattered. Doolin sought refuge under an assumed name on the ranch of Eugene Manlove Rhodes in the mountains of eastern New Mexico. The fugitive also attempted, without success, to negotiate a surrender in return for a reduced charge and sentence.

Suffering from rheumatism, Doolin finally sought relief at the bathing resort of Eureka Springs, Arkansas. Deputy federal marshal Bill Tilghman diligently followed the trail and on 15 January 1896 arrested him in the Davey Hotel. News of the apprehension attracted a multitude of spectators to Guthrie, Oklahoma Territory, where Tilghman had taken his prisoner. Doolin was taken on a tour of the town, during which he shook hands with hundreds of fascinated citizens.

Confined for the first time in his life, the notorious outlaw declined the offer of a fifty-year sentence in return for a plea of guilty to the killings at Ingalls. On the night of 5 July 1896, still awaiting trial, he joined thirteen other prisoners and broke out of the federal jail at Guthrie. The escapees quickly scattered; most were never recaptured.

Doolin hid on the Cimarron River near his wife and son, who were then living in Lawson (later Quay), a small community some ten miles east of Ingalls. A local informant furnished information on the fugitive's movements, and Deputy Federal Marshal Heck Thomas planned an ambush. Just after sundown on 24 August 1896 Doolin said goodbye to his wife and walked down a road, where the posse was waiting. A fusillade of shots brought an immediate end to the outlaw's life. He had never been convicted of any crime.

Bill Doolin was quietly buried at Guthrie three days later. For decades only a rusting buggy axle marked the grave. Marshal Thomas eventually collected only $1,435 of the promised reward, a sum that did not cover his expenses.

F.R.P.

Charles Arthur "Pretty Boy" Floyd, shown here in an FBI photo, became the subject of a ballad by Woody Guthrie.

CHARLES ARTHUR FLOYD

[3 FEBRUARY 1904–22 OCTOBER 1934]

*Back home, in the Cookson Hills of Oklahoma, they called him "Chock,"
because of his enthusiasm for Choctaw beer, a local brew. As far as his neighbors were concerned, he was just a good old boy. If he had an adversarial
relationship with the banks he robbed, well, weren't they just robbers themselves, foreclosing on farms throughout the Dust Bowl?*

*Woody Guthrie captured that sentiment in a ballad that helped foster Floyd's
Robin Hood image. There were outlaws who'd rob you with a six-gun, he noted,
and others who'd do it with a fountain pen. In one verse he has Floyd donate
a thousand dollars for a Christmas dinner "for the poor folks on relief"—
which probably never happened; still, it's hard to argue with him when he
points out that he's never known an outlaw to drive a family from its home.*

*Floyd's efforts had a discernible impact upon the banks; in one year he robbed
so many of them that insurance rates in Oklahoma doubled. His Robin Hood
image lost ground, though, after the Kansas City Massacre. Floyd, who never
denied his bankrobbing exploits, insisted to his dying day—indeed, with his
dying breath—that he'd had nothing to do with it.*

Here's Ma Joad's verdict on Floyd, from John Steinbeck's The Grapes
of Wrath*:*

> "I knowed Purty Boy Floyd. I knowed his Ma. He was full of hell,
> sure, like a good boy oughta be. He done a little bad thing an' they
> hurt 'im, caught 'im and hurt 'im, an' the next bad thing he done
> was mad, an' they hurt 'im again. An' purty soon he was mean-mad.
>
> "They shot at him like a varmint, an' he shot back, an' they run
> him like a coyote, an' him a-snappin' an' a-snarlin', mean as a lobo.
> . . . But the folks that knowed 'im didn't hurt 'im. He wasn't mad at
> them. Finally, they run 'im down and killed 'im. No matter how they
> say it in the paper how he was bad—that's how it was."

C harles Arthur Floyd, bank robber and killer, commonly known as Pretty Boy Floyd, was born in Bartow County, Georgia, the son of Walter Lee Floyd and Mamie Echols, farmers. The Floyd family lived in Georgia until 1911, when they moved to Sequoyah County, near the Cookson Hills, in the new state of Oklahoma. They settled first in Hanson and five years later relocated to Akins, near Sallisaw. Charles attended school and worked on the family cotton farm, earning the reputation of a prankster and the nickname "Choc," for illegal Choctaw beer. He was an athletic, friendly teenager who enjoyed hunting and fishing but had little interest in school.

In 1920 Floyd left home to find work in the harvests of the Great Plains. Soon attracted by the excitement of cities, he moved to Wichita, Kansas, and may have briefly attended barber college. Unfortunately the heavyset young man also became acquainted with the area's underworld. By 1922 Floyd was a bootlegger, gambler, and burglar. He often returned to visit family and friends in Akins and the Cookson Hills. In June 1924, in Sallisaw, Charles married Ruby Hardgraves, the attractive daughter of a tenant farmer. At the time of the marriage, she was three months pregnant, and a son was born in December.

Fatherhood did not slow Floyd's rapidly progressing criminal career. On 11 September 1925 Floyd participated in a payroll robbery in St. Louis, Missouri. Within days the ostentatious display of sudden wealth led to his arrest in Oklahoma. Floyd pleaded guilty and received a sentence of five years in the penitentiary at Jefferson City, Missouri. He proved to be an intelligent, average inmate who committed only minor infractions and became the eager student of experienced, older prisoners. In January 1929 his wife obtained an uncontested divorce; Floyd was discharged two months later.

During the next year Floyd was repeatedly arrested for armed robbery in Kansas City and served a brief jail sentence for vagrancy in Pueblo, Colorado. He also managed several visits back to Oklahoma, including one for the funeral of his father. According to legend, Floyd took revenge on Walter Lee Floyd's murderer. In fact, the killer was found to have acted in self-defense, moved to the West Coast, and died of natural causes.

On 5 February 1930 Floyd and four companions robbed the Farmers & Merchants Bank of Sylvania, Ohio, outside of Toledo. The following month alert police officers in Akron arrested the culprits. Floyd received a fifteen-year sentence in return for a plea of guilty. Then, on 10 December 1930, he made a daring escape from the train taking him to prison. He had been identified earlier as using the alias "Pretty Boy Smith," but after journalists made inquiries about the fugitive Floyd in Kansas City and a local madam volunteered the nickname "Pretty Boy," newspapers throughout the nation adopted and popularized the designation.

Floyd soon joined a gang of efficient bank robbers and killers. He was believed responsible for the murders of gangsters Wallace Ash and William Ash of Kansas City in March 1931. There followed numerous bank robberies in Kentucky, Ohio, Oklahoma, Missouri, and Mississippi. Floyd was also wanted for the killings of two local police officers, a federal Prohibition agent, and an investigator for the Oklahoma Crime Bureau. During one five-month period the "Phantom of the Ozarks" robbed six small Oklahoma banks, only to vanish into the Cookson Hills where friends and family members remained sympathetic and supportive.

In the fall of 1931 Floyd located his former wife and his son. Ruby had remarried, but she promptly rejoined her first husband, bringing their child. The reunited Floyd family lived quietly under assumed names first in Fort Smith, Arkansas, and then in Tulsa, Oklahoma. Floyd proved to be a loving father and husband but continued his career of crimes and gunbattles.

On 17 June 1933 Floyd, together with Adam Richetti and Verne Miller, carried out the infamous Kansas City massacre. On that day, the three gunmen attacked a team of federal agents and local police officers who were transporting a prisoner to the federal penitentiary at Leavenworth. The fight they initiated at Union Station left five dead and two wounded. After several months the Federal Bureau of Investigation identified Floyd, Richetti, and Miller as perpetrators of the massacre. Floyd always denied responsibility for the Union Station killings, however. Miller's mutilated corpse was discovered near Detroit in November 1933. Three months later a thousand lawmen and national guardsmen searched the Cookson Hills in one of the largest manhunts in U.S. history. Floyd and Richetti, however, had left the state several months before.

Floyd may have joined John Dillinger for a bank robbery at South Bend, Indiana, in June 1934. When that notorious bandit was killed the following month in Chicago, Floyd replaced him as the officially designated Public Enemy Number 1. Floyd and Richetti hid quietly in Buffalo, New York, until October 1934, when they determined to return to Oklahoma. On the way, they had an automobile accident near East Liverpool, Ohio. Police recognized Richetti and placed him in custody. Federal agents, led by Melvin Purvis, rushed to the scene and joined the hunt for Floyd. Eight lawmen located him hiding behind a corncrib; as the bandit ran up a hill, the officers opened fire, striking him twice. When Purvis reached the fugitive he said, "You're Pretty Boy Floyd." The man responded, "I am Charles Arthur Floyd," and died.

The man known as the Sagebrush Robin Hood was buried at Akins in a plot he had selected a year earlier. During the depression some people viewed Floyd as a hero, the enemy of the banks, and tens of thousands attended the funeral; dirt was stolen from the grave for decades. In 1938 Missouri executed Adam Richetti for his part in the Kansas City massacre. John Steinbeck portrayed Floyd sympathetically in *The Grapes of Wrath*, and fellow Oklahoman Woody Guthrie wrote a ballad in honor of the fallen Pretty Boy. Floyd's younger brother was elected sheriff of Sequoyah County and served with distinction for twenty years.

F.R.P.

Carlo Gambino, Cosa Nostra organized crime leader, is shown in the 1930s at the start of his rise to power.

CARLO GAMBINO

[24 AUGUST 1902–15 OCTOBER 1976]

Carlo Gambino may well have been the title character in Mario Puzo's The Godfather. *Cool and calculating, he kept a low profile and stayed out of trouble with the law in a manner subsequently emulated by Uncle Junior on* The Sopranos. *Blessed with frail health, Gambino would parry every attempt to deport him or put him on trial by suffering a heart attack or otherwise contriving to wind up in the hospital. When he did die, a cynical prosecutor suggested his tombstone bear the inscription* See? I told you I was sick!

Gambino disliked the dramatic, but in one case he was willing to make an exception. He objected to Joseph Colombo's Italian-American Civil Rights League, seeing it as counter-productive and only serving to increase the public perception of organized crime as an Italian stronghold. In contrast to his usual style, Gambino arranged to make his point by having Colombo hit at a public rally of his organization. While the hit, probably carried out by the Gallo brothers, fell short of killing Colombo, it effectively ended his career, and lacked nothing in the way of dramatic impact.

Gambino was less successful at picking his successor. His cousin and brother-in-law, Paul Castellano, took over upon his death, but died himself in another very public killing orchestrated by John Gotti.

Carlo Gambino, organized crime boss, was born in Palermo, Sicily, Italy. His parents' names are unknown, but his mother's maiden name was Castellano. (The date of his birth is uncertain; the *New York Times* obituary gives it as 1 Sept. 1902.) Gambino, who grew up during a time in which the Mafia was gaining prominence in Sicily, came to revere the suave, well-dressed men who controlled the section of Palermo where he lived, especially Don Vito Cascio Ferro, the leader of the so-called Sicilian Honored Society. By the time he left Sicily, Gambino had been initiated into organized crime. Joining the large numbers of Italians immigrating to the United States, Gambino in November 1921 stowed away on a freighter bound for Norfolk, Virginia. He soon moved on to Brooklyn, New York, where some of his mother's family lived. He resided for the balance of his life in the United States, although he never became an American citizen.

Upon his arrival in New York, Gambino's cousin, future crime boss Paul Castellano, offered Gambino a position at a garage he owned. Soon, however, the profitable world of organized crime took precedence over his day job, as he began defying Prohibition by selling liquor for Brooklyn's

Giuseppe "Joe the Boss" Masseria. Gambino was a successful bootlegger, making money for both himself and Masseria by satisfying the public's craving for spirits.

By 1932 Gambino had switched loyalties to join with the ambitious Salvatore Maranzano, who aspired to become *càpo di tùtti I càpi* (boss of all bosses). Maranzano's objective was achieved in 1931, after directing Lucky Luciano to execute Masseria. After becoming boss, Maranzano set about the task of organizing the somewhat disordered American Mafia, fashioning the concept of La Cosa Nostra (this thing of ours) and creating five New York "families." Gambino was named a *caporegime* (captain) in the family run by Vincent Mangano. Maranzano's rule was short-lived, however, as Luciano had him murdered just a few months later. Luciano ostensibly did away with the position of boss of all bosses and created a more democratic twelve-member commission to run the Mafia in the United States.

Luciano's reconstruction did not affect Gambino's standing in the family, as the quiet, affable Gambino assisted Mangano in governing the waterfront district, extorting money from shipping companies, shipowners, and dockworkers and stealing cargo. In addition, Gambino continued to market illegal liquor, even after the repeal of Prohibition, by providing a product that was economical and quite fortified. During World War II he made millions procuring and reselling ration stamps obtained either from bribable federal employees or by theft. He also held assorted business interests, both legal and illegal, investing in bakeries, nightclubs, restaurants, and meat markets, among other ventures. Becoming very wealthy, Gambino married his first cousin Kathryn Castellano in 1932; they had one daughter and three sons.

Since few resign or retire willingly from the Mafia, attrition usually occurs by assassination. In 1951 Albert Anastasia, the head of Murder Inc., a group officially unconnected to La Cosa Nostra that carried out contract killings, had Mangano killed, and Anastasia ascended to boss of the family, promoting Gambino to underboss. Gambino ran the waterfront with the occasionally unstable Anastasia until 1957, when the latter was shot in the head as he sat in a barbershop chair at the Park Sheraton Hotel in New York City. Though no one claimed responsibility for the murder, many believe that the shrewd and enterprising Gambino, who was soon named boss of the family, played a role in the shooting. He would be known for the rest of his life as "Don Carlo."

During Gambino's successful reign as boss, he made money for himself and the organization by retaining control of the waterfront, by assuming command of the unions that moved cargo out of Idlewild (in 1963 John F. Kennedy) International Airport in New York City, and by running gambling rackets. Some allege that he also was immersed heavily in heroin smuggling. Under Gambino's guidance the Mafia took control of trucking in the garment districts of New York and the private garbage disposal industry in the city, among other activities. He also retained his legitimate holdings, making a fortune with interests in supermarkets, meat-packing companies, and furniture retail. He even united with two partners to form a labor relations consulting firm, Saltzstein, Gambino & Schiller, charging $40,000 a consultation. By the late 1960s more than 1,000 people worked for Gambino; 400 were initiated members of the crime family, and the rest were businesspeople and union officials.

Gambino's style contrasted with that of other notorious organized crime figures such as Luciano, Joseph Colombo, and John Gotti. Never gaudy or ostentatious, he was dedicated to his wife and children, well mannered, charitable, and seemingly passive. He is said to be the archetype for Don Vito Corleone in Mario Puzo's best-selling novel *The Godfather* (1969; three years later made into an Oscar-winning film by Francis Ford Coppola), as he was known for holding court in Little Italy, greeting the people, and dispensing favors as he saw fit. Gambino never acquired a good command of the English language and spoke in a Sicilian dialect. Though possessing a reputation for being nonaggressive, he punished when the circumstances called for it, but, unlike the public hits ordered by some Mafiosi, in most cases Gambino's enemies just "disappeared."

The 1970s marked a personal and professional decline for Gambino. In 1970 he was charged in connection with the theft of several million dollars from an armored car, though he was never brought to trial because of ill health. In 1967 the Justice Department had failed in an attempt to force Gambino, an illegal alien, to leave the country. A few years later they tried again, but when Gambino learned the order had been issued, he was rushed to the hospital for treatment for a heart attack. In 1971 his wife died. Realizing the fragile state of his health, Gambino chose his cousin and brother-in-law Paul Castellano as his successor in 1975. He died at his summer home in Massapequa, Long Island. During his long, prominent career in crime, he had spent less than two years in prison.

Gambino's management style emphasized control and discretion. Until the end of his life he discouraged initiating new soldiers into the family, especially non-Italians, as he felt that increasing membership would make organized crime more vulnerable to authorities. His success must be attributed in part to his longevity, and his conservative approach doubtless played a key role in keeping him alive and out of jail for most of his seventy-four years. Gambino's legacy in organized crime is immense. Under his control, the New York Mafia became larger, wealthier, and more powerful than at any time in the twentieth century.

S.H.

A handcuffed Ed Gein (center) leaves the state crime lab in Madison, Wisconsin, in 1957.

EDWARD GEIN

[27 AUGUST 1906–26 JULY 1984]

It was Alfred Hitchcock's film adaptation of Robert Bloch's novel Psycho *that installed Edward Gein in the pantheon of American homicidal maniacs. The original's not much like what we see on screen. There was no Bates Motel in Ed Gein's world, no mummified mother upstairs, no knife-wielding crazy cutting short Janet Leigh's shower.*

When we imagine Gein, we are apt to envision a man for whom the act of killing was enormously exciting and satisfying. But that doesn't seem to have been the case, and what I find interesting about the wretch is that he killed because that was the simplest way for him to obtain what he wanted—i.e., body parts. Early on, in fact, he got what he needed by robbing graves, assisted by an elderly neighbor named Gus. It was only after Gus was shuttled off to an old folks' home that Gein decided a few seconds of work with a gun would save hours of labor with a garden spade.

The nature of the psychopathology is elusive. Gein seems to have had sexual identity issues, and may have dissected his first victims in an effort to find out what exactly was involved in being female. He soon made use of what he'd brought home, practicing a hideous taxidermy and, at least occasionally, cooking and eating portions of his victims. Parallels with Jeffrey Dahmer, another Wisconsinite, are hard to resist; both seem to have wanted to hold on to their victims, to keep them close even after death.

Edward Gein, whose ghoulish crimes became the basis for Alfred Hitchcock's classic terror film *Psycho*, was born in La Crosse, Wisconsin, the son of George Gein and Augusta Loehrke, farmers. In 1913 the family (which also included Gein's older brother, Henry) moved to a small dairy farm near Camp Douglas, forty miles east of La Crosse. Less than one year later, they relocated again—this time permanently—to a 195-acre farm six miles west of Plainfield, a remote, tiny village in the south central part of the state.

From all available evidence, Gein was subjected to a deeply pathological upbringing. His mother was a hostile, domineering, and fanatically religious woman (the family was Lutheran) who railed incessantly against the sinfulness of her own sex. His ineffectual father alternated between periods of sullen passivity and alcoholic rage. Gein's emotional suffering was undoubtedly exacerbated by the extreme harshness of the environment and the bitter isolation of his life. A pariah even in childhood, he was generally treated as a laughingstock during his school years (which ended with his graduation from eighth grade). Incapable of forming normal social relationships, he grew up in thrall to his ferociously strong-willed mother.

Gein's father died after a lingering illness in 1940. Four years later, Gein's brother perished under ambiguous circumstances while fighting a marsh fire on the family property. At the time his death was attributed to natural causes, though in later years many townspeople came to believe that—in addition to his other outrages—Gein was guilty of fratricide.

The most devastating loss to Gein was his mother's death from a stroke in December 1945. Living alone in the grim, ramshackle farmhouse, he began to retreat into a world of violent fantasy and bizarre ritual. Though he remained tenuously connected to the community—doing odd jobs for neighbors, plowing snow for the county, making occasional trips into town—he was in the grip of a deepening psychosis.

Two years after his mother's death, Gein began making nocturnal raids on local cemeteries, digging up the graves of recently deceased middle-aged or elderly women whose obituaries he had read in the newspapers. His necrophiliac activities continued for at least five years. In 1954 he murdered a middle-aged tavern keeper named Mary Hogan and brought her 200-pound corpse back to his farmhouse.

During this period, rumors started circulating that Gein kept a shrunken head collection in his bedroom, but these stories were dismissed as the colorful imaginings of the village children, who had begun to regard the Gein place as a haunted house. The truth—which proved infinitely more appalling than the hearsay—finally came to light in the fall of 1957.

On Saturday, 16 November (the opening day of deer-hunting season, when the bulk of Plainfield's male population was away in the woods), fifty-eight-year-old Bernice Worden disappeared from the hardware store she operated with her son. Suspicion immediately lighted upon Gein, who had been hanging about the store in recent days, paying unwelcome attention to the widow.

Breaking into the summer kitchen abutting Gein's house, police discovered Worden's gutted and beheaded corpse dangling by the heels from a rafter like a butchered farm animal. Inside the house itself, disbelieving investigators uncovered a large collection of unspeakable artifacts: chairs upholstered with human skin, soup bowls fashioned from skulls, a shade-pull made from a pair of lips, a shoebox full of female genitalia, a nipple-belt, faces stuffed with newspaper and mounted like hunting trophies on the bedroom walls, and a "mammary vest" flayed from the torso of a woman. Gein later confessed that, on various occasions, he arrayed himself in this vest and other human-skin garments and pretended he was his mother.

The discovery of these Gothic horrors in the home of a quiet, midwestern farmer during the proverbially bland Eisenhower era jolted—and transfixed—the country. In Wisconsin itself, Gein quickly entered regional folklore. Within weeks of his arrest, macabre jokes called Geiners became a statewide craze—possibly the first documented instance of what has since become a common phenomenon, the seemingly spontaneous appearance of "sick jokes" about particularly appalling tragedies and disasters. The media, which descended in droves on Gein's hard-pressed hometown, turned him into an instant celebrity. During the first week of December 1957, both *Life* and *Time* magazines ran features on Gein, the former devoting nine pages to his "House of Horrors." For a while, Gein's farmstead became a popular tourist attraction, an intolerable development as far as the outraged community was concerned. On the night of 20 March 1958 a mysterious fire broke out in Gein's house. It was not extinguished until the hated place had been reduced to ashes.

In custody, Gein admitted to grave robbing, a claim initially greeted with skepticism but later confirmed when several empty coffins were exhumed in the Plainfield cemetery. He confessed to killing both Mary Hogan and Bernice Worden, though he maintained that their deaths (both women had been shot in the head) were accidental. Diagnosed as schizophrenic, Gein was committed to Central State Hospital for the Criminally Insane in Waupun, Wisconsin. After a pro forma trial in 1968, he was returned to the mental hospital and, in spite of a 1974 effort to win release, remained institutionalized for the rest of his life. A model inmate, he died of cancer at Mendota Mental Health Institute in Madison and was buried beside his mother in Plainfield.

By the time of his death Gein had become a seemingly undying part of American popular culture. In 1959 horror writer Robert Bloch, who was residing in Wisconsin when Gein's story broke, used the sensational case as the basis for his novel *Psycho* (whose protagonist, Norman Bates, is explicitly likened to Gein at one point in the book). The following year, Alfred Hitchcock transformed Bloch's pulp shocker into his cinematic masterpiece. Insofar as *Psycho* initiated the cycle of so-called slasher movies, Gein is regarded by aficionados of horror as a seminal figure, the "Grandfather of Gore." He is the prototype of every knife-, ax-, and cleaver-wielding maniac who has stalked America's movie screens since. Tobe Hooper's midnight-movie classic *The Texas Chain Saw Massacre* (1975) was directly inspired by the Plainfield horrors, and "Buffalo Bill," the skin-suit-wearing serial killer of Thomas Harris's *The Silence of the Lambs* (1988), was in part modeled on Gein. Horror fan clubs formed around Gein, and his unsettling likeness adorned magazine covers, T-shirts, comic books, and trading cards.

H.S.

VITO GENOVESE

[21? NOVEMBER 1897–14 FEBRUARY 1969]

"You can get further with a kind word and a gun," Al Capone famously said, "than with a kind word alone." He'd have had no argument from Vito Genovese, who saw violence as a perfectly reasonable tool for achieving what he wanted in business and in his personal life as well.

While the death of his first wife doesn't appear to have been investigated, there was a widespread feeling among those who knew him that Genovese had killed her. A year later, he fell in love with a married woman and managed to convince her husband to meet him on the top floor of a New York high-rise. Genovese killed the man, along with a witness who had the bad luck to be there. Two weeks later, he married the grieving widow.

Genovese's recommendations for leading a respectable suburban life remind me of the words spoken in a film by a veteran agent provocateur, laying down the rules for getting along with members of a guerrilla band: "Give the men tobacco, and leave the women alone."

Vito Genovese, criminal entrepreneur, was born in Ricigliano, Italy, the son of Philip Anthony Genovese, a building trades worker, and Nancy (maiden name unknown). Genovese received the equivalent of a fifth-grade education in Italy before following his father to New York City in 1913. A petty thief and street tough in the Greenwich Village area of Little Italy, Genovese soon established a reputation for unusual cunning and violence. Frequently arrested on charges of assault and homicide, he was twice convicted of carrying a concealed weapon. More important, he became a collector for the illegal Italian lottery, an indication that he had attracted the attention of locally prominent underworld figures.

In the 1930s Genovese became increasingly prominent in New York criminal circles. While he established a legitimate company handling waste paper and rags, most of his attention seems to have been devoted to illegal enter-

In 1959 Vito Genovese was convicted on federal narcotics charges and sentenced to 15 years in prison.

prises, especially gambling and extortion. In association with Charles "Lucky" Luciano in 1931, he was involved in a series of murders later linked by law enforcement officials with a major power struggle within the Italian underworld. The death in 1931 of Genovese's first wife (name unknown), whom he had married in 1924, apparently attracted considerable attention among gangland associates. Genovese was almost certainly involved in the murder of Gerard Vernotico, whose widow, Anna Petillo, he married two weeks later on 30 March 1932 and with whom he had two children. Genovese's entanglement in an extortion plot in 1934 led to the murder of one co-conspirator, Ferdinand Boccia, and an ongoing police investigation. In 1936, when Thomas E. Dewey won his celebrated conviction of Luciano for compulsory prostitution, the special prosecutor reportedly indicated that Genovese was his next target. Apprehensive about the Boccia case and fearful of Dewey, Genovese fled to Italy in 1937, a year after he had been naturalized.

Genovese lived well in exile. According to one account, he took $750,000 with him when he left the United States. Anna Genovese, who reportedly managed his income in the United States, made frequent visits to Italy, bringing him additional funds. At Nola in southern Italy, Genovese financed the construction of a power plant and also contributed $250,000 for the building of a municipal structure. For these services, the Mussolini government awarded Genovese the Order of the Crown of Italy, a significant civilian honor. As the fighting in Italy ended, Genovese presented himself to the victorious American forces as an interpreter and facilitator. In 1944, however, he was caught in a U.S. army investigation of black marketing in postwar Italy and jailed. While he was incarcerated, word arrived that he had been indicted in the Boccia case. Although authorities returned Genovese to New York in 1945 to face murder charges, the killing of a key witness in the case ultimately led prosecutors to drop the charges.

Back in the United States in the late 1940s, Genovese and his wife joined the movement to suburbia. They purchased and decorated a luxurious house in Atlantic Highlands, New Jersey, which commanded an impressive view of the New York skyline. Genovese cultivated the image of a conservative and civic-minded businessman. He later advised another underworld figure that respectable life in the suburbs required an altered lifestyle. "Make the people in the neighborhood like you. . . . Give to the Boy Scouts and all the charities. Try to make it to church. Don't fool around with the local girls" (quoted in Peter Maas's *The Valachi Papers* [1968], p. 206).

Discord with his wife, however, contributed materially to Genovese's problems in the 1950s. Charging physical and emotional abuse, Anna Genovese sued her husband for separate maintenance and support. To buttress her case, she testified that Genovese had stashed large sums of money in European accounts and that he grossed between $20,000 and $30,000 a week from the Italian lottery. Her charges, reported in the tabloid press, brought considerable notoriety and embarrassment to Genovese. Ultimately, she won her case, and her husband sold their home and moved into a modest clapboard cottage in Atlantic Highlands. Genovese's discomfort was compounded by a series of congressional investigations into organized crime in the 1950s. After sensational televised hearings in 1950–1951, a special committee chaired by Senator Estes Kefauver of Tennessee concluded that Genovese was a major figure in the Mafia, a sinister national crime cartel controlled by Italian Americans. In the late 1950s a select Senate committee on improper activities in the labor-management field heard testimony that Genovese had amassed a fortune of up to $30 million, in part from his activities with corrupt unions.

Law enforcement officials also linked Genovese to a series of highly publicized gangland developments. In May 1957 a would-be assassin in New York wounded Frank Costello, said to be Lucky Luciano's successor in the underworld. In October gunmen killed the notorious Albert Anastasia, another widely feared gang leader, in a New York barbershop. Finally, in November state troopers apprehended Genovese and some sixty other underworld figures during an alleged mob convention in Apalachin, New York. While no compelling explanation for these developments was advanced, officials and reporters speculated that they involved either a major underworld power struggle or a debate over narcotics trafficking, possibly both. Genovese, said to be eager to assume Costello's mantle, was indicted shortly thereafter on federal narcotics charges. Convicted in 1959, he began serving a fifteen-year sentence in an Atlanta penitentiary in 1960. Events in prison led to more notoriety for Genovese. His cellmate and longtime subordinate, Joseph Valachi, became convinced that Genovese, paranoid and vindictive, suspected him of betrayal. Fearing for his life, Valachi agreed to cooperate with federal officials. In 1963 he testified before a congressional committee about the inner workings of organized crime. Valachi claimed that even in prison Genovese dominated an enormously powerful but mysterious Italian-American criminal organization called La Cosa Nostra. Valachi's testimony, largely taken uncritically, had a profound impact on law enforcement, policymakers, and popular culture. In the wake of the hearings, officials moved Genovese to federal facilities in Leavenworth, Kansas. He died of heart problems in a prison hospital in Springfield, Missouri.

W.H.M.

Charles Guiteau, assassin, wrote songs and poems in his prison cell.

CHARLES JULIUS GUITEAU

[8 SEPTEMBER 1841–30 JUNE 1882]

The tragedy of Charles Guiteau is that this disturbed young man could have such easy access to the president of the United States only sixteen years after the assassination of Abraham Lincoln. (The Secret Service, founded in 1865, was not given the job of protecting the president until after the assassination of William McKinley in 1901.)

Guiteau wrote poems and songs while awaiting execution, but they were mawkish quasi-religious efforts. He was not the author of "The Ballad of Charles Guiteau," a piece of authentic folk music which exists in at least three variations. Here's the one I like the best:

Come all you young people and listen unto me,
And likewise pay attention to these few words I say.
For the murder of James A. Garfield, I am condemned to die
On the thirtieth day of June, upon a scaffold high.

CHORUS:
My name is Charles Guiteau, that name I'll never deny.
I left my aged parents in sorrow for to die.
How little did I think, while in my youthful bloom,
That I'd be taken to the scaffold to meet my fatal doom.

'Twas down at the depot I tried to make my escape.
But, Providence against me, I found I was too late.
I tried to play insane; I found that would not do.
The people were against me, proved I was untrue.

My sister came to prison to bid her last farewell.
She threw her arms around me and wept most bitter and well.
She says, "My darling brother, tomorrow you must die,
For the murder of James A. Garfield, upon the scaffold high."

The hangman is a-waiting, it's a quarter after three.
The black cap's on my forehead, I can no longer see,
The black cap's on my forehead, I can no longer see,
But when I'm dead and buried, oh Lord, remember me.

They don't write 'em like that anymore . . .

Charles Julius Guiteau, assassin, was born in Freeport, Illinois, the son of Luther Wilson Guiteau, a businessman, and Jane Howe. Left motherless at the age of seven, he grew up a hyperactive, lonely child, dominated by his strict father, whose only passion was for the Perfectionist doctrine of John Humphrey Noyes, which taught that sin and therefore death were illusions. When Charles failed his preparatory exams for the University of Michigan in 1860, he took up his father's religion and joined the Perfectionist community at Oneida, New York, drawn there more by the sexual communitarianism it practiced than by the theology it preached.

Life among the Perfectionist saints proved disappointing to Guiteau, whom Noyes regarded as "moody, self-conceited, unmanageable." Unpopular in the community, Guiteau left in 1867, determined to fulfill some great destiny, perhaps even the presidency. For a time he toyed with the idea of establishing a religious newspaper in New York, although he was virtually penniless. Then he studied law in Chicago, trying only one case, which he lost disastrously. After that he specialized in collecting bad debts, but he tended to pocket the proceeds rather than sharing them with his clients.

An accomplished deadbeat, Guiteau left behind a trail of unpaid loans and boardinghouse bills before returning to New York in 1871. He was accompanied by his wife of three years, Annie Bunn, a timid YMCA librarian who had been attracted by his outward show of piety. She was soon so disillusioned by his violent temper and frequent consorting with "lewd women" that she sued for divorce in 1873; they did not have children.

In 1872 Guiteau tried his hand at politics, delivering a disjointed speech for presidential candidate Horace Greeley that, he was convinced, entitled him to be minister to Chile in a Greeley administration. With Greeley's defeat, he turned again to theology, after a brief stint in jail for fraud and a narrow escape from commitment to a mental asylum for chasing his sister with an axe. For three years he was an itinerant evangelist, preaching a revelation brazenly lifted from the works of Noyes.

In 1880 Guiteau again took up politics, publishing a cliché-ridden speech for James A. Garfield, the Republican nominee for president, and hanging around Republican headquarters, stealing stationery and trying to look important. For these services he expected to be rewarded with a suitable diplomatic appointment, preferably consul general at Paris. For months he badgered Garfield and Secretary of State James G. Blaine, who finally threw him out of his office in exasperation.

Shortly thereafter, on the evening of 18 May 1881, an inspiration, which he presumed to be divine, began to possess Guiteau with the conviction that the faithless president had to be "removed" in order to save the Republican party and avert another civil war. Unable to resist the "pressure" of this call, Guiteau purchased a .44 caliber, ivory-handled pistol (with borrowed money) and began to stalk his prey. Presidents were not yet protected by either the Secret Service or by bodyguards. Most Americans would have agreed with Garfield that "Assassination can no more be guarded against than death by lightning; and it is not best to worry about either."

Guiteau caught up with the president on 2 July 1881 at the Baltimore & Potomac railroad station. Garfield was in a festive mood: his patronage troubles with Roscoe Conkling, leader of the pro–U. S. Grant "Stalwart" wing of the party, were behind him; a vacation lay ahead of him. Garfield was waiting for his train, deep in conversation with Blaine about a forthcoming speech on southern affairs, when Guiteau stepped behind him and pumped two bullets into the president's back. Leaving his wounded victim lying on the waiting-room floor, Guiteau coolly headed toward a cab he had prudently hired to take him to the safety of the District of Columbia jail. Before he could reach it he was arrested by police officer Patrick Kearny, to whom he explained, "I am a Stalwart."

Throughout the summer of 1881 the weakened president slowly slipped away despite, or perhaps because of, the constant attention of a small army of physicians. He died at Elberon, New Jersey, at 10:35 on the night of 19 September and was succeeded by Vice President Chester Alan Arthur.

After Garfield's funeral, which was conducted amid scenes of unmatched national mourning, Guiteau's trial began. The trial lasted from 13 November 1881 to 5 January 1882. It soon degenerated into a tasteless circus, largely because of the bizarre antics of the defendant who sang, raved, and interrupted the proceedings at will. If this behavior was intended to support the defense's contention that Guiteau was insane, it failed to impress the jury, which ruled him guilty after deliberating for only an hour and five minutes. Behind the clowning, the trial contained some serious aspects. It served as a showcase for the infant discipline of psychiatry, and it underlined the deficiencies of the prevailing M'Naghten rule, which held that defendants could be deemed legally insane only if they failed to understand the consequences of their actions. By that standard Guiteau was clearly sane, despite his apparent derangement. He was hanged in Washington, D.C., on 30 June 1882 while reciting a childish poem he composed for the occasion entitled "I Am Going to the Lordy."

Guiteau's sad career was eagerly seized upon by advocates of civil service reform. In their propaganda, Guiteau's tangled web of delusions was reduced to the single strand of "disappointed office seeker," and in that guise he was transformed into a symbol of the evils of the spoils system, a gross oversimplification that has been imposed upon history ever since.

A.P.

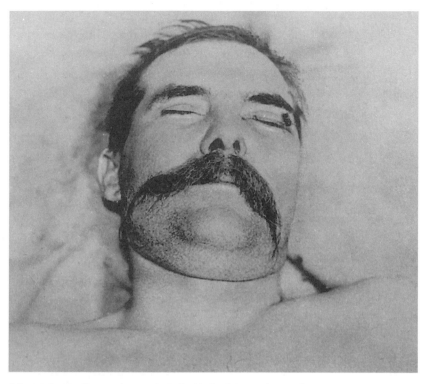

John Wesley Hardin was photographed after his death in an El Paso saloon.

JOHN WESLEY HARDIN

[26 MAY 1853–19 AUGUST 1895]

Ah, yes. John Wesley Hardin. You know the fellow. He was a friend to the poor, and traveled with a gun in every hand. He was never known to hurt an honest man, but on the contrary was always known to lend a helping hand. They could never prove a charge against him, either, and no man could track or chain him down, because, by God, the guy was never known to make a foolish move.

Sounds good, doesn't it? Except that's not John Wesley Hardin at all, as it turns out. That's John Wesley Harding, eponymous hero of Bob Dylan's bal-

lad, and attaching a superfluous G to the man's name is the least of the liberties the songwriter has taken with history.

Because a look at the man's life shows a racist, homicidal sociopath with no discernible redeeming qualities other than admirable hand-eye coordination. He killed a whole lot of people and lived a surprising length of time before another of nature's noblemen gunned him down.

John Wesley Hardin, gunman, was born in Bonham, Texas, the son of James G. Hardin, a Methodist preacher, and Mary Elizabeth Dixon. He attended school in Polk and Trinity counties in East Texas, where his father also taught school and practiced law. Though he owned no slaves in 1860 and opposed secession, the elder Hardin became an ardent supporter of the Confederacy. "Wes" Hardin imbibed his family's devotion to the cause as well as his father's lessons regarding "the first law of nature— that of self preservation" (Hardin, *The Life of John Wesley Hardin As Written by Himself*, p. 125). The Sixth Commandment and Methodist strictures regarding drinking and gambling seem to have made much less of an impression on him.

In 1868, at age fifteen, Hardin committed the first of his many homicides, shooting a Polk County freedman who had menaced him after being bested in a wrestling match. Unwilling to be tried in the Reconstruction courts for killing a black man, Hardin fled. He waylaid federal soldiers sent after him and claimed to have killed three of them. By early 1869 the fugitive had settled in Corsicana, Texas, where he taught school before hiring on as a cowboy. He became known for his marksmanship and his deep hatred of the Reconstruction regime. Hardin terrorized "impudent" freedpeople and tangled again with U.S. soldiers, killing one, according to his own account.

The identity of these early victims suggests that while Hardin has been remembered as "the most sensational gun-fighter of the gun-fighting Old West" (from the foreword of Lewis Nordyke's *John Wesley Hardin: Texas Gunman* [1957]), his criminal career had as much to do with the violent resistance of many conservative white southerners to the social and political consequences of emancipation and Reconstruction as with the lawlessness of a boisterous, lightly policed frontier. This postwar southern violence was particularly pronounced in Texas. Between 1865 and 1870 black Texans, Republicans, and military and civilian agents of the new order died by the score, often at the hands of night riders or of gunmen like Hardin. To fight such violence, the Republican state government established a racially integrated police force in 1870. Its members became Hardin's chief enemies. This body included some brutal scoundrels, but it is clear that the complexion as much as the character of the state police upset Hardin. He crusaded against what he termed "Negro rule," a phantasm conjured out of black Texans' exercise—together with whites—of state authority. Sought by the police, Hardin lay low in central Texas through the beginning of 1871. He was apprehended by lawmen several times but escaped in each instance by killing his captors.

In January 1871 Hardin settled among kin in Gonzales County. He worked as a cowboy and stockman and in 1872 married Jane Bowen. Initially Hardin kept his distance from the feuding that plagued the area—though it pitted the Taylors, an extended family of unreconstructed rebels, against a faction, designated the Suttons, that included members of the Reconstruction constabulary. He hardly eschewed violence, however. In September 1871 he murdered a black state policeman and wounded another. Black citizens raised a posse to run him down, but Hardin surprised and overwhelmed the force. The next summer, while selling horses in East Texas, Hardin shot several more policemen and was wounded himself before surrendering and being returned to Gonzales to stand trial. Because many county residents either admired or feared him, Hardin quickly escaped from jail and returned home, apparently unmolested. As he later explained, "In putting down Negro rule there, I had made many friends and sympathizers" (Hardin, p. 75).

At the same time he battled Reconstruction authorities, Hardin engaged in pursuits more befitting his Wild West image. In 1871 he drove a herd of cattle up the Chisholm Trail to Abilene, Kansas, where he defied marshal

James Butler "Wild Bill" Hickok's ban on carrying guns. In the course of this trip, Hardin appears to have killed ten men, including several Indians and five Mexican *vaqueros*. Other Hardin victims in these years included fellow gamblers and belligerent drunks. In every instance, Hardin claimed that he acted in self-defense. The sheer number of incidents, however, and the frequency with which his antagonists died suggest the decidedly pathological cast of Hardin's character. Contemporaries called him among the fastest and most accurate shots they had ever seen. Unfortunately for his enemies, Hardin usually aimed for the head.

By 1873 Hardin's luck, and the sympathy he enjoyed among some conservative whites, began to run out. A freshly elected Democratic legislature abolished the state police and other unpopular Reconstruction institutions, but Hardin became increasingly involved in the Sutton-Taylor feud. He helped kill a Sutton leader, former state policeman Jack Helm, and engineered the assassination of a second, William Sutton. With the installation of a Democratic governor in January 1874, Hardin's violent acts could no longer be regarded as blows against Reconstruction rule. Shortly after the William Sutton murder, Hardin started a herd of cattle north toward Kansas, stopping off in Comanche, Texas, to see his family. There, on 26 May 1874, he killed a deputy sheriff whom he said had drawn a gun behind his back. Local residents were not moved by Hardin's claims, however. He had to flee for his life, and mobs subsequently murdered his brother, four cousins, and three associates. The next time the Democratic legislature met, it offered a $4,000 reward for the "notorious murderer" Hardin.

Hardin escaped with his wife and child to Gainesville, Florida, then moved to Jacksonville, where he dealt cattle. After killing two detectives who had tracked him down, Hardin settled in southern Alabama. On 23 August 1877 Texas Rangers, having discovered his whereabouts, overpowered him on a train in Pensacola. Hardin was returned to Texas, convicted of second-degree murder, and sentenced to twenty-five years in prison for the killing in Comanche.

In prison in Huntsville, Hardin showed little remorse. Responsible, by his own count, for well over thirty deaths, he wrote his daughter that "the blood I have spilt is of that kind which can never stain" (14 July 1889, quoted by permission of Southwest Texas State University). After several early attempts to escape, however, he behaved well, studied law, and, ultimately, had nearly ten years shaved off his sentence. Hardin was released in February 1894 and shortly thereafter was pardoned by the state. His plans to lead a more settled life practicing law in Gonzales proved futile. His wife had died in 1892, and his three children were nearly grown. Few clients called, and he became involved in a bitter dispute with a figure from his outlaw days. After this man was elected sheriff, Hardin left Gonzales. In 1895 he married Callie Lewis in Junction, Texas, but his teenage bride left him almost immediately. Hired to handle a case in West Texas, Hardin ended up in El Paso, where he quickly resumed old habits—drinking, gambling, and gunplay. One summer night, another aging gunman, John Selman, shot him down in the Acme Saloon.

It has been difficult for those who romanticize outlaws to depict Hardin as a Robin Hood. He was not a robber or a friend to the poor. Instead— to employ historian E. J. Hobsbawm's typology of banditry—he was often pictured as an "avenger," a cruel man fighting even crueler oppressors. Attitudes toward Reconstruction have changed, however, and Americans take more seriously the dangers faced by African Americans and Republicans in postwar Texas and show more respect for the efforts of federal and state authorities to protect them. Viewed from this perspective, Hardin seems little more than a hate-filled miscreant with a penchant— and a genuine talent—for murder.

P.G.W.

Tom Horn holds the rope that he made in jail while awaiting execution by hanging.

TOM HORN

There's a wonderful photo in the collection of the Denver Public Library. It shows Tom Horn, a lock of hair falling down on his high forehead, looking down at the length of braided rope he's holding. The rope is identified as one he made in jail, and with which he was subsequently hanged.

Times have changed, I know, and I don't suppose they used to take a prisoner's belt and shoelaces from him, but the mind boggles at the thought of a man in jail being allowed to make himself a rope. And I have to say it looks like a rather frail rope for the use to which it was put. But then it's hard to know what Tom Horn did or didn't do, and the autobiography he wrote in his cell—when he wasn't braiding rope, I suppose—only confuses the issue.

While he was working for the Pinkertons, Horn allegedly brought in a bandit named Peg-Leg Watson, a train robber whom Horn found living alone in a remote cabin. After the two traded gunfire, Horn broke cover and walked across an open field, holding his rifle with the barrel pointed downward. Watson was so dumbstruck by this display of courage that he surrendered, and Horn brought him in single-handed.

Well, maybe. There's no evidence it ever happened, but then there's no evidence Horn committed the murder they hanged him for, and his confession would never be admitted in a modern courtroom. Still, it's hard to believe that Amnesty International didn't have better things to do than retry the case ninety years later.

Tom Horn, scout, detective, and assassin, was born near Memphis, Scotland County, Missouri. His parents, whose names are no longer known, were farmers. He attended school irregularly during winter months, did hard farm work, enjoyed hunting, and became an excellent marksman. At about age fourteen, after an argument and violent fight with his father, he ran away to Santa Fe and may have worked as a stage driver. While in that region, he learned to speak Spanish. In 1876 or so he went to Prescott, in Arizona Territory, where he met Al Sieber, the famous civilian chief of scouts for various U.S. Army units in the San Carlos area. Little is known of Horn's activities for the next several years. In 1882, according to Sieber, Horn worked as an army packer. He undoubtedly participated in the army pursuit of Apaches fleeing from the San Carlos Reservation. American cavalry units commanded by Tullius Cicero Tupper and William Augustus Rafferty, both captains, followed the Apaches into northwest Chihuahua, Mexico, and engaged them in April 1882 in a standoff at Sierra Enmedio, in Sonora.

In his autobiography, Horn claims that he learned to speak Apache fluently, but this assertion—often recorded as historical fact, like other boasts of his—may be doubted. In any event, he was one of some seventy-six packers with General George Crook during his 1883 expedition into the Sierra Madre mountains of Mexico, resulting in the return of the Apaches to the reservation. Although in his autobiography Horn contends that he played an important combat role under Crook, his name is not mentioned in any official report concerning the expedition. He evidently did, however, continue to work well under Sieber, who occasionally placed him in command of army scouts when he himself was absent. In 1885 Captain Emmet Crawford appointed Horn chief of scouts during the army's pursuit of Geronimo into the Sierra Madres. Mexican irregulars killed Crawford and wounded Horn in January 1886. Geronimo surrendered in September to Lieutenant Charles B. Gatewood, under General Nelson Appleton Miles's command, during which Horn was present. Although Horn later wrote that he was of central importance at the surrender, Gatewood reported that Horn acted only as a Spanish-English interpreter.

Once Geronimo was captured, Horn was no longer needed as a scout or an interpreter and became a prospector for gold in Aravaipa Canyon, Arizona. He says that he played a major role in the bloody Pleasant Valley War of 1886–1892. It involved fights by rival Tewksbury and Graham family members and their riders over cattle- and sheep-grazing lands in central Arizona. Horn says that he was ordered into the region to mediate the feud by Buckey O'Neill, sheriff of Yavapai County, and also that he was deputized by Commodore Perry Owens and Glenn Reynolds, sheriffs, respectively, of nearby Apache and Gila counties. However, O'Neill was not the Yavapai sheriff then, and there is no record that either Owens or Reynolds ever deputized Horn. In any event, he sided with the Tewksburys in 1887 and may have been responsible for the murder in July of Mart Blevins, a Graham man. Next, Horn is known to have won steer-roping events at rodeos in 1888 in Globe, Arizona, and in 1890 or so in Phoenix.

From 1890 to 1894 Horn was employed by the Pinkerton Detective Agency in Denver as a loner to track outlaws preying on banks, railroads, and mine payrolls. In 1894 the Swan Land and Cattle Company of Wyoming hired him as a stock detective. By this time, if not a little earlier, he may have become a hired gun. He boasted that in 1895 he killed two small-time ranchers near Laramie, Wyoming, for $600 each. After these jobs, he avoided possible legal consequences by working for a while as a ranch supervisor in Aravaipa. It is known not only that he wrote a letter late in 1896 to a Tucson marshal offering to destroy William Christian's gang of rustlers for pay, but also that William Christian was killed early in 1897 and Robert Christian disappeared permanently later the same year. During the Spanish-American War, Horn was employed as a packer in Tampa, Florida, from April to September 1898. Hired in 1900 as little more than a paid killer (now alias James Hicks), he waged a one-man war on suspected cattle rustlers in Brown's Hole, Colorado, shooting to death Madison M. Rash, a Cold Spring Mountain rancher, in July, and Isom Dart, an African-American rancher at Summit Spring, in October. By these acts he succeeded in scaring other possible rustlers out of the region.

In 1901 Horn resumed his work as a Wyoming stock detective. On 19 July William Nickell, age fourteen, was shot to death from long range in Wyoming's Iron Mountain area, and a few days later his father, Kels P. Nickell, was wounded, also by an unknown assailant. Horn, for some time an employee of John C. Coble of Iron Mountain, was a suspect in both incidents, but there was no proof. In January 1902 U.S. deputy marshal Joe LeFors baited Horn in Cheyenne about a possible job to rid rustlers from an area in Montana and enticed him to boast about his marksmanship. Horn, possibly drunk, hinted that he had killed the Nickell boy from a distance of 300 yards. Charles J. Ohnhaus, a court stenographer, was concealed in the next room and took down the "confession," which was used as evidence in Horn's subsequent trial for murder. Despite substantial defense funds from a never-identified source, Horn was convicted, and the Supreme Court of Wyoming upheld the verdict. In August he escaped, was quickly recaptured, and was executed by hanging. He never implicated his corrupt employers, either during his imprisonment or in the autobiography he wrote while awaiting execution.

Tom Horn has become a legendary figure of the Old West, part courageous hero, part brutal assassin, about whom the truth will never be known. In September 1993 a serious retrial was staged in Cheyenne by collateral descendants of Horn, who never married, and by forensic experts and Amnesty International. After detailed evidence was carefully presented, Horn was declared not guilty of killing the Nickell boy.

R.L.G.

JESSE JAMES

[5 SEPTEMBER 1847–3 APRIL 1882]

The myth of Jesse James was already very much in existence throughout his career, fostered by dime novels and newspaper articles. It grew exponentially with his death at the hands of the "dirty little coward" immortalized in the anonymous ballad, and endures to this day.

It doesn't bear scrutiny. Jesse was no Robin Hood, but then I don't suppose Robin Hood was, either. Like Willie Sutton, he robbed banks and trains because that's where the money was, and while he generously paid the country people who sheltered him from the law, that's not quite the same as robbing the rich and giving to the poor.

He started out as a teenager riding with Bloody Bill Anderson's detachment of Quantrill's Raiders. While he was too young for the raid on Lawrence, Kansas—probably the greatest single outrage of the Civil War—he was an enthusiastic participant in the massacre of seventy-five Union troops at Centralia, Missouri. After the war ended, it didn't take long for Jesse and his brother Frank to turn the skills they'd learned with Anderson into a criminal career.

For a man whose death was so thoroughly documented, with the precise circumstances so widely known (Jesse hanging a picture, Robert Ford shooting him in the back, then running out shouting that he'd done it, he'd killed Jesse James), it's remarkable how rumors flourished to the effect that someone else lay buried in his grave, that Jesse James was still alive.

It was different from the Elvis phenomenon. Nobody ran into Jesse buying peanut butter and bananas in the local Safeway. Instead, men kept turning up proclaiming themselves to be Jesse, with the first claimants appearing shortly after his death and the last popping up in 1948, insisting he was the 101-year-old Jesse James. (He couldn't explain how he'd regrown the tip of the finger which Jesse had shot off after the Centralia raid.) Some of these Jesses picked up a few dollars on the lecture circuit, the period's equivalent of a Vegas lounge act as an Elvis impersonator.

Outlaw Jesse James cultivated his image as an American Robin Hood.

Frank James, Jesse's older brother, is often portrayed in films as the more contemplative and less criminous sibling, and he did manage to parlay the public reaction to Jesse's murder into a free pass for the crimes he'd committed. Frank, it should be noted, was with Quantrill and Anderson at Lawrence, where the guerrillas hunted down every unarmed man and boy in town, killing them all and making the women of the town watch the slaughter.

Jesse James, outlaw, was born Jesse Woodson James in Clay County, Missouri, the son of Robert James, a Baptist minister who cofounded William Jewell college, and Zerelda Cole. His father died of cholera in 1850; his mother, after marrying and divorcing a second husband, married Reuben Samuel, a doctor, in 1855.

Raised in a rural Missouri county by slave-owning parents, Jesse James grew up experiencing at close hand the violent conflicts between antislavery elements in nearby Kansas and proslavery groups in Missouri before the outbreak of the Civil War. The Civil War intensified these conflicts, as the region experienced numerous atrocities carried out by rival guerrilla bands. After his parents were abused by Union soldiers and his mother imprisoned, James at seventeen joined his brother Frank James and several future criminal associates in "Bloody Bill" Anderson's Confederate guerrilla outfit and participated in several battles, earning a reputation for courage and skill.

What happened to Jesse James immediately following the war is uncertain. Widely accepted is the story that he was shot and left for dead when he surrendered to Union troops, giving rise to the belief that he became an outlaw because he was not granted amnesty. Many Confederate guerrillas, some more infamous at the time than James, did make the postwar transition to law-abiding citizen, making the tale seem more a convenient fiction than a historical fact.

James's first ventures into bank robbery probably began in 1866. It was not until December 1869, however, that he and his brother were publicly identified as suspects following a bank robbery in Gallatin, Missouri.

Popular feeling ran strongly against the James brothers, with a local news-paper reporting that, if captured, they "would be shot down in their tracks, so great is the excitement among citizens" (*Liberty [Mo.] Tribune*, 17 Dec. 1869).

Unlike most bandits, however, Jesse James recognized the power of public opinion and worked to shape it. An open letter published in the *Liberty Tribune* (24 June 1870) by the outlaw proclaimed his innocence and suggested he was the victim of political persecution by Radical Republicans in Missouri for his wartime service to the Confederacy. This was the first of several letters James published in local newspapers sympathetic to the Confederate cause, politicizing his criminality.

For the next ten years James and other ex-Confederates were glorified by the press and politicians of the Confederate wing of Missouri's Democratic party. Prominent editor John Newman Edwards was the prime force in shaping a "Robin Hood" image for James through numerous edi-torials and in his book *Noted Guerrillas* (1877). In one essay Edwards describes James and his band as "men who might have sat with Arthur at the Round Table, ridden in tourney with Sir Lancelot, or won the colors of Guinevere" (*Kansas City Times*, 29 Sept. 1872). James was cast as a righteous avenger who robbed from the wealthy railroads and banks vic-timizing the common folk. He was also presented, rather inconsistently, as an innocent victim of those who used the law illegitimately.

Edwards served as an able "campaign manager" for the James gang, but these outlaws also had a shrewd sense of how to construct a good public image. Beside writing letters to newspapers claiming innocence and con-demning the Republicans holding office, the bandits dramatized their rob-beries in meaningful ways. At an 1874 train robbery a written version of the event was given to passengers to distribute among the media, exag-gerating the height of the outlaws. Accounts of the robbery also indicated that the hands of passengers were examined so that working men would not be robbed. During a stagecoach robbery the valuables of a Confederate war veteran were returned. Through such actions, the gang fostered a Robin Hood image tinged with postwar politics.

In June 1874 the *St. Louis Dispatch* broke the news that the celebrated Jesse James had been snared at last, "his captor a woman, young, accomplished beautiful." James granted interviews and announced that he had married Zerelda "Zee" Mimms on 24 April "for love, and that there cannot be any . . . doubt about our marriage being a happy one." Papers throughout the land praised the outlaw for his style; with the appearance of the modern Maid Marian, and later two children, the portrayal of James as Robin Hood was easier to believe.

The event that generated popular sympathy more than any other was a raid on the James family home by Pinkerton detectives on 26 January 1875. An illuminating device tossed through a window exploded, killing James's nine-year-old half brother and shattering his mother's arm so badly that it required amputation. Receiving national attention, the incident was almost uniformly condemned. It was used by the Confederate wing of the Democratic party in Missouri as an excuse to propose an amnesty resolution before the Missouri House of Representatives describing James and his band as men who were driven into crime by Missouri Republicans and characterizing them as "men too brave to be mean, too generous to be revengeful, and too gallant and honorable to betray a friend or break a promise." The resolution also stated that "most if not all the offenses with which they are charged have been committed by others, and perhaps by those pretending to hunt them." Supported by every ex-Confederate in the legislature, the resolution narrowly missed the two-thirds majority needed to pass.

During the next year the Democratic and Republican presses warred. Republicans blamed Democrats for supporting outlawry; Democrats condemned Republicans for slandering the James brothers and attempted to revive the amnesty resolution. Jesse James, in a note to the *Kansas City Times* (23 Aug. 1876), charged the son of a prominent railroad official with engineering a phony robbery, denounced detectives, and asked for amnesty: "If we have a wise Congress this winter . . . they will grant us a full pardon. I will not say pardon for we have done nothing to be pardoned for. . . . If the express companies want to do a good act they can take all the money they are letting those thieving detectives beat them out of and give it to the poor." Outlawry remained a volatile political topic for several years because the Republican press and party persistently made Democratic support of the outlaws a political issue. Even out-of-state papers from regions competing with Missouri for trade and immigration increased the notoriety of Missouri's bandits.

Attempts to revive the resolution were dashed by the attempted robbery of the Northfield, Minnesota, bank on 7 September 1876. Things went badly: three robbers were killed, and three Younger brothers, known associates of the James brothers, were wounded and captured. Only two of the outlaws escaped, presumably Frank and Jesse James. The most important implication of the Northfield disaster was that it destroyed years of carefully worded denials of guilt by the James gang and its backers, a fact eagerly seized upon by the region's Republican newspapers.

With the virtual destruction of their criminal gang at Northfield, Frank and Jesse James turned to men with less skill and reliability in carrying on their trade. The robberies became more violent, and there began a cycle of betrayal and murder within the band, culminating in the assassination of Jesse James by Robert Ford and Charles Ford on 3 April 1882 in St. Joseph, Missouri. Even in death James's criminality continued to be politicized. Democratic governor Thomas Crittenden of Missouri, backed by railroad interests, publicly announced his role in the assassination plot and thus unwittingly implicated himself as an accessory to murder. Portions of the Democratic press, especially Edwards, led the condemnation. Six months later Crittenden accepted the surrender of Frank James and through a series of political maneuvers ensured that he would never be found guilty of any crime in a court of law in Missouri or elsewhere.

Jesse James is probably the most noted criminal in American history. On his death, the *New York Daily Graphic* 11 Apr. 1882) proclaimed him "the most renowned murderer and robber of his age." Unlike most habitual offenders, James received widespread adulation both in his own lifetime and in following generations. His notoriety resulted from several factors. First, he was supported through the media and in other ways by powerful friends in the Missouri political establishment. Second, he was helped by his identity as an ex-Confederate soldier from a respectable Missouri family. Other ex-Confederates from similar backgrounds also were glorified at the time, including Arthur McCoy, the Younger brothers, and Frank James. These social origins made it easier for segments of the population to identify with these brigands, and it also provided a network of support. Outlaws like Jesse James were undoubtedly protected by numerous otherwise lawful citizens in communities scattered throughout Missouri. As the editor of the *Sedalia (Mo.) Democrat* (14 Oct. 1882) observed, "Was it wrong for the Confederates of this state—when the war had closed—to look with some degree of gratitude upon men whose vigilance saved hundreds of rebel homes . . . from unmilitary desecration? . . . With their history as defenders of the faith, how natural it was for a generous people to extenuate the crimes that for seventeen perilous years have been charged to these men." It was the assassination of Jesse James, however, by the Missouri political establishment that established him as the most noted of Confederate guerrillas who turned to outlawry. Third, the social context of the 1870s made extralegal symbols of justice marketable to a broad audience. In addition to the political turmoil of Reconstruction politics in Missouri, there was an economic depression in the 1870s throughout the West that was widely blamed on banks, railroads, and land monopolies—the victims of outlaws of the time such as the James-Younger gang, Billy the Kid, and Sam Bass. Hundreds of books and articles have been written about Jesse James. He has been the feature of several popular Hollywood movies, and new ballads continue to praise and glorify him. He remains the archetypal American Robin Hood, a heroic criminal who in legend symbolized a form of "higher" justice than that represented by law.

P.G.K.

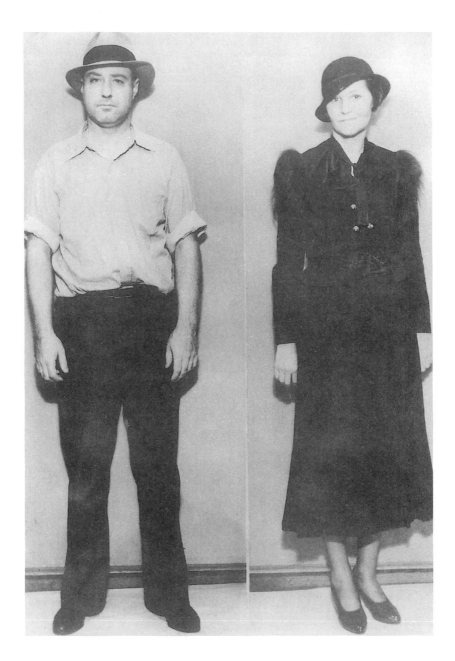

George "Machine Gun" Kelly and his wife, Kathryn Kelly, are photographed at police headquarters in Memphis, Tennessee, 26 September 1933. They were captured by police and federal agents for the kidnapping of Charles F. Urschel, a wealthy oil executive of Oklahoma City.

MACHINE GUN KELLY

[17 JULY 1895–17 JULY 1954]

Two nicknames, both fabricated, are largely responsible for the enduring legend of Machine Gun Kelly. Without them, I doubt we'd have heard of the man.

First, of course, is his own. "Machine Gun Kelly"—to hear the name is to see the man, the fearsome weapon in his hands, spraying a line of cops or bank customers with hot lead. The name and the image that goes with it conjure up the whole era of bank robberies, the lawless time between the two world wars.

It was, of course, a deliberate creation, bestowed upon George Kelly by his woman, Kathryn, along with the weapon itself, which she bought for him and trained him to use. Having named him, she gave him a persona to match.

Interesting woman. If she hadn't chosen crime, she might have made her mark in the emerging field of public relations.

The other nickname? It was coined not for Kelly but (as the legend has it) by him: "Don't shoot, G-Man!" Makes a nice story, and supplies a sobriquet for a whole generation of federal lawmen, but Kelly never said it, nor was it a G-Man who took him into custody. Ah, well. Give the credit to J. Edgar Hoover, someone else who might have done just fine in PR, if he hadn't gone into law enforcement.

Machine Gun Kelly, criminal, was born George Kelly Barnes Jr. in Memphis, Tennessee. Little is known about his parents, his childhood, or his early adulthood. He was a student at Tennessee A&M College, where he met Geneva Mae Ramsey. They were married in Clarksdale, Mississippi, in 1919. They evidently had no children. She divorced him in 1926 for desertion and because he was associating with persons of suspicious background and behavior. He is said to have been in Tennessee, New Mexico, and Texas. He served time in prison for bootlegging, vagrancy, and minor offenses. In 1929 Kelly married Kathryn Shannon Thorne, a 25-year-old "gun moll." They also evidently had no children. She had been married twice before, had been a prostitute, and had associated with known burglars. She bought a machine gun for $250 from a pawnbroker in Fort Worth, Texas, trained Kelly in its use, and nicknamed him "Machine Gun" Kelly after he allegedly wrote his name on a barn wall with bullets from it. The couple formed a criminal gang including friends from Texas and Minneapolis and St. Paul, Minnesota.

Already wanted on bank-robbery charges in four states in the Southwest, Kelly made himself even more notorious by especially vicious criminal activity in 1933. Among the crimes he was accused of that year were killing four police officers and a prisoner at the railroad station in Kansas City, Missouri, robbing the Federal Reserve bank in Chicago and killing a police officer there, and committing a murder in St. Paul. He was placed on the Most Wanted List of the Federal Bureau of Investigation. His most notorious crime occasioned his undoing. On 22 June 1933 Kelly, his wife (who was said to be the brains behind the plan), and Albert L. Bates kidnapped Charles F. Urschel, an oil millionaire and an influential political figure in Oklahoma City, Oklahoma. He was taken from his home by Kelly and Bates, both of whom were armed, was blindfolded and driven to a shack, and was held there for nine days. A ransom of $200,000 was demanded and was paid. Although Urschel heard a young woman arguing that he be killed, he was released unharmed.

Urschel gave details of a bumpy, fourteen-hour ride and of odors, weather conditions, the sound of two airplanes overhead daily with the exception of one day, and so on. These clues enabled FBI agents to locate the shack, which was on a farm in Paradise, Texas, owned by Robert G. Shannon, Kathryn Kelly's stepfather, and his wife, Ora. Shannon was an influence peddler in local politics, had contacts with the underworld, and was suspected of providing hideouts at a price for wanted criminals. Shannon and Harvey Bailey, another member of the gang, were arrested with some of the ransom money in their possession. They were tried and sentenced—under the 1932 Lindbergh law making kidnapping a federal crime—to life in prison.

On 26 September 1933 Kelly and his wife were apprehended in a small bungalow in Memphis, Tennessee. The dapper Kelly had dyed his dark hair a lemon yellow, and the couple had "borrowed" Geraldine Arnold, the twelve-year-old daughter of an itinerant worker, so as to present themselves to the world as a harmless little family. Young Geraldine, who sent messages that led the FBI to Kelly, later received some of the reward money. A legend promoted by FBI director J. Edgar Hoover had it that, at the time of his capture, an armed but cowering Kelly shouted, "Don't shoot, G-men, don't shoot!"—thus coining the term "G-men" for government agents. In truth, a Memphis detective, Sergeant W. J. Raney, entered the bungalow with a shotgun and caught Kelly, who was armed with an automatic. FBI agents remained outside as backup. In no time, G-men became heroes, however. In 1935 alone there were sixty-five movies featuring federal agents, the most famous being *G-Man*, starring James Cagney.

Machine Gun Kelly and his wife were tried, convicted, and sentenced to life imprisonment. Caught earlier in Denver, Bates was also tried, convicted, and given a life sentence; he died in Alcatraz. Later, FBI agents traced most of the ransom money to T. M. Coleman, Kathryn Kelly's grandfather, in Stratford, Oklahoma. It was determined that Coleman's ranch had been the Kelly gang's headquarters since the previous January. Kelly went to the federal prison in Leavenworth, Kansas (Oct. 1933), boasted that he would soon escape, and was transferred as a hardened criminal to Alcatraz (Sept. 1934). He was returned to Leavenworth (June 1951), where he made furniture until his death from a heart attack in the prison hospital. Having boasted that she would soon rendezvous with her husband, Kathryn Kelly was sent to a federal prison at Alderson, West Virginia. After a while she turned against Kelly and blamed him for "this terrible mess." She was later transferred to a workhouse in Cincinnati. She was granted a new trial in 1956 on a technicality and was released two years later without a second trial. She disappeared from recorded history.

R.L.G.

Criminal entrepreneur Meyer Lansky, shown here in 1949, made his mark in bootlegging and illegal casino gambling.

MEYER LANSKY

[28 AUGUST OR 4 JULY 1902–15 JANUARY 1983]

The image that endures is almost benign. Meyer Lansky was either a crimi-
nal genius or simply a man who applied modern business methods to areas
of enterprise—whiskey, gambling—which society chose to render illegal. By
the end of his long life, Prohibition was a distant memory, while gambling in
one form or another was legal (and often state-sponsored) in forty-eight states.
And Lansky, who'd survived most of his contemporaries, had somehow
morphed into a wise and gentle grandfather, so why did the Feds insist on
hounding this poor old man?

Well, he did kill a lot of people along the way. Lansky and Ben Siegel started
out supplying hot cars to gangsters and moved into murder for hire; it was
the Bugs and Meyer mob that, under Albert Anastasia, became known as
Murder Incorporated.

Was Siegel one of his victims? Hard to say, but if he didn't order the hit, it's
certain he at least signed off on it. "I had no choice," he's supposed to have said.

Meyer Lansky, bootlegger and gambling entrepreneur, was born Meyer
Suchowljansky in Grodno, Belorussia (then Russia), the son of Max
Suchowljansky, a garment presser, and Yetta (maiden name unknown).
Lansky's father immigrated to New York City in 1909 and brought the fam-
ily over two years later. Meyer, who left school in 1917 at age fourteen, was
fascinated by the street life and crap games of the Lower East Side and while
still a teenager associated with other hustlers, such as Bugsy Siegel and
Lucky Luciano.

With the coming of Prohibition in 1920, Lansky and Siegel entered bootlegging, backed initially by Arnold Rothstein and using a car and truck
rental company as a front. By the mid-1920s, in partnership with Luciano,
Lansky was bringing liquor across the Atlantic directly into New York and
New Jersey harbors. Soon his younger brother, Jake Lansky, was an active

partner and assistant in his enterprises. The contacts that Lansky made with other bootleggers on the East Coast and in the Midwest provided a network of associations that were central to his later career as a casino owner.

After Prohibition, Lansky became an entrepreneur of illegal and legal gambling casinos, especially in growing tourist centers. As early as the 1920s, he was probably involved in casino operations in Saratoga Springs, New York, during the August racing season, and by the late 1930s he, along with Frank Costello and Joe Adonis, owned the Piping Rock nightclub and casino there. His main focus, though, became the growing tourist trade in the Miami area. In the mid-1930s, along with Vincent "Jimmy" Alo, his closest Italian friend after the jailing of Luciano in the 1930s, Lansky invested in the Plantation casino in Hallandale (near Miami) and in other Florida gambling ventures. He also briefly operated gambling in Cuba through an association with Fulgencio Batista, the country's dictator.

Lansky reached the apex of his casino career in the decade and a half following World War II. In 1945, with Alo, Costello, and other investors, he remodelled and reopened the Colonial Inn in Hallandale; it was one of the most important illegal casinos in the country. Lansky also had interests in the Beverly Club outside of New Orleans, renewed his partnership with Costello in Saratoga Springs, and invested with Siegel and others in the construction of the Flamingo in Las Vegas. In June 1947 Siegel was killed, no doubt because some partners disapproved of his financial management of the Flamingo. Whether or not Lansky approved of the murder of his friend, he continued as an investor in the Flamingo. As the largest and most famous of the fledgling casino/hotels on the Las Vegas strip, the Flamingo helped to launch the city's development as a national center of legal gambling and entertainment. Although Lansky invested in other Las Vegas casinos, he remained in Florida and had little direct involvement in the city.

In October 1950 and March 1951 Lansky was called to testify before the U.S. Senate committee, chaired by Estes Kefauver of Tennessee, that was investigating interstate organized crime. Because the hearings identified

Lansky and other criminal entrepreneurs as central to a national coordination of "organized crime," he faced local investigations in Florida and New York (Saratoga Springs) that resulted in indictments and convictions for gambling and conspiracy in 1953 and the closing of his casinos. For the rest of his life, he was the subject of ongoing investigations by the Federal Bureau of Investigation, the Immigration Service, and the Internal Revenue Service.

Lansky's troubles in the United States coincided with the return to power in March 1952 of Cuba's Batista, who had retired in 1944. Lansky became Batista's adviser on the development of Cuban tourism through gambling. In 1955, he and Jake began running the casino at Havana's Hotel Nacional. Soon thereafter, investing his own money, Lansky built the Riviera, perhaps the largest hotel/casino in the world outside of Las Vegas. His days of glory ended abruptly after Fidel Castro took power in 1959. With the nationalization of the casinos in 1960, Lansky lost much of the money he had invested in Cuba.

Back in Florida, Lansky increasingly operated behind the scenes. By this time, he required frequent medical treatment for ulcers and a heart condition and was under the constant surveillance of law enforcement. For a while in the early 1960s he helped organize the skimming of profits from Las Vegas casinos for himself and others. He also arranged for the sale of his Las Vegas casino interests.

In May 1929 Lansky had married Anne Citron; they had three children (one son was physically handicapped). Anne Lansky increasingly soured on the marriage and divorced him in February 1947. In December 1948 Lansky entered into a happier marriage with Thelma "Teddy" Schwartz. Teddy had one child from a previous marriage, but she and Lansky had no children together. During World War II he assisted the U.S. government in contacting the imprisoned Luciano in order to secure his aid in having the New York waterfront unions guard against German sabotage. Although he was not an observant Jew, Lansky recognized a responsibility to Jewish causes and, after the war, gave money to aid the Israeli fight for independence. Frustrated by what he saw as U.S. government persecution, he moved to Israel in 1970 and applied for citizenship. By the time his application was finally denied in 1972, he faced several indictments in the United States. Leaving Israel on a long and highly publicized international plane trip, he sought asylum in Paraguay but wound up back in the United States. Over the next few years, he underwent a number of federal trials as well as heart bypass surgery. By 1976, he had beaten all charges and then went into retirement in Miami Beach. His medical and legal expenses, combined with the costs of caring for his increasingly handicapped son, drained much of the money he had acquired from selling his interests in Las Vegas casinos. After his death in a hospital in West Miami, the trust fund he had left for his wife and son proved to be almost worthless.

Lansky's importance derives from the central role he played among a group of criminal entrepreneurs, often ex-bootleggers from the 1920s, who developed illegal casino gambling in a number of American resort areas and who played a critical role in launching Las Vegas as the fastest-growing American city after World War II. It required considerable skill to assemble the capital required to start casinos, to negotiate deals with police and politicians, to hire and supervise a staff so that the casino would not go bankrupt through embezzlement, and to make wealthy customers feel at home while gambling. Although Lansky was often in the news because of a false perception that he was a money manager for an Italian-American mafia, he is properly understood as an independent entrepreneur whose reputation for business acumen and reliability encouraged others to invest in his projects. By the time he died, his world had vanished; the illegal casinos were gone, replaced in Las Vegas, Atlantic City, and other locations with legal casinos to feed America's fascination with gambling.

M.H.H.

Nathan Leopold, 19, far right, and Richard Loeb, 18, second from right, are seen during their arraignment in a Cook County courtroom with attorney Clarence Darrow, left, in July 1924.

NATHAN FREUDENTHAL LEOPOLD JR.
[19 NOVEMBER 1904–29 OR 30 AUGUST 1971]

AND RICHARD ALBERT LOEB
[11 JUNE 1905–28 JANUARY 1936]

The murder was sensational, not least of all because of who the killers turned out to be. They were children not only of enormous privilege, the sons of wealthy parents, but were gifted as well with towering intellects. After experimenting with minor crime, they decided to elevate lawbreaking to the level of an art form, kidnapping and murdering a boy they had nothing against, in the hope of ransom money they didn't need. They left clues at the crime scene and had an unconvincing alibi.

It took all the resources of the country's foremost courtroom wizard to keep them out of the electric chair, and the public howled when he pulled it off, contending that the boys' lives had been bought for them by their rich Jewish parents. The case had a sufficient hold on the popular imagination to make Meyer Levin's novel, Compulsion, *a best-seller thirty-two years after the murder, and two decades after Dickie Loeb's death in prison. (It was, not incidentally, a very good piece of work; it's been more than forty years since I read it, but I suspect it holds up well.)*

Loeb was probably a sociopath, Nathan Leopold a victim of his friend's unhealthy influence. Leopold blossomed in prison, and the extent of his rehabilitation would seem to argue that Clarence Darrow's efforts in sparing his life were not without value.

N athan Freudenthal Leopold Jr. and Richard Albert Loeb, criminals, were both born in Chicago, Illinois. Leopold was the son of Nathan Leopold, millionaire box manufacturer, and Florence Foreman; Loeb of Albert H. Loeb, the vice president of Sears, Roebuck and Company, and Anna Bohnen. As a child and young man, "Babe" Leopold enjoyed the customary comforts and advantages that derive from wealthy parentage. Yet he also suffered from glandular disorders that may have contributed to his psychological problems. Endowed with great intelligence—Clarence Darrow would claim that Leopold possessed "the most brilliant intellect I have ever met in a boy"—he early developed a passion for natural sciences, especially botany and ornithology. Like many other intellectually alert young persons of his time, he was also drawn to the philosophy of Friedrich Nietzsche. In 1923 at age eighteen he became the youngest graduate in the University of Chicago's history. In the ensuing months he studied for and passed the requisite entrance examination for the Harvard Law School, which he planned to enter in the fall of 1924. Loeb had graduated from the University of Michigan, also at age eighteen, the youngest graduate in the history of that institution, and was also planning to study law in the months ahead. Instead, the two friends were arrested on 31 May 1924 for the cold-blooded murder of fourteen-year-old Robert Franks in what soon came to be called "the crime of the century."

Unprepossessing in looks and demeanor, Leopold had met the more attractive, even wealthier, and much more self-assured "Dickie" Loeb while both were in their early teens. Although Leopold was the older of the two by nearly a year, he worshipped Loeb as a sort of Nietzschean superman. For several years, largely through the urgings of Loeb, the two committed petty crimes and misdemeanors but escaped apprehension. In late 1923 they began to plot a "perfect" crime that would involve kidnapping, ransom, and murder, although Leopold was reluctant to go as far as killing someone.

On the afternoon of 21 May 1924, Leopold and Loeb, after having rejected several prospective victims, lured Bobby Franks into their rented car. Since the Leopold and Loeb families were neighbors and friends of his own wealthy family, Franks was not suspicious. While Leopold was driving the car, Loeb suddenly killed the unsuspecting Franks with a chisel. They buried their victim near some deserted railroad tracks and later that evening called his parents, assuring them that their son was safe and that ransom instructions would follow. They did not receive the money, however, and the naked body of Bobby Franks was discovered the next day. A week later authorities arrested them largely because a pair of Leopold's glasses was found at the scene of the crime and the alibi the two had used was faulty. (The chauffeur for the Leopold family disputed the murderers' account of the whereabouts of Nathan's car on the day of the murder and also told authorities that he had seen the two friends trying to eradicate some red matter from the interior of the car the next day.)

The families of Leopold and Loeb retained Clarence Darrow, the nation's most famous trial lawyer, to defend their sons. Their guilt was never in serious question: both had confessed not long after their arrest. (Loeb briefly contended that Leopold had perpetrated the murder.) But their sixty-seven-year-old lawyer was determined to save their lives. Long an adamant foe of the death penalty, Darrow chose not to risk trial by jury for fear that the publicity and anger surrounding the crime would doom his clients. Instead, when the trial began on 24 July 1924, he entered a plea of guilty for them and asked for mitigation on the grounds that the defendants, while not insane, were mentally abnormal. Both the prosecution and the defense subpoenaed numerous witnesses, including psychiatrists. On 10 September Judge John R. Caverly rendered his decision. Announcing that he was moved more by the defendants' age than by other arguments, he sentenced them each to life imprisonment and ninety-nine years for the respective crimes of murder and kidnapping.

Between 1924 and 1958, Nathan Leopold remained incarcerated, occasionally at the Illinois State Penitentiary at Joliet, but mainly at nearby Stateville. During these years he received regular visits from family members. He also continued to see Loeb, until the latter's murder in early 1936 by a fellow prisoner who claimed that Loeb had made homosexual advances. More importantly, Leopold managed to fill these years with a variety of projects. He studied languages (including hieroglyphics), mathematics, and physics. (While involved with the last he wrote to Albert Einstein for advice on how best to study the subject; he received a reply that contained suggested readings.) Additionally, Leopold, who admitted that he had only begun to feel genuine remorse for his crime after serving some time in prison, worked zealously to benefit others. He brought organization to the Stateville library, for instance, and encouraged fellow inmates to pursue their education. At one point he learned Braille in order to teach it to a young inmate. During the mid-1930s he helped with an ambitious statistical study for predicting recidivism among parolees. Published as *Predicting Criminality* (1936), by Ferris F. Laune, a Stateville prison official, it drew recognition from both sociologists and criminologists. (Leopold originally was to be cited as coauthor, but the notoriety surrounding Loeb's murder earlier that year altered the decision.) During World War II, when fighting in the Pacific theater of operations raised public concern about malaria, Leopold immersed himself, both as a volunteer subject and as a technician, in an Army project that ultimately yielded pentaquine, one of the cures for the disease. A decade later, he wrote *Life plus 99 Years* (1958), an autobiography that recounted the Franks murder and subsequent trial but focused primarily on his prison experiences.

As the years went by, Leopold hoped that his exemplary prison record might earn him parole or a pardon from the state governor. After several rejections, however, he began to fear that "the crime of the century" would never be forgotten, thanks to periodic bouts of publicity about the event, most notably Meyer Levin's *Compulsion* (1956), an enormously popular fictionalized account of the crime. Nonetheless, in 1958 Leopold's fifth attempt at securing parole proved successful. Moving to Puerto Rico, he spent his remaining years most notably as the administrator of the island's sole leprosy hospital. In 1961 he married Trudi Feldman Garcia de Quevado, the widow of a local physician. Leopold died in San Juan.

R.M.

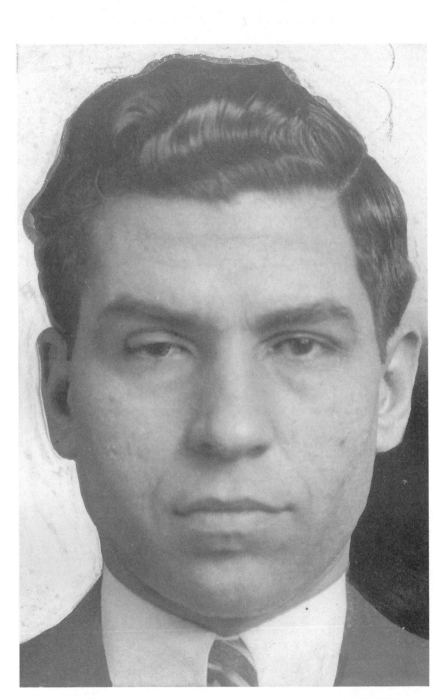

A scar from a knife wound contributed to Lucky Luciano's sinister appearance in this 1935 photo.

LUCKY LUCIANO

[11 NOVEMBER 1897–26 JANUARY 1962]

I think what I like most about Lucky Luciano is the way he got his name. He started out using it as an alias, then adopted it in earnest when he realized it was easier for the cops to pronounce. How many criminals would show that much consideration for the players on the other team?

Luciano has been called "the man who organized organized crime," and not without justification. The structure in which twenty or so crime "families" divvied up the country and cooperated with one another transformed American criminal enterprise along lines that exist to this day.

Luciano lived well and in style, with a suite at the Waldorf, until Dewey's investigation brought him down on what was probably a bogus charge of pimping. His service during World War II may or may not have been of considerable value—opinions differ—but it wasn't enough to keep him from being deported, and he spent the rest of his life longing to return to the States.

Toward the end, an American reporter interviewed him in Naples, asking him if he'd do things differently if given a second chance. "I'd do it legal," Luciano told him. "I learned too late that you need just as good a brain to make a crooked million as an honest million. These days you apply for a license to steal from the public. If I had my time again, I'd make sure I got that license first."

Lucky Luciano, founder of the Mafia in the United States, was born Salvatore Lucania in Lercara Friddi, Sicily, the son of Antonio Lucania, a miner and day laborer, and Rosalia Capporelli. Luciano's family immigrated to the United States in 1906 and settled on the Lower East Side of Manhattan. His attendance in school was erratic, and he was sent to a special school for truants in Brooklyn for two months in 1914. After his release, he dropped out of school with the equivalent of five years of education and became a delivery boy for a hat manufacturer—his only legitimate employment.

In June 1916 Luciano was arrested, pleaded guilty to opium trafficking, and was sentenced to one year in prison. After his release, Luciano formed a gang with Frank Costello, Meyer Lansky, Benjamin Siegel, Joe Adonis, and Vito Genovese to rob pawnshops, moneylenders, and banks on the Lower East Side. During Prohibition, the gang's fortunes grew dramatically. Luciano entered the bootlegging business with the financial backing and patronage of Arnold Rothstein, whose mythic reputation included unfounded claims that he had fixed the 1919 World Series. Luciano reinvested his bootlegging profits in a variety of other illegal enterprises, including labor racketeering and gambling. Luciano's rising fortunes gained the attention of New York's two Sicilian crime bosses, Giuseppe Masseria and Salvatore Maranzano, both of whom wanted a share of his bootlegging business. In 1927 Luciano sided with Masseria, becoming his chief lieutenant. It was while working for Masseria that Lucania, also called Charlie, adopted the names Lucky and Luciano. In the fall of 1928 he was arrested for robbery and used the alias Luciano. When he discovered that the police had less trouble pronouncing the alias than his real name, he adopted Luciano. The following year he was abducted, badly beaten, and left for dead in a deserted part of Staten Island. His wounds included a knife scar across his face that caused his eye to droop and gave him a sinister appearance. Because Luciano was the only person ever known to have survived the gangland ritual of being "taken for a ride," he adopted the nickname Lucky. Luciano never revealed the details of the incident, although many speculated that his attackers included Maranzano.

In 1931 Luciano seized on the growing rivalry between Masseria and Maranzano to enlarge his own power base. During the so-called Castellammarese wars, Luciano arranged the murders of both Masseria and Maranzano. He then took over the Italian underworld, setting up a syndicate that later became mythologized as the Mafia. In fact, Luciano's empire consisted of a series of informal relationships and business dealings with other underworld figures, mostly limited to gambling and part ownership in clubs at Sarasota Springs, rather than the formal structure described by law enforcement officials, who labeled him the "boss of bosses."

The first law enforcement official who had a vested interest in portraying Luciano as the nation's leading crime boss was Thomas E. Dewey, who in 1935 was appointed a special district attorney in Manhattan. Dewey launched his reputation as the nation's most fearless racket buster by prosecuting Luciano in 1936 for running a prostitution ring. Although the evidence was weak and Dewey's techniques were questionable, he won a conviction because of the charged atmosphere of the era. Luciano was given a thirty-to-fifty-year sentence, the longest for that type of crime in New York State history.

World War II broke out while Luciano was serving his sentence at the Dannemora prison in upstate New York. Naval intelligence authorities, concerned about German espionage along the docks of New York City, sought Luciano's help in gathering information among dockworkers. Luciano was transferred to the state penitentiary at Comstock near Albany so that he could consult with his allies, including Joseph "Socks" Lanza, the labor racketeer who controlled the Fulton Fish Market. The most visible success of the underworld operation was the arrest in June 1942 of eight German agents, who had been landed by U-boats. The agents had explosives, $170,000 in cash, and maps and plans for a two-year attack on defense plants, railroads, and bridges along the East Coast. Luciano also provided names of sources who helped the Allied invasion forces in Sicily. All this was later denied by the U.S. government for political reasons.

In exchange for Luciano's cooperation with the navy, Dewey, who had since become New York's governor, granted him executive clemency. Luciano, who never became a U.S. citizen, was deported to Italy on 10 February 1946. A year later he moved to Cuba, where Lansky and other allies owned gambling casinos. Federal authorities, led by U.S. Bureau of Narcotics director Harry Anslinger, pressured Cuban authorities to send Luciano back to Italy, which they did in March 1947. Anslinger claimed that Luciano was a major drug trafficker who hoped to use Cuba as a base for shipping heroin into the United States. Anslinger continued to insist that Luciano headed an international drug syndicate that shipped heroin into the United States, but Luciano was never tried on the charges.

Luciano died in Naples. Some newspapers claimed he had married Iges Lissoni, a dancer, in 1949, but the evidence for that remains questionable. Luciano's siblings brought his body back to the United States and interred it in the family vault at St. John's Cemetery in Queens in February 1962.

Luciano's importance stems in part from his larger-than-life persona as the founder and supposed head of the Mafia in the United States. In fact, organized crime always has been loosely structured, localized, and more ethnically diverse than the stereotypes suggest. Sicilians were just one ethnic group involved in organized crime, as Luciano's own links with Jews, such as Lansky and Siegel, indicate. Chroniclers also have credited Luciano with being the first crime boss to create modern rackets, organized along corporate lines with layers of middlemen. In fact, the trend toward modernization began much earlier. Rothstein, for example, organized his gambling and bootlegging operations using business techniques before Luciano. Still, Luciano and his partners furthered these trends, in part because of the fortunes they amassed during Prohibition. In the process, they created powerful crime syndicates that also played an important part in the nation's folklore.

M.M.S.

Ebenezer Mackintosh helped lead the Stamp Act riots in 1765.

EBENEZER MACKINTOSH

[20 JUNE 1737–1816]

To the victors belong more than the spoils. They get to write the history, and their perspective not only determines whether one is deemed a patriot or a traitor, but also transforms episodes of thuggery into acts of heroism.

Ebenezer Mackintosh has been largely forgotten by history—although New Hampshire has a highway marker to memorialize him. Its legend reads

"Born in Boston and a veteran of the 1758 Battle of Ticonderoga. As a known participant in the Boston Tea Party, for his own and his children's safety, he walked to North Haverhill in early 1774. He later served in Northern Army under Gen. Gates in 1777. He was a shoemaker by trade and practiced his vocation here for the rest of his life. He is buried nearby in Horse Meadows Cemetery." A more careful look at the record suggests he was a roughneck and a rabble-rouser, not vastly different from the troublemakers who started the 1863 Draft Riot in New York.

Then again, stripped of its historical context, the glorious Boston Tea Party looks like little more than an exercise in petty vandalism, while the indignities of the Stamp Act mob appear pointlessly brutish and wanton and violent. Yet there might well have been no American Revolution without such acts, and such men.

Ebenezer Mackintosh, shoemaker and mob leader, was born in Boston, Massachusetts, the son of Moses Mackintosh, who served on occasion as a soldier during the 1730s and 1740s, and Mary Everet. The family name has also been spelled MacIntosh, McIntosh, and McKintosh. Mary died in 1751, and Moses left town, leaving young Ebenezer in the care of his uncle Ichabod Jones, a shoemaker to whom he was apprenticed. Ebenezer enrolled in the militia in 1754 and served on the British-colonial expedition to Fort Ticonderoga in 1758.

In 1760 the young cordwainer joined Fire Engine Company No. Nine in Boston's South End. In that capacity he rose to be leader of the South End Mob, which each year on 5 November—Guy Fawkes Day or "Pope's Day"—fought with the rival North End Mob over their respective effigies of the Pope, which the winners burned. The riot of 1764 was unusually violent, resulting in many injuries and the death of a young boy whose head was crushed by a cart bearing a "pope." Mackintosh and others were arrested but never tried, their bonds provided by members of the Loyal Nine, a political club that soon played a key role in Boston's revolutionary movement as a liaison between the crowd and upper- and middle-class groups like merchants' associations and the Sons of Liberty. In addition to escaping punishment for the Pope's Day violence, in 1765 Mackintosh was elected sealer of leather, an unpaid town office. Eager to ensure crowd leaders' loyalty to the cause, former tax collector Samuel Adams sued the shoemaker for approximately £12 in back taxes in July 1765, perhaps to remind Mackintosh that he needed the patriots to keep him out of legal trouble. The debt was not collected.

Mackintosh more than repaid the debt by his leadership of the Stamp Act mobs. On 14 August 1765 he probably headed the mob that pulled down a small building that Andrew Oliver, recently chosen stamp master of the province, had erected on Oliver's Wharf. Oliver was then compelled to declare that he would not exercise his office. Twelve days later, Mackintosh was present when a mob destroyed the Boston mansion of Lieutenant Governor Thomas Hutchinson, forcing him to flee for his life, dismantling his possessions, stealing his money, and scattering his collection of manuscripts and his uncompleted history of Massachusetts in the streets. The offices and residences of customs officials William Story and Benjamin Hallowell were also vandalized. Historians have disputed whether Mackintosh and his fellows acted autonomously, moving beyond the orderly protests favored by leading citizens, or whether upper and lower orders acted in tandem, as Loyal Nine member and merchant Henry Bass suggested when he wrote: "We do everything in order to keep this . . . private, and are not a little pleased to hear that Mackintosh has the credit of the whole affair" (Massachusetts Historical Society, *Proceedings* 44 [1910–1911]: 609). In any case, prominent Whigs prevented Suffolk County sheriff Stephen Greenleaf from holding Mackintosh after his arrest by promising that order could be maintained in Boston, but only if Mackintosh were free.

Later that year, the North and South End mobs, led by "General" Mackintosh, combined forces to parade rather than riot, discarding their popes for effigies of contemporary representatives of tyranny such as the Earl of Bute and George Grenville, author of the Stamp Act. In December Oliver's written resignation as stamp master being deemed insufficient, Mackintosh and his followers escorted Oliver to the Liberty Tree and forced him to abjure his office publicly. Observers noted that the town militia refused to protect Oliver and that many of them marched in the procession headed by Mackintosh, "arm in arm" with Colonel William Brattle, the militia's commander.

Mackintosh, it seems, could command a crowd with a whisper or gesture, and, in order to demonstrate the popular will, sometimes marched as many as 2,000 people in orderly, quiet files past the general court while it sat. Peter Oliver, Andrew's brother, fellow loyalist, and justice of the superior court, remarked that Mackintosh was "sensible and manly" and, referring to the town's radical leaders, said he "performed their dirty jobs for them with great éclat." Lieutenant Governor Hutchinson termed him "a bold fellow and as likely for a Massianello [a Sicilian revolutionary] as you can well conceive. When there is occasion to hang or burn effigies or pull houses these [the "rabble"] are employed" (Hutchinson to Thomas Pownall, 8 Mar. 1766, Massachusetts Archives 26: 207–14).

However, though the town meeting again elected him sealer of leather in 1766, 1767, and 1768, Mackintosh by 1769 had been eclipsed as a crowd leader. The reasons are unclear, but George Mason, a British informer, suggested his relationship with the revolutionary leadership had soured. Because Mackintosh knew "more of their Secret Transactions than the whole of what they call the Torys put together," Mason claimed that leaders of the Sons of Liberty had "threatened [Mackintosh] with Death in case he should inform" (quoted in George Pomeroy Anderson, "A Note on Ebenezer Mackintosh," pp. 360–61). Mackintosh was not reelected sealer of leather in 1769, spent time in debtors' prison the following year, and eventually disappeared. Peter Oliver thought him dead. In fact he had moved to Haverhill, New Hampshire, where he was living by September 1774. He served that town in his old position as sealer of leather (1782–1784), having enlisted for two months in the army to oppose British General John Burgoyne's invasion of New York in 1777.

Mackintosh had married Elizabeth Maverick in August 1766; his seventeen-year-old brother-in-law, Samuel, was one of the Boston Massacre's victims in 1770. The couple had two children, one of whom, Paschal (or

Pasquale) Paoli, was named for the Corsican freedom fighter then leading his ethnically Italian island in revolt against the French. Elizabeth died in 1784; Mackintosh subsequently married a widow, Elizabeth Chase, with three children. Three more children followed. A number of Mackintosh's progeny moved to Ohio. At age sixty-five, he walked there and back to visit them. In old age he claimed to have led the Boston Tea Party, which is unlikely, given his earlier rift with the patriots, but not impossible. Ironically, this fighter for liberty had to sell his services to the overseer of the Haverhill poor farm in 1810–1811 in order to survive. When he died in Haverhill, New Hampshire, he was buried in the local cemetery, where he is erroneously identified as Philip McIntosh and credited with leading the Boston Tea Party.

An obscure shoemaker who briefly made history in 1765 and 1766, Mackintosh's leadership shaped crowd violence in pre-revolutionary Boston. Called a dupe by the loyalists, he nevertheless seems to have been a sincerely committed patriot, as the naming of his son in 1770 suggested. Director and symbol of the lower-class Bostonians without whom the American Revolution would never have occurred, he deserved better than the poverty and mislabeled tombstone that marked the end of his days.

W.P.

Owney Madden leaves the District Attorney's office in New York City, 1934.

OWEN VICTOR MADDEN

[1891–24 APRIL 1965]

What I find most interesting about the career of Owney Madden is the way he managed to retire from it. In his Hell's Kitchen days, warring with the Hudson Dusters and terrorizing anyone who made the mistake of hitting on a girl who interested him, Madden seems to have been a murderous hothead with poor impulse control. Before he was forty years old, he relocated to Hot Springs, Arkansas, where he lived for another thirty-plus years without getting into trouble with the law. You'd think the man would have to have had some sort of conversion experience to manage such a transformation.

Well, maybe not. Few would contend that Owney steered clear of criminal activity in Hot Springs, only that he stayed out of trouble. In those years, Hot Springs was an easy place to avoid trouble, if you were well-connected and stayed out of the limelight. Still, he enjoyed a comfortable and serene retirement rarely achieved in his line of work.

There's a clue in a journal he wrote out for a New York newsman who asked him how he got through the days. Here's what he wrote:

"Thursday. Went to a dance in the afternoon. Went to a dance at night and then to a cabaret. Took some girls home. Went to a restaurant and stayed there until 7 Friday morning.

"Friday. Spent the day with Freda Horner. Looked at some fancy pigeons. Met some friends in a saloon early in the evening and stayed with them until 5 in the morning.

"Saturday. Slept all day. Went to a dance in the Bronx late in the afternoon, and to a dance on Park Avenue at night.

"Sunday. Slept until 3. Went to a dance in the afternoon and another in the same place at night. After that I went to a cabaret. . . ."

Clearly the fellow had a knack for amusing himself. If he could kick back and relax like this while he was busy killing people in New York, retirement in Hot Springs must have come easy to him.

·

Owen Victor Madden, criminal entrepreneur, was born in Leeds, England, the son of Irish immigrants Francis Madden, a factory laborer, and Mary (maiden name unknown). After Madden's father died, in 1902 his mother moved the family to New York, where they settled in the West Side Irish slum area known as Hell's Kitchen. As a teenager Madden became an archetypal delinquent, combining mugging, burglary, and racketeering with gang battles to build a reputation as a fearsome street fighter. First as a member and then a leader of the Gophers, a major Irish gang in Hell's Kitchen, Madden's skill with firearms earned him the nickname "The Killer." He was responsible for at least three murders by 1914. Madden was one of several New York City street toughs who managed to build successful careers in bootlegging and entertainment (including nightclubs, prizefighting, and gambling) during the first half of the twentieth century. While still a gang member he married Dorothy Roberts in 1911. A daughter was born before they separated in 1913. They were divorced in 1934.

Although members of the Gophers enjoyed a degree of protection from Tammany Hall because of their help in winning elections on the West Side, the gang's notoriety eventually was its undoing. Madden's personal immunity ended in 1915 with his conviction on a charge of first-degree manslaughter. Sentenced to serve ten to twenty years, Madden's good behavior while in Sing Sing prison earned him an early release in 1923.

Madden had missed the early days of Prohibition, but a combination of good luck, a shrewd business sense, and a reputation as an honest man (among his criminal peers) enabled him to build a very successful career in bootlegging and associated enterprises during the 1920s. Forming a long-term partnership with George Jean DeMange, another West Side street tough, Madden began his bootlegging career as a highjacker of other people's liquor supplies. He quickly moved on, however, to other areas in the business of bootlegging, joining a partnership with Bill Dwyer and Frank Costello that smuggled whiskey from England and rum from the West Indies into New York. He also established an illegal brewery to manufacture beer.

Unlike some of his criminal contemporaries, Madden also displayed a flair for legal and quasi-legal business activities. Bootleggers were avid customers for the numerous nightclubs that proliferated in New York during the 1920s, a fact that Madden used to his advantage. In a partnership with DeMange and Arnold Rothstein (a major underworld figure of the era), Madden bought a nightclub in Harlem called the Club DeLuxe. Renaming it the Cotton Club, Madden turned it into one of the era's most famous entertainment centers. By the end of the 1920s Madden owned interests in several other major nightclubs, and he had become an important bene- factor in show business, sponsoring figures such as George Raft, Mae West, and Duke Ellington.

Madden simultaneously pursued another passion, prizefighting. During the 1920s he invested in partnerships that controlled the careers of five championship boxers, including Primo Carnera and Maxie Rosenbloom, both of whom became world champions.

Madden's connections with Hot Springs, Arkansas, which would become the focus of his post-Prohibition career, began in the spring of 1931. He had come under increasing scrutiny from diverse law enforcement agen- cies, including Judge Samuel Seabury, who was investigating corruption in New York City, and the New York State Parole Board, which was under political pressure to investigate whether or not Madden had violated the terms of his parole. These inquiries into his affairs may have prompted Madden to think of safer places to conduct his business, and Hot Springs had a long-deserved reputation for providing political protection to its local gambling and prostitution entrepreneurs who catered to the town's many tourists. On this first visit he met Agnes Demby, the daughter of the local postmaster, in her tourist shop. Madden and Demby married in 1934; they had no children.

In the summer of 1932 the parole board sent Madden back to Sing Sing for a year. After his release, he launched a new career as an investor in major gambling operations, following an emerging national pattern among for- mer bootleggers. He moved to Hot Springs, where he became the local rep- resentative of an investment syndicate composed of himself, Frank Costello, and probably Meyer Lansky in several Hot Springs casinos. Madden also invested in race tracks in California and Florida.

The remainder of his career was comparatively peaceful and, no doubt, profitable. A steady stream of entertainment and underworld friends visiting from Hollywood, New York, and Chicago guaranteed his local celebrity status and helped sustain Hot Springs's reputation as a major tourist attraction through the mid-1940s. He also spent considerable time cultivating a good reputation with the local citizens through charitable contributions. In the early 1940s he became a U.S. citizen.

Beginning in 1947, a decade-long struggle between reformers and corrupt politicians made prosperity somewhat more difficult and less predictable for Hot Springs's underworld, but Madden proved adroit at maintaining good relations with whomever happened to be in charge of local government.

In the late 1950s the slow decline of Hot Springs as a tourist attraction combined with national indignation over corrupt relations between the underworld and local politicians to force Madden out of business. Like many of his former bootlegger peers, Madden was getting old; his generation was passing from the scene, and it probably did not require much thought for him to decide to retire. He sold his remaining gambling interests in 1961 and spent the remaining four years of his life quietly in Hot Springs, where he died.

Although Madden never gained national notoriety of the sort associated with men like Bugsy Siegel or Frank Costello, he exemplified a particular kind of criminal entrepreneur. Criminals like Madden, who had reputations for toughness and honesty, built very successful careers by satisfying public demands for legal and illegal entertainment during and after Prohibition.

D.R.J.

SAMUEL MASON

[C. 1750–JULY 1803]

Because most of what I know about the early years of the American Republic I learned in elementary and high school, I had no idea what a hazardous place the frontier was. Wild animals were the least of it; predatory humans, of the sort to be found hiding out in Cave-in-Rock, were a far greater danger.

Micajah and Wiley Harpe (Big Harpe and Little Harpe respectively) were brothers, North Carolina Tories who headed west after the Revolution, preying on settlers and travelers in the Mississippi Valley. They were bearded giants dressed in buckskin, wearing scalps on their belts and much given to swooping down on passersby, screaming, "We are the Harpes!" and butchering all within reach. When a posse trapped them in 1799, Wiley escaped; Micajah was shot down and his head sawn off while he was still alive. The posse members carried off his head, perhaps in hope of a reward, but wound up boiling it for soup one night when rations ran low. They nailed his skull to a tree and it stayed there for years.

According to some sources, the "John Setton" who brought in the head of Samuel Mason was actually Wiley Harpe. Others identify him as a bounty hunter named Bill Setton, and maintain that hanging him as Harpe was yet another miscarriage of frontier justice, as Little Harpe continued preying on the local populace for several years, until he disappeared and was presumably eaten by wolves.

They didn't teach me any of this in Mr. Green's eighth grade history class. . . .

Samuel Mason, outlaw and pirate, was born in Virginia of unknown parents. Virtually nothing is known of his early life, although historian Samuel Draper noted that he was "connected by ties of consanguinity with the distinguished Mason family of Virginia, and grew up bad from his boyhood." Mason first appeared in historical records during the American Revolution, during which he served as a captain in the militia

Cave-in-Rock, Illinois, was a known haven for Samuel Mason and other river pirates.

of Ohio County, Virginia (now West Virginia). He fought in several engagements against Native Americans in 1777 and served at Fort Henry in the upper Ohio Valley until the autumn of 1779. Retiring from active service, he retained his captaincy in the militia until at least May 1781 and apparently also ran a tavern in the vicinity of present-day Wheeling, West Virginia.

Prosperous enough by this time to own slaves, he had also begun a criminal career at some time prior to the war by stealing horses in Frederick County, Virginia. Following the Revolution, he drifted down to what is today eastern Tennessee and occupied (in squatter fashion) some cabins belonging to General John Sevier. There Mason and a band of companions apparently engaged in petty thievery and otherwise made such a nuisance of themselves that Sevier summarily evicted them. By 1787 Mason was in western Kentucky, possibly to claim a land grant that was a reward for his wartime service. Although he had signed a petition in 1790 (along with 114 other "respectable citizens") urging the creation of Logan County in what is today southwestern Kentucky, his veneer of respectability was apparently insufficient to sustain him in the community, and by 1794 he had removed to Henderson, Kentucky, where he dwelt among "horse thieves, rogues, and outlaws." In 1795 a disagreement between Mason and the local constable, John Dunn, led to Mason (with four others) physically attacking Dunn in ambush and leaving him for dead. While making his headquarters in Henderson County, Mason, his family, and his gang also stole slaves and were parties to at least one murder.

By 1797 Mason and his ensemble had moved once again, to Cave-in-Rock, Illinois. A large natural cave that overlooked the Ohio River in Hardin County, Illinois, the site was long noted as a haven for criminals as well as a temporary shelter for travelers. Numerous river pirates preyed on the slow-moving flatboats that brought settlers and supplies down the river during the period, and Mason ranked among the most successful of the lot. Operating under the alias of Wilson, he opened "Wilson's Liquor Vault and House for Entertainment" in the cave to lure unsuspecting passersby. The site offered an excellent long-distance view of the river in both directions, thereby giving Mason and his associates early warning of both potential victims and militias sent to curtail Mason's activity. Some flatboats were lured to shore by the use of a man or woman (posing as a stranded settler) hailing the boats from the riverbank as they passed. While some of the captured crewmen were killed to ensure their silence, Mason always promoted himself as a robber who only killed when necessary. As a result he frequently forced his victims to join his gang in lieu of murdering them.

Ever restless and fearing the repercussions that were likely to follow his growing notoriety, Mason moved his operation southward, establishing a base on Wolf Island in the Mississippi River (about twenty-five miles south of the mouth of the Ohio). In March 1800 he applied for and received a passport to the Spanish-held western bank of the Mississippi in New

Madrid, Missouri. This passport, he hoped, not only would allow him to purchase land in Spanish-held territory but also would allow him to concentrate his operations on the eastern (American) side of the river and use the western bank as a safe haven. In the latter part of his career Mason continued to rob riverboats on the Mississippi and also turned highwayman by expanding his operations to the Natchez Trace. Using agents in places like Natchez to inform him concerning movements of mule trains on the trace, Mason plundered trade moving through the two major thoroughfares of the Mississippi Valley.

Mason's continued notoriety led to his capture at Little Prairie, Missouri (about thirty miles south of New Madrid), in January 1803. Along with his four sons, a daughter-in-law, three grandchildren, and a man with several aliases (John Taylor, John Setton, and Wells), he was questioned at length by the Spanish commandant Don Henri Peyroux de la Coudreniere. Don Henri then sent the band under guard to his superior in New Orleans, Intendant Manuel Salcedo. After arriving downriver, the gang was questioned by Salcedo. Although unable to prove any criminal activity within Spanish territory, the intendant suspected that infractions had been committed on the American side, and arrangements were made to turn Mason over to the American authorities in Natchez. Leaving New Orleans by boat, the party traveled upriver until a broken mast forced a repair stop and provided Mason with his chance. On 26 March 1803 Mason grabbed a rifle from his captors and escaped with the rest of his band, with Captain Robert McCoy dying during the attempt from gunshot wounds. News of Mason's escape traveled quickly, and a reward of $1,000 was soon offered by the Americans for his recapture. Sometime in July 1803 Mason was killed by two members of his gang, John Setton and James May. The two men cut off Mason's head and attempted to collect the reward money in Mississippi but were recognized as members of the gang and were put on trial. During the trial it came to light that John Setton was actually the notorious Wiley "Little" Harpe, who with his reputed brother Micajah "Big" Harpe had cut a murderous swath through Kentucky and Tennessee several years earlier. Following the trial, the two men were executed by hanging on 8

February 1804 at Old Greenville (no longer in existence), Jefferson County, Mississippi. The disposition of Mason's gang is unclear, but he was survived by his wife (name and date of marriage unknown) and four sons.

During his years of operations on the Ohio and Mississippi rivers and the Natchez Trace, Mason was a widely known and feared individual. His gang made early journeys through these regions more perilous.

E.L.L.

Gaston Bullock Means was the co-author of a best-seller in 1930.

GASTON BULLOCK MEANS

[11 JULY 1879–12 DECEMBER 1938]

Gaston Means got through the First World War as a German spy and propagandist. Then he latched onto a rich widow, stole a good portion of her inheritance, and shot her in the head.

Then he turned bad.

What a remarkable swindler he was! He kept getting into trouble, and deservedly so, but it seemed to roll off him. Perhaps his most noteworthy feat came on the heels of a prison sentence. He collaborated with May Dixon Thacker, a True Confessions *writer whose brother, Thomas Dixon, wrote* The Klansman, *the novel D. W. Griffith filmed as* Birth of a Nation. *Together they produced a completely spurious work out of whole cloth that charged President Warren Harding's widow with having murdered her husband. Means, who never even met Mrs. Harding, claimed in the book to have served as her private investigator, breaking into Harding's mistress's apartment to steal diaries and love letters.*

Means had something to work with here. Harding died during a national speaking tour, ostensibly as a result of ptomaine poisoning from tainted crabmeat. No one else showed symptoms, not even an aide who shared the crab with the president, and Mrs. Harding was the only person with him when he died. She refused to allow an autopsy, and none was performed. (Try to imagine a president dying suspiciously today, and being interred without an autopsy. The mind boggles.)

So Means may have been on to something, but what he wrote was pure invention nevertheless. The book became a best-seller, but the hoax was soon discovered, and Means shrugged and moved on. His Lindbergh swindle reached new heights of chutzpah when he claimed the kidnapped infant of the famous aviator was still alive even after the grieving father had already identified his dead son.

Gaston Bullock Means, spy, swindler, and detective, was born in Blackwelder's Spring, North Carolina, the son of William Gaston Means, an attorney, and Corallie Bullock. Means grew up in Concord, North Carolina, in a family that had lost most of its considerable wealth during the Civil War. He left the University of North Carolina in 1900, early in his third year, and served for two years as the superintendent of the elementary schools in Stanly County, adjacent to Concord. In 1902 he took a job as a salesman for the Cannon textile mills, living in New York City and traveling widely. Means married Julie Patterson in 1913; two children would later be born to them. In 1914 he took a job in New York as an investigator with the William J. Burns detective agency. Before U.S. entry into World War I, Means served as a German spy, relaying information about armaments and ship movements. He was agent E-13 and reported directly to the assistant naval attaché at the German embassy in Washington, D.C. Means placed German agents in U.S. shipyards that were building submarines for shipment to England and France so that they could obtain information to demonstrate that the United States was violating neutrality laws. Means also served as a German propagandist, operating an organization he called the American Peace Society and circulating stories about Americans supplying British ships in New York harbor, also a violation of the neutrality statutes.

Means's subsequent career was marked by bizarre and sensational acts of skullduggery as well as by the probable murder of a millionaire heiress. In 1917 Maude King, the widow of a lumber baron, became the first major victim of Means's extraordinary ability to work his way into a person's confidence. Means's wife, before her marriage, had known King. When the acquaintance was renewed, Means began to gain the widow's confidence and to manage her finances. She apparently began to suspect that he had bled some $400,000 of her fortune for his own benefit. In August 1917 Means invited King to Concord, North Carolina, purchased a gun, allegedly for her, and took her on a barbecue outing that was to include rabbit hunting. Means's tale was that King was killed when she removed the loaded weapon from a tree limb where he had placed it and accidentally shot herself. Authorities in New York were convinced that Means had murdered King. They were, however, unable to have the trial transferred. A Concord jury acquitted Means, despite ballistic evidence that it was impossible for King to have shot herself in the back of her head. In part, the jury appears to have been irritated by the presence in the courtroom of "Yankee" prosecutors monitoring the proceedings.

Despite this episode, William Burns appointed Means as an agent in 1921 when Burns was named head of the newly created Bureau of Investigation in the federal Department of Justice. Soon Means was shaking down criminal suspects, promising that for a payoff he would fix their cases. He also solicited bribes to have liquor released from federal warehouses. Often he failed to deliver on these promises, but his victims were in no position to protest formally. Though earning only $7 a day from the government, Means employed three servants in his house and went about in a chauffeur-driven Cadillac.

Means was suspended by the bureau in February 1922 but was employed by the Treasury Department as a customs agent. In March 1924, while under indictment for federal offenses, Means testified before the Senate committee investigating the conduct of the attorney general of the United States. He brought with him two huge accordion cases that allegedly contained diaries of his government work but that actually had recently been concocted with the assistance of several secretaries. When he later was asked to deliver his materials to the committee, he said that he had given three large suitcases and a trunk containing his records to persons who represented themselves as Senate sergeants-at-arms. Nothing was ever found, undoubtedly because it never existed.

In June 1924 the government began the much-delayed prosecution of Means for violations of Prohibition law. His conviction in this trial and a subsequent one for extortion led to a sentence of four years in prison. At the federal penitentiary in Atlanta, rather predictably, Means worked his way into the good graces of the warden and served his term in cozy quarters with privileges accorded only a few inmates.

Once out of prison, with the collaboration of May Dixon Thacker, a writer and the wife of a prominent southern evangelist, Means wrote a best-seller, *The Strange Death of President Harding* (1930), maintaining that Warren G. Harding had been poisoned by his wife (Florence Mabel Kling DeWolfe Harding) so that she could protect his reputation against allegations that when he was an Ohio newspaper publisher he had fathered a child with Nan Britton, a young admirer. The book is striking for its inventive genius and puts on display Means's talent for providing explicit details regarding trivial matters, such as clothing and house furnishings, and ostensibly verbatim quotations from people who were no longer alive. Such information, all secondhand, was intended to show the intimate connection Means enjoyed with the inner White House circle, though in truth he had never met Mrs. Harding. After authorities ridiculed the tale and Means could not supply the supporting documents he had claimed to possess, Thacker wrote, "with humiliation," that she had been duped by Means and that the book was a "colossal hoax."

When renowned aviator Charles Lindbergh's baby boy was kidnapped in 1932, Means thrust himself into that case by persuading Evalyn Walsh McLean, an extremely wealthy woman and a friend of the Lindberghs, that for $100,000 he would get the kidnappers to return the child. Subsequently, Means had a friend impersonate a gangster and demand another $4,000 from McLean. McLean traveled with Means to El Paso, Texas, to pick up the baby, but she reneged, fearing for her life, when he insisted that they proceed to Mexico to establish contact with the kidnappers, whom he said had become suspicious and left the United States. For stealing the $100,000, which never was recovered, Means was sentenced to ten years in prison and to an additional five years for extorting the $4,000.

Means's activities are often viewed as amusing episodes, perhaps because his victims, often shamefaced about their own gullibility, sought to downplay his thoroughly despicable behavior. Edwin P. Hoyt's biography of Means is titled *Spectacular Rogue* (1963), while a *New York Times* (15 May 1932) editorial portrayed him as "incurably romantic," noting, "He belongs to the half-world of facts and fancy, never knowing which is which." In her autobiography, McLean indulgently called Means "a fat and deeply dimpled scoundrel." But Means also can be seen as an unconscionable predator, meanly exploiting those whom he was able to ensnare in a web of deceit, and on at least one occasion he was very likely a cold-blooded murderer. In his tale of Harding's death, Means wrote that he was "entirely aware of the fact that I am regarded as a consummate liar" but then noted defensively that "it is difficult for the lay mind to distinguish between trained dissimulation and lying." Means often would lie even when it might be to his disadvantage to do so. In a later, even more frantic attempt to get attention, he claimed that he himself had kidnapped the Lindbergh baby. Means died at the Medical Center for Federal Prisoners in Springfield, Missouri, where he had been transferred from the federal penitentiary at Leavenworth, Kansas, to undergo a gallbladder operation.

G.G.

This engraving from an 1847 biography of John Murrell shows the legendary thief stealing a slave, a crime for which he was sentenced to ten years of hard labor.

JOHN ANDREWS MURRELL

[1806?–1 NOVEMBER 1844]

There is, as a reading of the following essay quickly reveals, very little that was noteworthy about John Murrell. He was a small-time criminal of no great distinction, jailed for ten years at age twenty-eight, and was dead of tuberculosis not long after his release. What's noteworthy is not what the man did but what was done with him. While Murrell set about being a model prisoner in Nashville, Virgil Stewart's fabrication spurred vigilante action that claimed dozens of lives.

Interesting, too, is how the legend persisted. Bloodletters and Badmen, *Jay Robert Nash's encyclopedia of American crime, tends to err somewhat on the side of legend, but in this instance Nash seems to have swallowed Stewart whole. He reports as fact conversations between the two men in*

which Murrell boasted of an extensive career of murder and robbery, and
his plans to form a slave army that would take over the city of New Orleans
and, eventually, the states of Louisiana and Mississippi. Through Stewart's
good offices Murrell was captured, whereupon "his abortive slave revolt
began without a leader and soon collapsed following a number of murders
along the Natchez Trace."

John Andrews Murrell, archcriminal according to legend but in reality a
minor thief, was born in Lunenburg County, Virginia, and raised from
infancy in Williamson County, Tennessee, the son of Jeffrey Murrell and
Zilpha Andrews, farmers. He was the third of eight children; his three brothers also became felons, and at least one sister married a criminal. The reasons for this moral collapse are obscure. Jeffrey Murrell was a respectable,
hard-working farmer who owned 146 acres and as many as three slaves.
His estate, however, was frittered away in court costs, confiscated bail money,
and other expenses connected to the villainy of his sons. Shortly after his
death in 1824 the family was reduced to penury.

Nothing is known of Murrell's education, but he was literate and wrote
in a fine copperplate script. He first ran afoul of the law at the age of sixteen and was in and out of difficulty thereafter. By the age of twenty-one
he had already served three years in jail for stealing a horse, for which he
was also whipped at the public pillory and ordered branded on the thumb.
In 1829 he married Elizabeth Mangham from a neighboring farm family,
and they had two children. By 1831, after first moving to Wayne County,
Murrell had shifted residence to Madison County near the tiny hamlet of
Denmark in western Tennessee, where he claimed to be a farmer but seems
to have continued to excel as a wastrel. There is good reason to believe
that he was an occasional counterfeiter, but it was for the crime of slave
stealing that he was sentenced to ten years hard labor in 1834. After one
attempt to escape he settled down and became a model prisoner at the
Nashville penitentiary, where it was reported that he found Jesus, learned
the blacksmith's trade, and contracted tuberculosis (not necessarily in

that order). He died of tuberculosis, and his body was interred at Pikeville, Tennessee, where he had worked quietly as a blacksmith during the six months between his release and his death. According to one story, his body was dug up after burial, the head removed for use as a carnival exhibit, and the remainder left to be eaten by hogs.

This historical Murrell bears little resemblance to the legendary figure who has occupied a place in standard reference works and been the subject of several popular histories and novels. The legendary Murrell was a demonic figure who, after he was whipped and jailed as a youth, swore vengeance against respectable society. He traveled widely, murdering, stealing, and making the acquaintance of desperate men like himself all over the South. Eventually, the legend continued, he presided over a criminal conspiracy that stretched from Maryland to Louisiana, the Mystic Clan of the Confederacy, whose members were bound together by horrid oaths. The clan's purpose was to provoke slave uprisings throughout the region. Taking advantage of the chaos, Murrell and a band of followers would steal as much money as possible and then escape as troops marched from the North to suppress the rebellion.

The legendary—and bogus—Murrell was the creation of Virgil A. Stewart, an informer (possibly Murrell's confederate) whose testimony had sent Murrell to prison for slave stealing. Shortly after the trial, a small pamphlet appeared; the author's name, Augustus Q. Walton, appears to have been a pseudonym for Stewart. It described the conspiracy of the Mystic Clan in lurid detail, promoted Murrell to the status of master criminal—"the Great Western Land Pirate"—and presented Stewart as the savior of the South because he had been instrumental in ending Murrell's career before the conspiracy had had a chance to develop (at great personal risk—the pamphlet described several harrowing attempts on Stewart's life by furious henchmen). Although Stewart's motives are obscure, they certainly included, in descending importance, large measures of self-justification, self-aggrandizement, and the hope of monetary gain.

The pamphlet was greeted with derision in west Tennessee, where Murrell was seen as a thieving nuisance but singularly ill-suited for the grandiose role of archfiend. It found a more receptive audience in the Delta region of Hinds and especially Madison County, Mississippi, where Stewart began hawking the pamphlet in June 1835. Cotton lands had been recently brought under cultivation by large gangs of slaves, plantations were scattered, settlements were few, and the white population, outnumbered and fearful, was particularly susceptible to tales of an insurrection conspiracy.

Convinced that Murrell's henchmen were determined to go ahead with the scheme despite their ringleader's imprisonment, whites in the area around Beattie's Bluff and Livingston in Madison County began an inquisition of slaves already identified as troublemakers. Under torture they implicated white men, virtually all of them outsiders or men of low status. So-called committees of safety were formed, and whippings and hangings began in earnest. Panic spread into neighboring counties and west to Louisiana, and patrols were stepped up over much of the South. Most of the killing occurred in Mississippi; seven white men were hanged by the committees of safety, and at least as many were murdered by spontaneous mobs. Several dozen were whipped and banished. The number of blacks who were hanged or otherwise killed can only be estimated but may have exceeded fifty. Gamblers, viewed as rootless and disreputable, also fell under suspicion. In Vicksburg five were hanged, and the rest were expelled; as July progressed, towns along the Mississippi River, from Cincinnati to New Orleans, were purged of the gaming fraternity.

Stewart claimed that Murrell had often expressed antislavery views as a way of gaining the confidence of slaves he intended to kidnap and then sell in other parts. The ruse acquired significance later in July 1835 when the Anti-Slavery Society began flooding the South with antislavery tracts. The entire regions responded as if threatened by foreign invasion. The mobbing of individuals who circulated the tracts and the mobbing of "Murelites" merged in the public mind, and Murrell acquired his true infamy. His career seemed to confirm the southern view that abolitionism was fraudulent while at the same time undermining the superior moral claims of antislavery proponents.

Little is known of Virgil A. Stewart, but his handiwork inspired one of the most bizarre outbreaks of mob violence in American history. Stewart's vogue was brief; even in the Mississippi Delta he was widely considered to be a charlatan a decade after the panic of the summer of 1835 had subsided. His creation, however, has lived on in popular histories and novels and standard reference works, including the *Dictionary of American Biography*.

J.L.P.

PHILIP MARIANO FAUSTO MUSICA

[12 MAY 1884–16 DECEMBER 1938]

Until he was almost forty years old, Philip Musica was a fairly ordinary sharp-ster, bribing customs agents, borrowing huge sums against worthless assets, and selling bootleg whiskey. Then he launched a swindle on such a grand scale and with so long a run of success that he essentially became respectable—until it all caught up with him.

In light of some of the corporate scandals of recent years, Musica looks less remarkable. He didn't leave hundreds of workers with worthless pensions, didn't bankrupt his stockholders. His acts were criminal, certainly, and his punishment assured, but I wonder if it wasn't depression more than a realis-tic assessment of his future prospects that led him to kill himself.

He was, it should be noted, almost obsessively neat about it. He shot himself in the bathroom of his Connecticut home, and was careful to position himself so that he would fall into the marble tub, thus leaving no bloodstains on the carpet.

Philip Mariano Fausto Musica, swindler, alias William Johnson and Frank Donald Coster, was born in New York City, the son of Antonio Musica, a barber, and Assunta Mauro, both recent immigrants from Naples, Italy. Musica attended public schools on the Lower East Side of Manhattan, where he was reportedly a good student with a somewhat depressive nature. After one or two years of attending high school, he left to help his father oper-ate a modest grocery store.

As A. Musica and Son, the small business began importing fine cheeses—a venture Philip promoted in hopes of earning large profits. Unwilling to wait for the family to accumulate enough wealth to live comfortably, the younger Musica began bribing New York customs agents to lessen the duties the business paid on its imports. In 1909 New York officials began con-ducting routine, periodic investigations of the customs offices, and Musica's fraudulent activities were discovered. He pleaded guilty in court in order

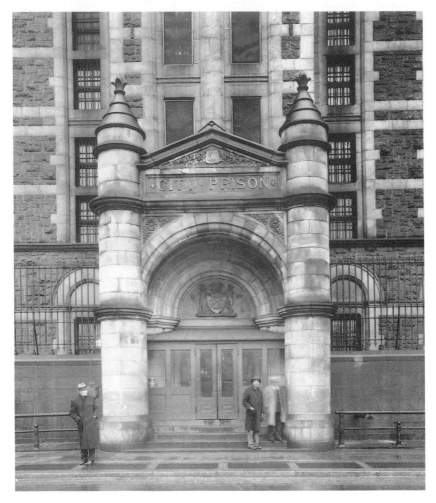

Philip Musica spent three years in the Tombs, a New York City jail, awaiting sentencing and spying on his fellow prisoners.

to protect his father from prosecution; he served five months of a one-year sentence at the Elmira Reformatory before family friends (including the Italian ambassador to the United States) pressured President William Howard Taft to commute the sentence.

Released from jail, Musica soon established the United States Hair Company, a firm that utilized his father's expertise as a barber. The company imported human hair, mainly from Italy and China, for use in the elaborate hair designs that were popular for women at the time. Musica's firm proved prosperous, and he took to dressing elegantly and to frequenting New York's best nightspots, particularly the Metropolitan Opera.

During the summer of 1912 Assunta Musica and her three youngest children visited Italy, where she collected poor-quality pieces of hair (chiefly barbers' scraps) and sent them to Philip in New York. By borrowing money against these fraudulent assets, Philip Musica generated huge profits for his family, amassing enough wealth to enter the United States Hair Company on the New York Stock Exchange (a dream of Philip's) in October 1912. However, in March 1913 another investigation at the New York customs offices revealed that the Musicas were guilty of falsifying their importing records.

Several days before investigators arrived on 17 March, the six family members living in the United States attempted to flee to Honduras, where extradition was difficult, if not impossible. Burns Detective agent Dan Lehon followed the Musicas to New Orleans, where they were apprehended with close to $70,000 in cash and $20,000 in jewels. The men were charged with grand larceny and tried on 11 April 1913; only Philip pleaded guilty, so that his father and brothers could go free. Philip Musica had in fact swindled some twenty-two New York–area banks out of $600,000 by repeatedly borrowing money against the fraudulent hair shipments from Italy.

Musica spent the next three years years awaiting sentencing at the Tombs in New York, where he became valuable to police authorities. He was found to be a careful and hardworking spy who reported on other prisoners' activities, including their conversations with their lawyers. When Musica was freed in March 1916, his entire family was reunited in a lavish home in the Bay Ridge section of Brooklyn. Soon thereafter, Musica began work as an investigator for the New York district attorney's office. He worked under the name William Johnson, uncovering acts of sedition and sabotage perpetrated by German spies in New York. The job came to an end in March, however, when Musica was found to have induced a witness to commit perjury in a trial concerning the murder of Barnet Baff. Musica jumped bail and spread a rumor that he had fled to South America and was killed there; in reality, he continued to reside in New York.

In 1920, as Frank Costa, Musica opened the Adelphi Pharmaceutical Manufacturing Company of Brooklyn with $8,000 borrowed from his mother, who mortgaged her property and pawned her jewels. The company purported to manufacture furniture polish and hair tonics, but it was primarily a bootleg liquor supplier. Musica's two partners in the firm were Mary and Guiseppe Brandino, a brother and sister who used rough business tactics and who blackmailed Musica for the remainder of his life (he paid them to conceal his true identity). In 1922 the Adelphi Company was closed when federal officials discovered that it was bootlegging liquor; it is believed that Musica anonymously turned in the company to dissolve his troubled partnership with the Brandinos.

Early in 1923 Musica, alias Frank D. Coster, began Girard and Company, a drug manufacturing firm in Mount Vernon, New York. Besides hiring a legitimate chemist with a Ph.D. from the University of Heidelberg, Musica also employed his brothers George and Robert. The company sold drugs legally and liquor illegally, reporting sales of $2 million in 1925. Musica hired Price, Waterhouse and Company as the firm's accountants, and he studied their reporting methods closely. He noted particularly that accountants checked company inventories only on paper, almost never entering warehouses; Musica later employed this knowledge in his most grandiose case of swindling.

By the spring of 1925, Musica was using the name F. Donald Coster and claiming to have earned a Ph.D. and an M.D. from the University of Heidelberg. He solicited the advice of an investment banker, Julian F. Thompson, and asked that Thompson show him how to build up Girard and Company's assets so that it could be listed on the New York Stock Exchange. Thompson, who worked for Musica's company (first as an adviser, later as an employee) for the rest of his life, was impressed with Musica's dedication, diligence, and ingenious intelligence. In late 1925 Musica, with the aid of equally impressed bankers in Bridgeport, Connecticut, purchased a large abandoned factory in Fairfield, Connecticut, and moved Girard and Company there so that he could more easily bootleg liquor into New England. In the spring of 1926 Musica bought out the prestigious and well-respected drug manufacturing firm of McKesson & Robbins and merged the company with Girard and Company. Again, bankers in Bridgeport, as well as in Waterbury, helped Musica with the necessary loans, some even investing their personal funds. Also in 1926, Musica, as Coster, married Carol Jenkins Hubbard; they had no children.

Under the respectable guise provided by the McKesson & Robbins name, Musica ran legitimate drug wholesaling activities as well as illegitimate ventures. He retained his brothers George and Robert as employees, renaming them George and Robert Dietrich and giving them high-ranking positions; George became the assistant treasurer of the firm. Musica and George ran the crude drug department from Fairfield. This division of McKesson & Robbins bought large quantities of exotic raw materials from around the world to use in the production of drugs. In order to increase the firm's assets and his own financial worth, Musica began falsifying the quantities of crude drugs actually purchased and held in warehouses (reportedly all in Canada) for McKesson & Robbins. Musica devised an ingenious, elaborate scheme to prevent the Price, Waterhouse accountants from questioning the validity of the drug firm's purchases. The firm's common stock value rose steadily with Musica in control, and as a 10 percent shareholder, he prospered. Musica hired a third brother, Arthur, alias George Vernard, to aid the scheme; he fronted a bank that acted as a clearinghouse for Musica's falsified financial records.

Musica's illegal dealings proceeded smoothly until early 1937, when the company treasurer, Julian F. Thompson, requested that the crude drug department sell off some of its assets to help the less successful departments in McKesson & Robbins. Musica promised to do so but actually did the opposite, amassing more false inventories for his section of the firm. Thompson then became suspicious for the first time and began a private inquiry into Musica's department. Thompson pursued his investigation from March to late November 1938, when he confronted Musica with his complaints. The two men discussed the matter, and Musica, confessing nothing, placed the company in receivership on 5 December 1938, one day before Thompson and the board of directors had threatened to do so.

The ensuing investigation of fraudulent activities in the crude drug department led to the arrests of Musica and his three brothers. The charge was grand larceny, and federal authorities prosecuted the case because mail fraud was involved. On 11 December a New York district attorney's employee (and former colleague of Musica's in that office) recognized a newspaper picture of F. Donald Coster as being Philip Musica. On 15 December a positive identification was made by New York authorities using Coster's fingerprints.

During the proceedings Musica, free on bail, remained at his Fairfield home, obviously distraught. Shortly after noon on 16 December, as federal authorities stood on his doorstep waiting to rearrest him as Philip Musica, Musica shot himself in the head in his upstairs bathroom. A suicide note was found, pleading his innocence. Although Musica had earned more than $3 million from his reworking of the inventories at McKesson & Robbins, he had spent most of it by 1938—some on local charities, some on his manor-like home, and much to pay off relatives and blackmailers.

Philip Musica was temporarily successful at concocting and deploying one of the most elaborate corporate frauds in U.S. history. While posing as Frank Donald Coster he was admitted into the highest social circles of Fairfield County, Connecticut, and enjoyed a most comfortable life until his illegal activities were discovered.

P.E.S.

BONNIE PARKER

[1 OCTOBER 1910–23 MAY 1934]

AND CLYDE CHESTNUT BARROW

[24 MARCH 1909–23 MAY 1934]

It's hard to get past the movie: Bonnie and Clyde, *with Faye Dunaway and Warren Beatty in the title roles, great supporting performances by Gene Hackman, Estelle Parsons, and Michael J. Pollard, a brilliant screenplay by David Newman and Robert Benton, all under the direction of Arthur Penn. It was a spectacular film, and managed to elevate what were essentially a couple of small-time bank robbers into icons of the American experience.*

Bonnie Parker would have loved it.

Her poetry, quoted below, shows her propensity for self-dramatization, evident as well in the habit she and Barrow had of abducting people, driving them around for a few hours, then letting them off with a quotable quip.

She wanted to be somebody, and armed robbery was her ticket to celebrity status. Imagine her, if you will, not gunned down as she actually was but somehow captured and briefly jailed, writing poems in prison, then queening it on talk shows (or that era's equivalent) after her release.

She had the looks for it, too. The photos that survive show she was no Faye Dunaway, but then she didn't have a Hollywood studio furnishing her wardrobe and seeing to her hair and makeup.

She'd have enjoyed the role, but it wasn't to be. By all accounts, the movie got the ending right; the two of them drove into a trap and their car was riddled with bullets. They never had a chance to surrender, and that would probably occasion a public outcry nowadays, but police ambushes were fairly standard then—e.g., Dillinger in Chicago—and lawmen felt less compelled to give their quarry a chance to surrender. It ended, then, just as Bonnie predicted in her poems. While I doubt she welcomed the fusillade, perhaps she died with the satisfaction of having gotten it right.

Bonnie Parker had a talent for self-dramatization.

Bonnie Parker and Clyde Chestnut Barrow, bandits known as Bonnie and Clyde, were born, respectively, in Teleco and Rowena, Texas. Clyde was the son of Henry Barrow and Cummie (maiden name unknown), farmers; Bonnie, the daughter of Charles Parker, a brick mason, and Emma (maiden name unknown). One of eight children, Clyde Barrow grew up in extreme poverty. His parents were tenant farmers until 1921, when they moved to the Dallas area, where neither his mother nor his illiterate father managed to significantly improve the family's prospects. Never a devoted student, Clyde quit school at age sixteen and followed his older brother Ivan "Buck" Barrow into delinquency and petty theft. In 1926 the two were arrested when a police officer observed a flock of stolen turkeys jumping about in the back seat of their automobile. Buck claimed full responsibility and served several days in jail; Clyde was released. By 1929 Clyde and Buck were robbing filling stations and cafés around Dallas. That year Buck was sentenced to four years in the Huntsville State Prison for burglary, and Clyde received a suspended sentence for car theft.

In January 1930 Clyde met Bonnie Parker, probably at the home of a mutual friend in Dallas. Her father's death in 1914 had brought difficult times for Bonnie, her mother, and her two siblings, but nevertheless as a young girl she was a successful student, winning prizes for essays, spelling, and recitation. At the age of sixteen she married Roy Thornton. They lived together only sporadically and separated permanently after he received a five-year prison sentence for robbery in 1929. Her 13 January 1928 diary entry summed up her dissatisfaction with a life she saw as dull and empty: "Sure am blue. Everything has gone wrong today. Why don't something happen. What a life!" Bonnie, as she later put it, was "bored crapless."

Clyde represented deliverance to Bonnie, and the two moved into a small furnished room in Dallas. Within a few months police arrested Clyde for the robbery of a Waco grocery; he was convicted of robbery and sentenced to two years in the Waco jail. In early March 1930 he escaped with the aid of a pistol probably smuggled in by Bonnie. Soon recaptured, Clyde was sent to the notorious Eastham Prison Farm. Paroled on 8 February 1932, he reportedly vowed, "I'll die before I ever go back into a place like that." Later that month he wrecked a stolen car while being chased by police after the burglary of a hardware store in Kaufman, Texas. He escaped, but Bonnie was caught and spent three months in jail before being released on the basis of insufficient evidence. In the intervening months Clyde committed a number of armed robberies, several accompanied by Ray Hamilton, an acquaintance from his childhood gang. In a holdup of a jewelry store in Hillsboro, Texas, Clyde or an accomplice killed the proprietor. In July he and Hamilton killed a sheriff and his deputy outside a barn dance in Atoka, Oklahoma.

Exploits of the late summer and fall of 1932 brought Bonnie and Clyde, now reunited, national notoriety. In Carlsbad, New Mexico, they took captive a local sheriff who had begun investigating their stolen car. In what would become a pattern, they abused him verbally, locked him in his own handcuffs, and took him for a long ride before releasing him frightened but otherwise unharmed. "Tell your people that we ain't a bunch of nutty killers, sheriff," Clyde reportedly told him, "just down home people tryin' to get through this damned Depression with a few bones." October raids on a bank and the National Guard armory in Abilene, Texas, were widely attributed to the gang. During a grocery store robbery in Sherman, Texas, Clyde killed the resistant proprietor.

That December, Clyde killed a man in Temple, Texas, who attempted to stop the gang from stealing his Ford. In January he killed a Dallas deputy sheriff. Shortly thereafter the gang took as a hostage a Missouri state trooper who had pulled them over for a traffic violation. When the gang dropped him off a hundred miles away, unharmed, Bonnie advised him, he told reporters, to find a "new line of work where you won't meet such dangerous people as us."

In March 1933 the gang was joined by Clyde's brother Buck, on parole, and his wife, Blanche. Their reunion turned violent on 13 April when Joplin, Missouri, police, acting on a tip, raided their apartment. Two detectives were killed during a fierce shoot-out, and the gang careened away in a stolen car. Inside the hideout police discovered a large arsenal, jewelry from a recent robbery, and, more important to the gang's subsequent fame, a poem by Bonnie and two rolls of snapshots of the gang posing playfully with a variety of menacing weapons. Among the photos was one of Bonnie holding a shotgun on a "captured" Clyde. Even more widely published in the nation's newspapers was a shot of a cigar-champing Bonnie, revolver in hand, leaning casually on one of the gang's stolen cars. (Later, oddly regretful about this particular violation of conventional propriety, Bonnie told a captive to "tell the public that I don't smoke cigars. It's the bunk.")

Bonnie's poem, "Suicide Sal," the tale of a heroic outlaw woman, was widely published in the nation's press, after which she responded with more verse, which she mailed to several newspapers:

> You have heard the story of Jesse James,
> Of how he lived and died.
> If you are still in need of something to read,
> Here's the story of Bonnie and Clyde.

Her epic managed to be at once boastful:

> . . . those who squeal
> Are usually found dying or dead.

self-justifying:

> If they try to act like citizens,
> And rent them a nice little flat,
> About the third night they are invited to fight,
> By a submachine gun, rat-tat-tat.

and mawkish:

> Some day they will go down together,
> And they will bury them side by side.
> To a few it means grief,

To the law it's relief,
But it's death to Bonnie and Clyde.

Literary abilities notwithstanding, Bonnie and Clyde had become celebrity criminals of the first order.

Adding to the gang's notoriety was yet another hostage exploit in late April 1933. An undertaker in Ruston, Louisiana, attempted to prevent Clyde from stealing his new Chevrolet. The gang took the undertaker and his girl-friend captive, driving them for several hours into Arkansas. After Bonnie learned his occupation, the man later told reporters, she said to him, "When the law catches us, you can fix us up."

Fame intensified the gang's encounters with law enforcement. Clyde, Buck, or William Daniel Jones killed the town marshal of Alma, Texas, while he was pursuing the gang after the robbery of a local bank. Shortly thereafter, in July, a posse of about a dozen men surrounded the gang in a cabin camp in Platte City, Missouri. A barrage of fire enabled the gang to make its escape. Buck Barrow, however, was seriously wounded by a gunshot to the head, and most of the others received minor injuries. The gang was soon sighted near Dexter, Iowa, and a force of lawmen, a National Guard unit, and vigilantes, numbering about one hundred, converged on the gang in a deserted amusement park. Bonnie and Clyde escaped a withering fusillade, but Buck was mortally wounded and Blanche taken into custody.

On 16 January 1934 the gang was believed to have aided the escape of Ray Hamilton, Henry Methvin, and several other convicts from the Eastham Prison Farm. Bonnie and Clyde, now the most notorious and sought-after fugitives in the country, eluded a force of hundreds of lawmen and vigilantes near Muskogee, Oklahoma, in February. Reacting to the death of a guard wounded at Eastham, prominent Texans called for drastic meas-ures. Lawmen received considerable support in their call for a $2,500 "Wanted Dead" reward to be posted for the two; Clyde in particular was considered a "mad dog" who deserved no better. More moderate voices prevailed, however, and a $2,500 "Dead or Alive" poster was issued.

In February 1934 the head of the Texas prison system hired Frank Hamer, a former Texas Ranger with a reputation for ruthless efficiency, to hunt the pair down. His manhunt came to fruition on 23 May. Methvin, seeking immunity from prosecution, aided Hamer in setting up a trap along a road near Gibsland, Louisiana. When Bonnie and Clyde arrived at the site, Hamer and his five-man posse poured 167 rounds of ammunition into their vehicle, killing the pair instantly.

A penchant for killing—especially lawmen—and a flair for appealing to the emotions of working people contributed to the notoriety of Clyde Barrow and Bonnie Parker far more than their monetary gain: their largest haul was probably less than $1,500. Americans had long been both appalled and enthralled by outlaws, and Bonnie and Clyde fascinated a public tuned into the mass media and the new culture of celebrity. Their deeds and words—in addition to Bonnie's poetry, Clyde reportedly wrote a famous testimonial to Henry Ford extolling the virtues of the Ford V-8 for people in his "business"—captured the public imagination as effectively as the public relations campaign of any Hollywood star. Americans were fascinated by the shattering of conventional gender rules personified by Bonnie—a petite, attractive, fashionable blonde who robbed banks, was photographed smoking cigars, and had a man's name tattooed on her thigh. Moreover, the deep depression of the early 1930s undoubedly contributed to the seductiveness of a pair of young lovers who defied the powerful forces of a hostile world.

D.E.R.

William Quantrill led a band of guerrillas on a bloody trail of destruction in Civil War–era Kansas and Missouri.

WILLIAM CLARKE QUANTRILL

[31 JULY 1837–6 JUNE 1865]

Quantrill is remarkable not merely for the atrocities he instigated but for the motley crew he assembled to carry them out. Of the gunfighters, train robbers, and all-around hard cases who flourished in the years following the Civil War, a considerable number first made their bones as Quantrill's Raiders.

Apologists for the outlaws often cited this as a mitigating circumstance. These boys, it was argued, served the Confederate cause and served it nobly. Now, oppressed by the banks or the railroads or the Reconstruction government, what could they do but fight back in the only way they knew how? The argument falls apart when you consider that most of Quantrill's band of guerrillas were hardly choirboys to start with. The war simply gave them an opportunity to disguise murder and looting as patriotism. Long before the guns sounded at Fort Sumter, their leader had begun terrorizing the Border states for personal profit. Posing as an abolitionist jayhawker, he raided farms, carried off slaves purportedly to free them, and promptly sold them to other slaveholders. In one well-publicized incident, he enlisted five young Quakers to raid the farm of a Missouri slaveholder; then, before the raid, he tipped off the slave owners and led the Quakers into an ambush in which three of them were killed. Then he informed the slaveholders that the Quakers had killed his brother, and that he'd finally managed to track them down.

There are alternate versions of Quantrill's end at the hands of Union soldiers in Kentucky. One holds that he didn't die later of his wounds, but that he died on the battlefield, shot in the back while running away.

William Clarke Quantrill, pro-Confederate guerrilla leader, was born in Canal Dover (now Dover), Ohio, the son of Thomas H. Quantrill, a tinsmith and teacher, and Caroline Clarke. After acquiring a better-than-average education for the time and place, and following his father's death in 1854, Quantrill taught school in Canal Dover and various other towns in the Midwest before moving to Kansas in 1857. During the next three years he engaged in various occupations—farming, teamstering with an army expedition to Utah, gold prospecting in Colorado—before again teaching school, this time in Stanton, Kansas. In 1860 he moved to Lawrence, Kansas, where under the alias of Charley Hart he became a jayhawker (best defined as a bandit with professed abolitionist sympathies). In December 1860, facing arrest in Lawrence for his criminal activities, he betrayed a group of jayhawkers into an ambush at the farm of Morgan Walker in Jackson County, Missouri, thereby gaining the confidence of the people of that locality, to whom he represented himself as being a native of Maryland and proslavery. After the outbreak of the Civil War he served with Confederate forces in Missouri. Late in 1861 he returned to Jackson County, where he soon became the leader of a guerrilla band, which he led in a series of raids into Kansas and against pro-Union Missourians. Having helped regular Confederate forces capture Independence, Missouri (11 Aug. 1862), he received a captain's commission as a partisan ranger. By this time he was the most notorious of the many "bushwhackers" operating in western Missouri.

The climax of his career came on 21 August 1863 when he led more than 400 guerrillas in a raid on Lawrence, Kansas, that resulted in the destruction of the business district and the massacre of 150 men and boys. This was the most atrocious event of its kind during the Civil War, making Quantrill the most famous, and infamous, guerrilla chieftain of that conflict. On 6 October 1863 his band massacred nearly 100 Union troops at Baxter Springs, Kansas, while on its way to spend the winter in Texas. Thereafter, however, he had a downturn of fortune. First, Confederate military authorities in Texas, outraged by depredations being committed by the Missouri bushwhackers, tried in vain to arrest him and suppress his band. Then, after returning to Missouri in the spring of 1864, he quarreled with his chief lieutenant, George Todd, with the result that Todd supplanted him as leader.

During most of the remainder of 1864 he hid out in Howard County, Missouri, with his teenage mistress, Kate King. Late in 1864, following the death of Todd and the defeat of a Confederate invasion of Missouri, he resumed command of some of the surviving bushwhackers, whom he led into Kentucky in January 1865. On 10 May 1865 a party of "Federal guerrillas" that had been assigned to hunt him down surprised his band at a farm near Louisville, mortally wounding and capturing him. Nearly a month later he died at a military prison hospital in Louisville. Both a product and producer of the turmoil that reigned along the Kansas-Missouri border during the Civil War era, Quantrill was an exceptionally able and daring, but also unscrupulous and opportunistic, bandit who left behind a well-deserved reputation as "the bloodiest man in American history."

A.C.

RAILROAD BILL

[?–7 MAR. 1896]

It's not surprising that Railroad Bill became a creature of folklore. The name alone is almost enough to guarantee it. And there's something about a man who avoids capture in the face of overwhelming odds that appeals strongly to the imagination. Living off the land, sustained by secret sympathizers—something makes us want to root for guys like that. Even Eric Rudolph, the murderous anti-abortion activist with precious little in the way of redeeming qualities, acquired some degree of folk-hero status by remaining free in the Carolina hills for as long as he did. It's the appeal of the underdog, I suppose, irrespective of what a sonofabitch he may be.

A fascinating note in Railroad Bill's saga is just how many times he was killed, and in how many guises. I was reminded of the story of the big-city police department that broadcast a "Man Wanted" circular, with six photographs of the criminal. They received a wire from a backcountry sheriff: "Pleased to report we have four of the fellows in custody and expect to capture the other two within the week."

Railroad Bill, thief and folk hero, was the nickname of an African-American man of such obscure origins that his real name is in question. Most writers have believed him to be Morris Slater, but a rival candidate for the honor is an equally obscure man named Bill McCoy. But in song and story, where he has long had a place, the question is of small interest and Railroad Bill is name enough. A ballad regaling his exploits began circulating among field hands, turpentine camp workers, prisoners, and other groups from the black underclass of the Deep South, several years before it first found its way into print in 1911. A version of this blues ballad was first recorded in 1924 by Gid Tanner and Riley Puckett, and Thomas Dorsey, a blues singer from the 1920s took Railroad Bill as his stage name. The ballad got a second wind during the folk music vogue of the 1950s

A ballad about Railroad Bill's exploits first circulated among turpentine camp workers and other groups from the black underclass of the Deep South in the early 1900s.

and 1960s, and in 1981 the musical play *Railroad Bill* by C. R. Portz was produced for the Labor Theater in New York City. It subsequently toured thirty-five cities.

The name Railroad Bill, or often simply "Railroad," was given to him by trainmen and derived from his penchant for riding the cars as an anonymous nonpaying passenger of the Louisville and Nashville Railroad (L&N). Thus he might appear to be no more than a common tramp or hobo, as the large floating population of migratory workers who more or less surreptitiously rode the cars of all the nation's railroads were labeled. But Railroad Bill limited his riding to two adjoining South Alabama counties, Escambia and Baldwin. Sometime in the winter of 1895 he began to be noticed by trainmen often enough that he soon acquired some notoriety and a nickname. It did not make him less worthy of remark that he was always armed, with a rifle and one or more pistols. He was, as it turned out, quite prepared to offer resistance to the rough treatment normally meted out to tramps.

An attitude of armed resistance from a black man was bound inevitably to bring him into conflict with the civil authorities, who were in any case inclined to be solicitous of the L&N, the dominant economic power in South Alabama. The conflict began on 6 March 1895, only a month or two after trainmen first became aware of Railroad Bill. L&N employees discovered him asleep on the platform of a water tank in Baldwin County, on the Flomaton to Mobile run, and tried to take him into custody. He drove them off with gunfire and forced them to take shelter in a nearby shack. When a freight train pulled up to take on water he hijacked it and, after firing additional rounds into the shack, forced the engineer to take him farther up the road, whereupon he left the train and disappeared into the woods. After that, pursuit of Railroad Bill was relentless. A month to the day later he was cornered at Bay Minette by a posse led by a railroad detective. A deputy, James H. Stewart, was killed in the ensuing gunfight, but once again the fugitive slipped away. The railroad provided a "special" to transport Sheriff E. S. McMillan from Brewton, the county seat of Escambia, to the scene with a pack of bloodhounds, but a heavy rainfall washed away the scent.

In mid-April a reward was posted by the L&N and the state of Alabama totaling $500. The lure of this reward and a rumored sighting of the fugitive led Sheriff McMillan out of his jurisdiction to Bluff Springs, Florida, where he found Railroad Bill and met with death at his hands. The reward climbed to $1,250, and the manhunt intensified. A small army with packs of dogs picked up his scent near Brewton in August, but he dove into Murder Swamp near Castelberry and disappeared. During this period, from March to August, the legend of Railroad Bill took shape among poor blacks in the region. He was viewed as a "conjure man," one who could change his shape and slip away from pursuers. He was clever and outwitted his enemies; he was a trickster who laid traps for the trapper and a fighter who refused to bend his neck and submit to the oppressor. He demanded respect, and in time some whites grudgingly gave it: Brewton's *Pine Belt News* reported after Railroad Bill's escape into Murder Swamp that he had "outwitted and outgeneraled at least one hundred men armed to the teeth." During this period a Robin Hood–style Railroad Bill emerged, who, it was said, stole canned goods from boxcars and distributed them to poor illiterate blacks like himself. Carl Carmer, a white writer in the 1930s, claimed that Railroad Bill forced poor blacks at gunpoint to buy the goods from him, but Carmer never explained how it was possible to get money out of people who rarely if ever saw any. Railroad Bill staved off death and capture for an entire year, a virtual impossibility had he not had supporters among the poor black population of the region.

Sightings became infrequent after Murder Swamp, and some concluded Railroad Bill had left the area. The "wanted" poster with its reward was more widely circulated. The result was something like open season on vagrant blacks in the lower South. The *Montgomery Advertiser* reported that "several were shot in Florida, Georgia, Mississippi and even in Texas," adding with unconscious grisly humor, "only one was brought here to be identified." That one arrived at Union Station in a pine box in August, escorted by the two men from Chipley, Florida, who had shot him in hopes of collecting the reward. Doubts about whether he remained in the area were answered on 7 March 1896, exactly a year and a day after the affair at the water tower when determined pursuit began. Railroad Bill was shot without warning, from ambush, by a private citizen seeking the reward, which by now included a lifetime pass on the L&N Railroad. Bill had been sitting on a barrel eating cheese and crackers in a small grocery in Atmore, Alabama. Perhaps he was tired as well as hungry.

Railroad Bill's real name probably will never be known. At the time of the water tower incident and up to the killing of Deputy Stewart he had only the nickname, but in mid-April the first "wanted" posters went up in Mobile identifying Railroad Bill as Morris Slater, who, though the notice did not state it, had been a worker in a turpentine camp near Bluff Springs,

Florida. These camps were often little more than penal colonies. They employed convict labor and were heavily into debt peonage. People were not supposed to leave, but Slater did, after killing the marshal of Bluff Springs. When railroad detectives stumbled on this story their interest was primarily in Slater's nickname. He had been called "Railroad Time," and "Railroad" for short, because of his quick efficient work. The detectives quickly concluded, because of the similarities in nicknames, that Slater was their man. The problem, of course, is that the trainmen called their rider Railroad Bill precisely because they had no idea who he was and well before railroad authorities heard about Slater. If the detectives were right, then it follows that the same man independently won strangely similar nicknames in two different settings, once because he was a good worker, and again because he was a freeloader.

No one from the turpentine camp who had known Slater identified the body, but neither the railroad detectives nor the civil authorities involved questioned the identification. The body was taken to Brewton, on its way to Montgomery, where it would go on display for the public's gratification, but it was also displayed for a time in Brewton and recognized. The *Pine Belt News* reported that residents recognized the body as that of Bill McCoy, a man who would have been about forty, the approximate age of the corpse, since he had been brought to the area from Coldwater, Florida, as a young man eighteen years earlier. McCoy was remembered as a town troublemaker who two years earlier had threatened T. R. Miller, the richest man in town, when he worked in Miller's sawmill and lumberyard. He had fled the scene hastily, not to be seen again until his corpse went on display as Railroad Bill. But, apart from the local newspaper stories, no one disputed the Slater identification, and the local Brewton people seem to have concluded that Morris Slater must have been a name used by Bill McCoy after he fled the town. The problem with that conclusion is that when the incident at Miller's sawmill occurred Morris Slater had already earned the nickname "Railroad Time" in a Florida turpentine camp.

J.L.P.

A farmer by day, Stephen Renfroe rode with the Ku Klux Klan by night. This 1872 engraving, "Visit of the Ku Klux Klan," shows a Klan member threatening an African American family with a rifle.

STEPHEN S. RENFROE

[1843–13 JULY 1886]

Kids who grow up playing cops and robbers are secure in the knowledge that one is either one or the other, a good guy or a bad guy, a cop or a robber. If, when they're older, they look deeper into the subject, they're apt to find that the distinctions aren't always that clear-cut. It is often the same socioeconomic group that furnishes a city's cops and criminals, and it's not unheard of for cops to go bad, or for crooks to take a turn as lawmen.

This was especially true on the frontier, when a man could ride a few hundred miles and change his life. Such prominent lawmen as Wild Bill Hickock and Wyatt Earp just narrowly avoid being classed as outlaws, while others like Tom Horn straddled the line for years.

As Sheriff of Sumter County, Alabama, Stephen Renfroe seems to have turned bad almost immediately. According to a local newspaper, he "committed robbery, twice, of his own office—drinking, arson, blackmails, thieving and other almost inconceivable outrages." Addison G. Smith, a local lawyer and friend of Renfroe, added the following: "It is well established that while he was sheriff he burned the clerk's office, robbed himself of money he had collected for other people, embezzled money, used trust funds, turned prisoners out of jail, committed an unprovoked assault with intent to murder, and was guilty of various thefts."

When that's what your friends say about you, you're probably not going to win any Good Citizenship awards.

Renfroe's end came at the end of a rope, and he seems to have been lynched not because his crimes were so heinous, or because anyone hated him all that much, but because he was deemed incorrigible. He wouldn't stop committing crimes, and no jail seemed equal to the task of holding him, so what else were they supposed to do with him?

Stephen S. Renfroe, noted Alabama outlaw, was born in Georgia, the son of J. G. and M. A. P. Renfroe, farmers. The family moved to Butler County, Alabama, around 1853. Poorly educated but intelligent, Renfroe was quick-tempered, handsome, powerful, and athletic. An expert shot and accomplished horseman, he served as a private in the Civil War, was wounded, and then deserted in 1864.

In 1865 he married Mary E. Shepherd of Butler County. He and his wife lived in Lowndes County with Mary's sister and her husband, who was a physician. During a family argument in 1867, Renfroe shot and killed his brother-in-law. He fled to Livingston in Sumter County. A Black Belt county bordering Mississippi, Sumter County had become a Republican stronghold after the war. The county's native white Democrats fought bitterly with northern whites ("carpetbaggers") and their local white allies ("scalawags"), although former slaves provided the Republicans' real voting strength.

Renfroe's wife died, and in 1869 he married Mary M. Sledge. After his second wife's death (1871), he married Cherry V. Reynolds of nearby Meridian, Mississippi, in 1873. Their son was born the following year. Meanwhile, Renfroe became a respected farmer by day, but at night he rode with the Ku Klux Klan in opposition to Radical Reconstruction leaders. Renfroe was involved in Klan beatings, murders, and intimidation of Republican voters that made a tangible contribution to statewide Democratic victories in 1870. The Republicans won in 1872, however, and the Klan's excesses led to its demise. Nevertheless, Renfroe remained a hero to many white Democrats.

In 1874 Renfroe and two other men were arrested for murder in violation of the Enforcement Acts. Tried in Mobile, the men became martyrs. When all charges were dropped due to a lack of evidence, Renfroe returned home in triumph. In statewide elections the Democrats won political control of the state. Renfroe resumed farming, and in 1877 he was elected sheriff of Sumter County. Within a year the sheriff's courthouse office was robbed. Renfroe was suspected, but no charges were made. By 1880, Renfroe had burned the county clerk's office, embezzled money, misused trust funds, released prisoners, and committed an assault. On 19 April, he was indicted and imprisoned. Although friends posted bond, Renfroe's behavior resulted in his re-arrest.

On 19 June, he cut a hole through the outside wall of his cell and escaped. He hid out in the heavily timbered flatwoods bordering Mississippi. By letter he formally resigned as sheriff and awarded his property to his wife. In 1881 Renfroe allegedly joined the Harrison Gang, a band of robbers who operated in Louisiana and Mississippi. He secretly visited his family and, hoping to reform, returned to Livingston in 1884 and surrendered to authorities. Friends raised his bond, but again Renfroe began drinking and fighting and was locked up. His attempted escape caused authorities to transfer him to a more secure jail at Tuscaloosa. The resourceful ex-lawman burned his way out of this jail, making a brilliant escape on 7 July 1884.

Renfroe fled to New Orleans and from there to Texas and Mexico. He returned to Sumter County in 1885 but then decided to go to Central

America. Before leaving, Renfroe stole a horse and saddle. After he left Alabama, a detective tracked him through Mississippi and arrested him at Slidell, Louisiana. Renfroe was returned, physically debilitated, to Livingston's new jail (an unacknowledged tribute to him). An escape effort failed, and in August 1885 Renfroe pled guilty to two charges and received a five-year sentence. Under Alabama's notorious convict lease system he was consigned to the mines of a coal company near Birmingham. On 3 October, he broke out, eluded pursuers, and fled to the flatwoods. A massive manhunt failed to locate him, even as Renfroe gave out interviews to newspaper reporters.

Rewards for his capture were offered when he was accused of stealing horses and mules, and in July 1886 three farmers wounded and captured him near Meridian. Renfroe was returned to Livingston on 13 July and, when interviewed, asked that his wife change his son's last name. After dark, a small group of armed but undisguised men appeared before the jail and took charge of Renfroe. They marched with him down the main street, stopping south of town at the Sucarnatchie River. A noose was placed around the stoical Renfroe's neck, and he was hanged from the limb of a chinaberry tree. He was buried later in a pauper's grave in Livingston. The lynchers were well known, but no arrests were ever made. The incorrigible but able Renfroe has become an Alabama legend.

W.W.R.

ARNOLD ROTHSTEIN

[1882–6 NOVEMBER 1928]

As Meyer Wolfsheim, Arnold Rothstein has a cameo role in F. Scott Fitzgerald's masterpiece, The Great Gatsby, *identified as the man who fixed the 1919 World Series. It's hard to say just what prompted the author to include the scene, and my own best guess is that Fitzgerald, hardly a stranger to Manhattan nightlife, had been in the same speakeasy as the gambler. Someone must have pointed out and identified Rothstein, and the instant must have made an impression.*

By all accounts, the man was extremely slick and sophisticated, a genius with numbers, and a master at profiting hugely from crime while staying clear of the law. All of this makes his sudden decline and fall in 1928 difficult to understand.

Apparently he had some sort of breakdown. Always well-dressed and perfectly groomed, he turned overnight into an unkempt man with shaking hands and a pallid face. Gambling had always been profitable for him, and now he suddenly turned into a man who couldn't win for losing. Finally, at an epic poker game at the Park Central Hotel, Rothstein lost $320,000 in a matter of hours.

He left, saying he'd pay later, then repudiated the debt on the grounds that he'd been cheated. Eventually a phone call drew him back to the hotel, where he was shot to death, ostensibly because of his refusal to pay what he owed.

A rnold Rothstein, prominent gambling entrepreneur and the suspected fixer of the 1919 World Series, was born in New York City, the son of Abraham Rothstein and Esther Kahn. The father was a successful businessman in various phases of the garment industry, and both parents were observant Jews, greatly respected within the Jewish community of the city. Unlike his siblings, Rothstein was a rebellious youth who disdained school, and he was fascinated by the excitement and gambling that he found

By the late 1920s, Arnold Rothstein spent most afternoons at his office in midtown Manhattan.

in the street life of the city. By his mid-teens he was a pool shark and was running his own dice games. He left home at age seventeen and worked briefly as a traveling salesman, but by the time he was twenty he was building the career that would lead him to a central role as the major intermediary between the underworld and upper world of New York.

By 1902 Rothstein had become a bookmaker, taking bets on horse racing, prizefighting, and elections. By 1907 he was taking lay-off bets from other bookmakers and was increasingly respected so that big time bettors placed their bets with him. In 1904 he went to Saratoga Springs to make book during the August racing season, and in 1907 he opened a gambling house there. At the same time he operated high stakes crap games in New York City and opened a string of gambling houses. Rothstein was himself a high roller, making bets on various sporting events and becoming the owner of a stable of racing horses. As a result of his growing prominence in gambling, he made friends among the big bettors from the legitimate world and the underworld. He was or would become an associate of men like Charles Stoneham, owner of the New York Giants baseball team, newspapermen such as Bayard Swope and Damon Runyon, major figures in the underworld, and many people in theater and entertainment. Equally important, his close ties with Tim Sullivan, Charles Murphy, Jimmy Hines, and other leaders of Tammany Hall meant that by the end of World War I he was the chief coordinator between the worlds of sports, gambling, and politics.

With the famous "Black Sox" scandal of 1919, in which the favored Chicago White Sox threw the World Series to the Cincinnati Reds, Rothstein achieved an unwanted notoriety. Yet whether he directly participated in the fix remains unclear. Abe Attell, a former featherweight champion and a member of Rothstein's entourage, was in Cincinnati at the beginning of the series along with Rachel Brown, Rothstein's chief accountant. Attell bet heavily on each game and was in regular contact with the players to whom he eventually gave money. Joseph "Sport" Sullivan, a Boston sports gambler who knew Rothstein, contacted the players in Chicago. Rothstein certainly knew about the fix, as did many knowledgeable people in the gambling world, and he probably won bets on the series. For nearly a year following the World Series, Major League leaders and sportswriters carefully protected the good name of baseball rather than seek out the facts about a scandal that many knew about and many more suspected. When a grand jury in Cook County, Illinois, finally undertook an investigation, Rothstein declared: "There is not a word of truth in the report that I had anything to do with the World Series of last fall" and testified voluntarily. The grand jury indicted Attell, Brown, Sullivan, and eight White Sox players. (Because the confessions of the eight players were later "lost," no one was convicted, although the players were later banned from baseball for life.) Thereafter Rothstein, although not indicted, was branded as the man who fixed the World Series, and he came to symbolize the shadowy connections between crime and power in the nation's largest city. He was the person upon whom F. Scott Fitzgerald based the character of Meyer Wolfsheim in his 1925 novel *The Great Gatsby*.

As the baseball scandal unraveled in 1920, Rothstein announced his retirement from gambling. Although he gradually dropped his gambling houses, he remained the bookmaker for big bettors, took part in high stakes poker games, bet on the races, and sought out other opportunities for profitable bets. He also used his contacts and power to expand his business interests. With the coming of Prohibition, Rothstein provided the money and political protection that helped a number of bootleggers to launch their careers. These included Jack "Legs" Diamond, Waxey Gordon, Bill Dwyer, and Frank Costello. For a while Rothstein took an active part in bootlegging but soon largely withdrew. Nevertheless, his involvement in bootlegging led to the smuggling of opiates into the United States, and at the time of his death he had money invested in the purchase of drugs in Europe. By the early 1920s Rothstein had also entered into various shady stock market activities, including the fencing of stolen securities and the sale of worthless stocks. He also established real estate companies for investments in Manhattan real estate, and he played an important role in the labor and business racketeering that had become an important part of the garment industry in New York City.

By the 1920s Rothstein generally worked in his office in midtown Manhattan in the afternoon. In the evenings he had a regular public place where he hung out, such as the Knickerbocker Hotel or Lindy's restaurant. There he engaged in quiet conversations with people of all walks of life who knew where to find him and who wished to talk business. Rothstein did not drink, avoided profanity, and had little of the flamboyance often associated with underworld figures. Although he often had a mistress, his chief emotional support came from his wife, Carolyn Greene Rothstein, whom he had married in August 1909; they had no children. By 1928, despite his many business investments, Rothstein seemed to face a cash shortage and became uncharacteristically lax in paying off his gambling debts. On 4 November 1928 he was shot in a room in the Park Central Hotel and was found after he stumbled down to the employees' entrance. The shooting was assumed to stem from his failure to make payment on a debt. He died in a New York City hospital.

M.H.H.

Dutch Schultz waits for the verdict in one of the income tax cases against him in 1935.

DUTCH SCHULTZ

[6 AUGUST 1902–24 OCTOBER 1935]

"*Delirious and ranting, Schultz died in a Newark hospital the following day.*"

I suppose a fair number of those who live and die by the sword die delirious and ranting, but Dutch Schultz's deathbed ravings have gained for their author a certain immortality. By a happy accident, they were taken down by police quizzing Schultz in an effort to find out who killed him. There's a surreal quality to the Dutchman's rant that elevates it to the level of poetry, albeit an elusive sort of poetry. Here's an excerpt:

"Oh, oh, dog biscuits and when he is happy, he doesn't get snappy. . . . Frankie, you didn't meet him, you didn't even meet me. The glove will fit what I say. . .

"I don't know who shot me. Don't put anyone near this check. You might have. Please do it for me. Let me get up, he? In the olden days, they waited and they waited. Please give me shot. It is from the factory. . .

"No, no. There are only ten of us. There are ten million fighting somewhere of you, so get your onions up and we will throw up the truce flag. Oh, please let me up. Please shift me. Police are here. Communistic—strike—baloney— honestly this is a habit I get. Sometimes I give it and sometimes I don't. Oh, I am still in. That settles it. Are you sure? Please let me get in and eat. Let him harness himself to you and then bother you.

"Please don't ask me to go there. I don't want to. I still don't want him in the path. It is no use to stage a riot. The sidewalk was in trouble and the bears were in trouble and I broke it up. Please put me in that room. Please keep him in control. My gilt-edged stuff and those dirty rats have tuned in. . .

"Then pull me out. I am half crazy. They won't let me get up. They dyed my shoes. . .

"Look out for Jimmy Valentine for he is an old pal of mine. Come on, come on, Jim. Okay, okay, I am all through. Can't do another thing. Look out, mama, look out for her. You can't beat him. Police, mama, Helen, mother, please take me out. I will settle the indictment. Shut up, you got a big mouth! Please help

me up, Henry. Max, come over here. French-Canadian bean soup. I want to
pay. Let them leave me alone."
    Hard to argue with that. . . .

Dutch Schultz, gangster and underworld entrepreneur, was born Arthur
Flegenheimer in the Bronx, New York City, the son of Herman
Flegenheimer, a glazier and baker, and Emma Neu. Before the boy completed the sixth grade, his father either deserted the family or died. Arthur's
mother then took in laundry to support the family, and he quit school to
sell newspapers, run errands, and work as an office boy, printer's appren-
tice, and roofer. While he proudly retained his roofers' union card as evidence of his working-class respectability, he was pulled into the gang world
of the Bronx slums. In 1919 he was convicted on a burglary charge and
was sent to a reformatory for fifteen months. This police record, plus his
cultivation of a reputation as a hardened tough, led to his calling himself
Dutch Schultz, the name of a well-known former street brawler in the area.

After several years of odd jobs and brushes with the law, Schultz became
a partner in an illegal Bronx saloon in 1928. Newspaper reporters sensa-
tionalized the bootlegging wars and assorted violence that soon flared
between the gangs of Schultz, Jack "Legs" Diamond, and the exceptionally
reckless Vincent "Mad Dog" Coll. Schultz hired a small army of gunmen
that protected his beer trucks and destroyed or hijacked those of his com-
petitors. He also succeeded in purchasing police protection by generous
backing of New York political figures. By the early 1930s Schultz was the
most powerful bootlegger in the Bronx and upper Manhattan.

Journalists and law enforcement officials sometimes drew comparisons
between Schultz and such celebrated gangsters as Al Capone of Chicago.
Indeed, in 1939 Schultz's attorney, J. Richard "Dixie" Davis, remembered
him as cultivating gangster slang and that "the girls" thought he looked like
"Bing Crosby with his nose bashed in." Despite his reputation for outbursts
of calculated violence, Schultz was a mousy and frequently secretive individual. Although he was widely feared, few in the underworld seem to

have had any affection for him. His frugality, especially in the purchase of apparel, became legendary. "Only a sucker," Schultz told *New York Times* reporter Meyer Berger in 1935, "will pay $15 or $20 for a silk shirt." Berger observed that the drab gangster had the appearance of an "ill-dressed vagrant." Sometime in the mid 1930s Schultz entered into a common-law marriage with Frances Maxwell, who bore him two children. Schultz's real genius lay in his sense of business and political leverage. Assembled during the beer wars of earlier years, his gang directed its energies in other directions by the early 1930s. Schultz's operatives used threats of violence to muscle their way into food servicing unions; once in control, they embezzled union funds and extorted "protection" money from the restaurants. The organization's links to Tammany leader James J. Hines (who in turn exercised considerable control over the police) neutralized appeals to law enforcement by either unions or restaurants.

The ties to Hines apparently were critical to Schultz's dramatic takeover of large portions of the black-run Harlem policy game. Commonly called "numbers," these gambling operations appealed to many people, mostly poor, and employed as many as 15,000 street runners, or "collectors." The Harlem numbers racket was in some chaos at the time, the result of a series of reform exposés as well as rapid growth during the depression. In early 1932 the Schultz organization began to threaten black policy bankers with violence and then to squeeze them from control of the lucrative racket. Resistance seemed useless because of Schultz's payoffs to Hines. Soon the Harlem numbers were dominated by the Schultz combination, which prosecutors later estimated grossed as much as $20 million annually.

As part of a long-term campaign aimed at industrial racketeering in New York, U.S. Attorney Thomas E. Dewey in 1933 initiated an income tax investigation of Schultz. While the investigation proceeded, Schultz went into hiding for more than a year. By 1935, however, he had surrendered and was tried twice, once in Syracuse and once in the village of Malone, New York. In Syracuse, Schultz and his attorney won a hung jury; in Malone, he was acquitted after a whirlwind public relations effort possibly influenced the jury.

Schultz's acquittal, however, did not mark the end of his ordeal. Dewey's office continued a broad-gauged investigation into the restaurant and numbers rackets and into Schultz's evasion of New York state taxes. Meanwhile, underworld rivals, apparently counting on Schultz's conviction, moved in on his holdings in New York City. Alarmed, Schultz retaliated against deserters from his ranks and allegedly planned to assassinate Dewey. In the midst of a major underworld power struggle, Schultz and two subordinates were gunned down in a saloon in Newark, New Jersey. Delirious and ranting, Schultz died in a Newark hospital the following day.

Although the subsequent corruption trial of Hines and the writings of Dixie Davis provided substantial information on Schultz's work as an underworld entrepreneur, the details behind his killing remain clouded. Ultimately, gunman Charles Workman served twenty-three years in prison for the shooting, but he revealed little about his motives. In the 1960s and 1970s some writers speculated that Charles "Lucky" Luciano, putative leader of a secret Sicilian-dominated criminal cartel, had ordered Schultz's killing. A number of later motion pictures, including *The Cotton Club* (1984) and *Billy Bathgate* (1991), also present a highly mythologized portrait of Schultz's career.

W.H.M.

BUGSY SIEGEL

[1906–20 JUNE 1947]

He couldn't stand the nickname, and you were ill-advised to say it to his face. Yet he seems to have come by it honestly, back in his teenage years, and it stayed with him all his life. He was by all accounts an excitable man, a man given to sudden rages.

Even when his explosive temper was not a factor, Ben Siegel was a dangerous man, who had no discernible compunctions about committing murder. His early partnership with Meyer Lansky, the Bugs and Meyer mob, specialized in contract killings and ultimately grew into Murder, Incorporated. It's impossible to say how many murders Siegel committed personally, but there were a good many of them, and he had plenty of blood on his hands by the time a gunman cut short his career as the creator of Las Vegas.

While criminals have acquired folk-hero status for centuries, Siegel was the first American criminal to attain the kind of glamour that got him taken up by Hollywood celebrities. He was evidently quite charming and personable, and famously soothed his new friends by proclaiming himself as dangerous only to other criminals. "We only kill each other," he assured them.

A generation after Siegel's death, Joey Gallo had a similar edgy appeal for a subset of New York celebrities. The press reported his literary observations—he preferred Camus to Sartre because the former was more of a survivor—and recounted his quips. (After Albert Anastasia was gunned down in a barber's chair at the Park Sheraton Hotel, Gallo said, "I suppose you could call us the Barbershop Quartet.") An actress friend of mine knew Gallo then, and became quite close to him; she has a canvas on her wall that he painted during a stretch upstate in Green Haven, and she was present at Umberto's Clam House the night he was killed. "If you could get your mind around some of the things he did," she said, "he was a perfectly nice fellow, and a good friend."

Bugsy Siegel, shown here in 1940, had a reputation as a charming killer.

Bugsy Siegel, gangster, was born Benjamin Siegel in Brooklyn, New York, the son of parents whose lives remain obscure. As a youth Siegel joined one of the many gangs that were so common on New York's Lower East Side in the early years of the twentieth century. His volatile personality, which combined intelligence with charm, generosity, irrational rages, and violent behavior, earned him his nickname of "Bugsy" early in life.

As with so many other major underworld figures, Siegel owed his eventual prominence to a combination of his own ability, key relationships, and good luck. While still a teenage hoodlum, he formed a lasting friendship with Meyer Lansky that became the basis for much of Siegel's personal success and notoriety.

Prohibition provided the first major opportunity for Siegel and Lansky to create significant careers in crime. With the financial backing of Arnold Rothstein, New York's premier underworld figure at the time, they established a car and truck rental company on Cannon Street on the Lower East Side. Eschewing the more dangerous aspects of bootlegging, the two partners offered transportation facilities to bootleggers seeking ways to deliver their products to thirsty customers around the city. By controlling such a crucial aspect of the bootlegging business, Siegel and Lansky became major figures in the distribution of alcohol in the New York region. By 1929 their organization was regarded as one of the Big Seven, an informal title for the seven most important illegal liquor operations in the northeastern United States. In 1929 he married Esther Krakower. They had two daughters.

Like many other bootleggers, Siegel continued his association with liquor when Prohibition ended, but in strictly legal ways. He invested with Lansky, Joe Adonis, and Frank Costello in Capitol Wines and Spirits, one of the larger liquor distributors in New York. Siegel also participated in another favorite post-Prohibition activity among former bootleggers by investing in gambling. In the early 1930s he operated crap games and a bookmaking business. At a time when several other major underworld figures such as Lansky and Costello were experimenting with gambling ventures in Florida, Arkansas, Kentucky, and Louisiana, Siegel decided to explore the investment possibilities in southern California. George Raft, one of his lifelong friends from the Lower East Side, provided an entrée into high society in Hollywood, which Siegel first visited in 1933. In 1935 or 1936 Siegel moved permanently to Hollywood, where he initially made his living by investing in floating crap games in private homes, in bookmaking at the Santa Anita track, and in gambling ships off the California coast. These business activities introduced Siegel to many members of southern California's gambling fraternity, men who had developed successful careers independent of their more famous East Coast peers.

Siegel is perhaps most remembered in popular crime lore as the inventor of the Flamingo, supposedly the casino that transformed Las Vegas into America's gambling playground. His claim to fame in this instance is not well supported by the known facts.

Siegel's initial acquaintance with Las Vegas developed from his bookmaking interests. In 1939 or 1940 the Al Capone syndicate in Chicago founded Trans-America, a wire service for bookies, and Siegel agreed to develop the West Coast market for the new company. He visited Las Vegas in 1941 as Trans-America's representative and established several partnerships with local bookies.

Since Siegel also invested in a casino called the Colonial Inn in Hallandale, Florida, with his old friend Meyer Lansky in the early 1940s, he may have developed a simultaneous interest in owning a Las Vegas casino. His desire to expand this aspect of his business activities to Las Vegas first emerged in 1943, when he attempted unsuccessfully to buy El Rancho Vegas, which had been built by California gambling entrepreneurs in 1941, and which was the first major luxury hotel-casino in Las Vegas. Two years later he formed a syndicate consisting of California and East Coast associates (including Lansky) to buy El Cortez, a casino in downtown Las Vegas.

The opportunity to build the Flamingo occurred only because its original developer, Billy Wilkerson, needed money to complete his dream. Wilkerson was a major figure in Hollywood, owning a newspaper and several famous restaurants. He was also an important figure in the gambling fraternity, and it was Wilkerson who conceived of the Flamingo as a new kind of casino featuring major Hollywood stars as one of its prime attractions. When his grandiose plans outran his financing, Wilkerson sought help from additional investors.

Siegel used Wilkerson's plight as his own opportunity. He persuaded his partners in El Cortez to sell out and invest their handsome profits in the Flamingo. Once in control (the Siegel syndicate owned 66 percent of the Flamingo), Siegel proceeded to embellish Wilkerson's original concept in an extravagant fashion that cost his partners much more money than they had intended to spend.

The Flamingo opened for business on 26 December 1946 and promptly suffered huge losses. Business was so bad that the casino had to close at the end of January 1947. Siegel promptly sought further funding from his partners, but they reputedly had run short of patience with his extravagance. The Flamingo reopened successfully in March, but Siegel's managerial deficiencies continued to threaten the economic well-being of his partners. When an unknown assassin murdered Siegel in Beverly Hills, California, his partners immediately assumed control of the Flamingo's management and turned it into a premier Las Vegas attraction.

Unlike his friend Meyer Lansky, Siegel lacked the temperament and skills to be a major innovator in the world of illegal enterprise. His reputation as a charming killer (who boasted that he had murdered twelve men) and, more importantly, as a close associate of Lansky, enabled Siegel to enjoy a relatively successful criminal career. But his stewardship of the Flamingo revealed his fundamental inability to manage a major project in a manner that could satisfy the strict accountability standards of his peers.

D.R.J.

In this 1939 photo, a sign on the Hangman's Building in Virginia City, Montana, invites visitors to "see the original gallows used by vigilantes" like those who hanged Joseph Slade in 1864.

JOSEPH ALFRED SLADE

[1829 OR 1830–10 MARCH 1864]

But for drink, Jack Slade might have led a blameless life. He was never a criminal, never stole or murdered, and in fact behaved heroically on the side of the law. The incident at the core of his reputation for ruthlessness, the killing of Jules Beni, was hardly unprovoked; Beni shot Slade five times at close range with a shotgun, and was almost lynched on the spot by witnesses, who held off only when Slade amazed everyone by getting to his feet. Beni was spared on the condition that he leave the state. He returned within the year and was preparing an ambush when friends of Slade caught him and lashed him to the corral post.

When Slade drank, he lost it. At the very end, he was ordered out of Virginia City, and agreed to leave town. But on the way out he stopped for a drink. . . .

Joseph Alfred Slade, reputed "bad man," was born in Carlyle, Illinois, the son of Charles W. Slade, a founder of Carlyle, an Illinois assemblyman, and a U.S. congressman, and Mary Kane. Little is known about Slade's childhood or education. In May 1847 he joined the volunteer army and served in the Mexican War, primarily as a teamster, detailed to protect the supply lines to the Santa Fe Trail. Honorably discharged on 16 October 1848, he soon obtained a veteran's land warrant for 160 acres and returned to Carlyle. From there he fled west, possibly to California, after killing a man with a rock in 1849. The deed may have been justified, for when he returned to Carlyle for a visit in the spring of 1863, he was not arrested.

In the late 1850s, Slade was in the employ of Russell, Majors & Waddell as a freighter and wagon-train boss and gained a considerable reputation as a cool and fearless fighter. When that firm established a passenger and mail service in the autumn of 1859 under the name of the Central Overland California and Pike's Peak Express Company, Slade replaced Jules Beni at the Julesburg station in the northeastern corner of Colorado and was charged to bring peace to the stagecoach divisions stretching along the southern border of present-day Wyoming. With gun and rope, he moved vigorously against Indian predators, horse thieves, and highwaymen and in so doing became involved in a feud with Jules Beni, who once caught Slade unarmed and unaware and riddled him with bullets and buckshot. Slade recovered, swore vengeance, and eventually trapped Beni. One legend has it that he tied him to a corral snubbing-post and slowly shot him to death in a most cruel manner, although there are discrepancies and disputes about virtually every aspect of this celebrated incident. It is a fact, however, that Slade cut off Beni's ears and carried them to the day of his own death.

When Russell, Majors & Waddell became insolvent in 1862, Ben Holladay, who took over some of its operations, continued to employ Slade but moved him to division headquarters at Virginia Dale in northern Colorado. Slade's indulgence in liquor increased, and he became a dangerous hell-raiser. After U.S. Army authorities complained about his destructive spree at Fort Halleck, located at the foot of the Medicine Bow Mountains, Holladay fired him near the end of 1862.

Slade and Maria Virginia (his wife either by formal ceremony or common law) and an Indian boy who lived with them moved to the Fort Bridger area in southwestern Wyoming, where Slade engaged in the freighting business on his own. From there he followed the gold rush to Virginia City, Montana, arriving in June 1863. He acquired mining claims, established two ranches—Ravenswood and Spring Dale—in Madison County, and engaged in freighting. He might have prospered had he not again succumbed to drunken rowdyism, shooting up saloons and stores and terrifying the citizenry of Virginia City and nearby towns. But he did not commit murder or theft and often made restitution for his destructiveness. A final spree during which he defied the People's Court and threatened the judge was his undoing. Vigilantes at Virginia City and the nearby mining camp of Nevada hanged Slade. His widow put his body in alcohol in a zinc coffin and buried him in Salt Lake City.

So ended the career of one of the West's gunmen. Reputedly he had claimed twenty-six lives, but he had never robbed or stolen and had risked his life many times so that passengers, supplies, and mails might travel in safety. The Montana editor of the *Madisonian* (quoted in John B. McClernan's *Slade's Wells Fargo Colt* [1977], p. 7) noted that five years after the hanging of Jack Slade, "another gunman, 'Wild Bill' Hickok, who had gone down in history as a great peacemaker and marshal, was known as 'the Slade of western Kansas.'"

"Jack" Slade's army discharge papers described him as five feet, six inches tall, with dark complexion, black eyes, and light hair. Mark Twain, who met him at the Rocky Ridge station, east of South Pass, noted that he was "rather broad across the cheek bones" with lips "peculiarly thin and straight" and "the most gentlemanly appearing, quiet and affable officer" he had found along the road.

M.L.S.

Belle Starr was photographed with the outlaw known as Blue Duck in the 1880s.

BELLE STARR

The woman outlaw, beautiful and dangerous, is a compelling and enduring figure. In the post–Civil War West, Belle Starr found herself cast in that role, and the legend assumed heroic proportions.

Belle was said to have borne Cole Younger's daughter. Her marriage to Jim Reed was supposed to have been performed on horseback by another member of the gang. And, like just about everyone who ever picked up a gun, she was credited with robbing the rich and giving to the poor.

And of course she was beautiful.

Well, we know that last wasn't the case. Photos survive, showing a woman who fits the contemporary description: "bony and flat-chested with a mean mouth; hatchet-faced; a gotch-toothed tart."

Woody Guthrie's ballad is the most wonderfully fanciful, with this eloquent opening:

> *Belle Starr, Belle Starr, tell me where did you roam?*
> *Since old Oklahoma's sandhills you did roam?*
> *Is it Heaven's wide street now you're trying your reins?*
> *Are you single-footing somewheres below?*
>
> *Eight men, they say, combed your black wavy hair;*
> *Eight men knew the feel of your dark leather waist;*
> *Eight men loved your tan leather circling skirt;*
> *Eight men heard the bark of the guns that you wore.*

The eight lovers Guthrie credits to Belle's account include Cole Younger, Blue Duck, Jim Reed, Cole's brother Bob Younger, William Clarke Quantrill, Frank and Jesse James, and yet another Younger brother, Jim.

Belle Starr, outlaw, was born Myra Belle Shirley in Carthage, Missouri, the daughter of John Shirley, a wealthy innkeeper, and Eliza Hatfield. In 1863 her brother, a Confederate guerrilla, was killed by Federal troops. In 1864 she moved with her family to Scycene, Texas (near Dallas), to avoid the turmoil of the border war in Missouri. She married Jim Reed, a former Confederate guerrilla from Missouri, in 1868; the couple had a daughter in 1869 and a son in 1871. Reed engaged in various criminal enterprises, including robbery and horse theft. The family fled to Los Angeles after Belle Starr's remaining brother was killed in a Texas gunfight and her husband murdered a man in Missouri. She returned with her family to Texas after federal agents in California began closing in on her husband's counterfeiting operations. In April 1874 Jim Reed robbed a stagecoach, and Belle Starr was charged as an accessory to the crime (although charges were later dropped). Jim Reed was killed by a deputy sheriff near Paris, Texas, on 6 August 1874.

In 1876 Starr sold her farm in Scycene and lived with various relatives for a while. In 1878 she moved to Youngers' Bend, Indian Territory (now Oklahoma), and for a time lived with Bruce Younger, a relative of the Missouri outlaw Cole Younger. This liaison probably helped perpetuate the myth that she carried on a lengthy affair with Cole Younger and had a child (Pearl) by him. On 5 June 1880 she married Samuel Starr, a Cherokee Indian. Belle and Sam Starr were found guilty of horse theft in 1883. Because it was the first conviction for both, they were given a lenient one-year sentence by Isaac "Hanging Judge" Parker at Fort Smith, Arkansas, but they served only nine months. After their release they presumably continued to rustle horses and engage in armed robbery. Starr was indicted several times but was never tried for the crimes. She was arrested again in 1886 for robbery but was released for lack of evidence. Her cabin in Indian Territory was reputedly a refuge for Jesse James and other noted regional outlaws, and she became a local celebrity because she consorted with lawbreakers. In a lengthy interview with the *Dallas Morning News* (7 June 1886) Starr denied that she dressed in male attire and "led a party of three men who robbed." But she did show the reporter a pair of revolvers and commented, "Next to a fine horse I admire a fine pistol." She concluded the interview by stating, "You can just say that I am a friend to any brave and gallant outlaw."

In December 1886 Sam Starr was killed in a gunfight. To hold onto her homestead in Indian Territory, Starr invited an Indian named Bill "Jim" July to live with her in 1887. She was shot and killed in ambush near her home in Youngers' Bend. The identity of her murderer was never determined, although speculation included her husband and even her son, James Edwin (Edward), with whom she was rumored to have an incestuous relationship.

Belle Starr's notoriety stemmed from her loose affiliation with other more famous Missouri outlaws, namely, members of the James-Younger gang, and the fact that she was a female engaged in criminal enterprises otherwise monopolized by males. Her national career was launched by the *National Police Gazette* in 1889 as part of its efforts to expose and capitalize on the popularity of western outlaws. Beginning in the late 1890s Starr became a biological "model" for popular criminology books, such as Richard Dugdale's *The Jukes* (1910) and Henry Goddard's *The Kallikak Family: A Study in the Heredity of Feeblemindedness* (1912), in which crime and other "social defects" were mapped out as hereditary and traced through highly entertaining family histories. The Italian physician Cesar Lombroso, often hailed as the "father" of modern criminology, featured Belle Starr in his work, *The Female Offender* (1895). She has been alternatively cast as a relative carrying the crime-ridden genes of other Missouri outlaws and as the mother of a "dynasty of outlaws." Her son, Edward, was a bootlegger who died in a saloon fight in 1896. Her daughter, Pearl, achieved notoriety as a prostitute in Fort Smith. According to legend, her genes eventually "yielded" the noted Oklahoma bandit Arthur "Pretty Boy" Floyd. More recently, she has been revived in popular culture as a nineteenth-century feminist figure.

P.G.K.

WILLIE SUTTON

[30 JUNE 1901–2 NOVEMBER 1980]

The fellow was slick. In an era when bank robbery demanded little more than a resolute spirit and an inability to recognize that actions have consequences, Willie "The Actor" Sutton brought planning, disguise, misdirection, and general resourcefulness to the pursuit. He was an artist, albeit in an antisocial medium, and his artistry won him a fair amount of respect—grudging respect from law enforcement professionals, and a less equivocal admiration from a public ever ready to acknowledge a stylish criminal.

The one blot on the Sutton escutcheon was the murder of Arnold Schuster, the observant Brooklynite whose tip led to Sutton's capture. Schuster was no criminal, just a law-abiding citizen, and he had in no sense betrayed a trust; Sutton was as unlikely to hold a grudge against him as against the officers who apprehended him or the judge who pronounced sentence.

But Albert Anastasia, head of Murder Incorporated, evidently saw Schuster on television and threw a fit, announcing that no squealer deserved to live. He ordered a hit, and some contract killer, never identified, carried it out. Sutton, according to all reports, was understandably horrified.

Willie Sutton, bank robber, was born William Francis Sutton Jr. in the tough waterfront district of Brooklyn, New York, the son of William Francis Sutton Sr., a blacksmith, and Mary Ellen Bowles. Both parents were Irish immigrants. Sutton grew up fascinated by the rough-and-tumble street life of the Brooklyn docks. He graduated from grammar school at age fifteen, the first of his family to do so. But he later admitted that he had been engaging in various petty thefts since age nine, starting with the rifling of the cash box of a local grocery. After grammar school Sutton held a number of manual labor jobs, alternating bouts of work with robberies. In 1921 he was implicated in a murder. In that same year he encountered Eddie Tate, an underworld character known as Dr. Tate, who became his criminal mentor.

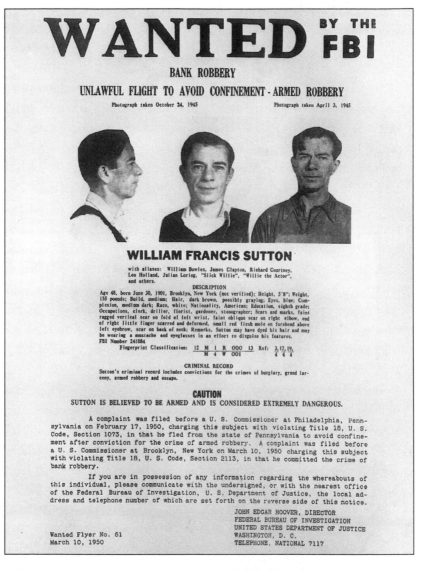

This FBI wanted poster from 1950 shows three portraits of the notorious bank robber Willie Sutton.

Tate, who dressed in banker's striped pants, frock coat, and gloves, was well educated and to Sutton a "criminal genius." Sutton said he had been an amateur until he was taken in hand by Tate and taught the finer points of safecracking. Sutton operated safely for the next several years. In April

1926, however, he was found guilty of burglary and grand larceny and sentenced to five to ten years, first at New York State's Sing Sing Prison and later at Dannemora Prison.

Sutton emerged from prison in 1929 intending, he insisted, on going straight. That same year he married Louise Leudemann; they had one child. They were divorced in 1947, and later a woman named Jeanne Courtney claimed to be his second wife. In his autobiography Sutton admitted that "banks continued to have a strong appeal for me (and) I never was able to pass one without automatically, almost unconsciously, looking it over." One day on New York City's Broadway he noticed a simple piece of business that changed his life. Two uniformed messengers rang the bell of a bank. They were immediately admitted. Sutton was sure the guard had never looked in their faces. He used a phony drama school letterhead to rent a messenger's uniform. He then carefully "cased" a bank, noting the comings and goings of employees. One day he showed up with what he said was a telegram. When the bank guard took it in both hands, Sutton lifted his gun and informed him a robbery was in process. The career of Willie "The Actor" Sutton, bank robber, was launched.

Over the next few years Sutton perfected his technique of careful preparation and playacting. He appeared at banks as, from time to time, a policeman, a postman, and even a window cleaner, in a career during which it was estimated he stole more than $2 million. One of Sutton's trademarks was to dissuade employees from resistance by assuring them insurance would pay for all losses. Sutton also committed jewel robberies, fencing his loot through the notorious Dutch Schultz. It was for one such robbery that Sutton was convicted and in June 1931 returned to Sing Sing Prison.

In prison Sutton applied his talents to escape. He succeeded in 1932 and fled to Philadelphia, where he returned to bank robbery, was captured, and was sent to Eastern State Penitentiary in Pennsylvania. Over the next eleven years he repeatedly tried to escape prison, once spending a year carefully crafting a dummy to place in his bed to convince guards he was asleep. He eventually did escape from Eastern State Penitentiary but was free only for a matter of hours. On 9 February 1947, however, he succeeded in his most famous escape, from Holmesburg County Prison outside Philadelphia, in a blinding snowstorm. At large for the next several years, Sutton worked quietly as a handyman while his fame skyrocketed and he was admitted to the FBI's Most Wanted list. In 1950 he reemerged, robbing a bank in Sunnyside, Long Island City, New York.

In February 1952 Sutton was recognized on a subway by Arnold Schuster, a tailor shop presser, who was later interviewed on television. Schuster hailed police, who despite the innumerable reports of Sutton's location investigated. Much to the astonishment of local officers Sutton was identified and arrested. When Schuster was gunned down and killed not long afterward, Sutton denied any involvement.

At the time of his arrest Sutton owed New York and Pennsylvania between 126 years and three lifetimes plus 99 years, depending on how his debt was totaled. After a number of appeals in which he distinguished himself as an astute jailhouse lawyer, on Christmas Day 1969 Sutton was released from New York's Attica Prison. He lived quietly with a sister in Florida and devoted royalties from the sale of his story to a fund to help ex-convicts. He noted that robbery had been his business, nothing more, and that he had never been "a big-shot criminal, only a notorious criminal." He died in Spring Hill, Florida.

Sutton was, in the words of one of his captors, the "Babe Ruth of bank robbers." He single-handedly lifted bank robbery out of the era of blazing machine guns and speeding getaway cars and made it an art, to the fascination of the American public. Sutton was credited with having uttered the most familiar quotation in American criminal history. When asked why he robbed banks, he supposedly responded, "because that's where the money is." Sutton later denied having made the remark, but he was astute enough to know that in the business of newspaper headlines a good legend beats the truth every day, and he accepted the attribution with grace, riding on his exploits and his quotability to became one of America's most notable, even admired, outlaws.

B.H.

HARRY KENDALL THAW

[1 FEBRUARY 1871–22 FEBRUARY 1947]

It's hard to put a rich man in jail, or to keep him there once you do. Even when it's abundantly clear that's where he belongs.

The murder of Stanford White by Harry Thaw was the sort to swell tabloid circulation figures. White, the preeminent architect of his day, made an enduring mark on the city of New York; in his private life he was an unprincipled rake with a boundless appetite. Thaw, the erratic scion of a railroad millionaire, killed a man he'd never met because he'd been his wife's former lover. And Evelyn Nesbit, to be known forever as the Girl in the Red Velvet Swing, never took her eye off the main chance; when she became pregnant during Thaw's imprisonment, she insisted that he'd fathered the child after having bribed prison employees to facilitate an unauthorized conjugal visit.

Thaw's money got him Nesbit for a bride; his mother's money kept him out of the electric chair, and eventually got him out of prison. (A bizarre psychiatric diagnosis led to his commitment in a mental facility; when he was pronounced sane, he was released.) Money kept him out of jail for the rest of his life, a life that remarkably persisted until his mid-seventies.

Harry Kendall Thaw, heir to an industrial fortune who became notorious for his murder of the renowned New York architect Stanford White, was born in Pittsburgh, Pennsylvania, the son of William Thaw, a railroad executive, and Mary Sibbet Copley, a socialite. Raised in the opulent style of the Gilded Age nouveau riche, Thaw approached neither his studies nor any other potentially gainful pursuit with evident seriousness. Though he never completed a college degree, he attended Western University of Pennsylvania (now the University of Pittsburgh) for several semesters, later transferring to Harvard University, where he was enrolled briefly as a special student before being expelled for "moral turpitude."

Journalists and lawyers congratulate Harry K. Thaw (seated, left) on his release from a mental hospital on 14 April 1924.

Upon his father's death in 1893, Thaw inherited $3 million along with a substantial share in the family's coke-producing properties. Although William Thaw had structured his will to allow Harry access to only a small portion ($2,400) of his bequest each year, Mary Thaw exerted her considerable influence over the estate's trustees to advance him $80,000 annually. Hosting lavish parties in the United States and Europe, Thaw sought to use this largess to purchase entrée into elite society. Instead, he gained a reputation as a grasping and pretentious spendthrift, unduly preoccupied with his family's wealth and the power to which he perceived it to entitle him. That same presumptuousness can be seen in Thaw's attempts to use money as a means of extricating himself from the myriad legal disputes in which he found himself embroiled, a tendency that persisted throughout his lifetime.

When Thaw visited New York, his social calendar included regular attendance at the theater, where he avidly courted attractive young actresses and chorus girls. In 1901 he first encountered Evelyn Nesbit, a striking and ambitious sixteen-year-old who was then appearing in the popular musical *Florodora*. Nesbit had, by this point, already achieved considerable prominence as a result of the numerous sketches and photographs in which she had been featured since moving to New York the year before. After pursuing her for some months, Thaw finally convinced Nesbit of his merits as a suitor. Like most of his endeavors, however, their relationship was tumultuous from the start. Tormented by thoughts of Nesbit's prior relationship with Stanford White, Thaw was often hostile and abusive, on occasion engaging in acts of sexual violence that may have been drug induced. Yet, in spite of these conflicts, the two were married in 1905.

On 25 June 1906 Evelyn Nesbit and Harry Thaw attended the premiere of a new musical, *Mamzelle Champagne*, at the rooftop theater of the old Madison Square Garden. Stanford White, who had designed the structure, was also in attendance. In the midst of the performance, Thaw approached White's table and, without warning or provocation, shot him three times at close range, killing him instantly. He was arrested at the scene and was charged with murder in a case that became an instant cause célèbre. Thaw spent the months leading up to his trial imprisoned in New York's infamous Tombs, where officials relaxed the rules to accommodate Thaw's many demands, allowing him catered meals, unrestricted visitation rights, and similar privileges. Thaw's mother invested heavily in Harry's defense, hiring numerous respected trial attorneys and expert witnesses, as well as a publicist who was assigned the responsibility of shaping public opinion in a manner most favorable to her son.

The first trial, in which Thaw pleaded not guilty, began in January 1907 and lasted approximately four months. Covered extensively by the growing local and national press corps, it was the first trial in American history to become a genuine media event. Opposing the respected District Attorney William Travers Jerome, Thaw's defense team argued that he was suffering from a rare form of mental strain they termed "dementia Americana," an ailment to which chivalrous American men bent on protecting their wives' virtue were supposedly prone to suffer. When the jury was unable to reach a verdict, a new trial was ordered. After being retried in early 1908, Thaw was found not guilty by reason of temporary insanity and was committed to the Matteawan State Hospital for the Criminally Insane, where he remained for five years.

Throughout Thaw's stay at Matteawan, his mother worked tirelessly to secure his release. When her attempts proved unavailing, Thaw finally escaped in 1913, apparently with the assistance of at least one person inside the institution. Eventually captured in Canada, he was extradited to New York, where he stood trial on conspiracy charges before being returned to Matteawan. After being pronounced sane by a jury in 1915, Thaw was finally released. The following year he divorced Evelyn Nesbit, having denied paternity of the child to whom she had given birth while he was in custody. Nesbit remained adamant throughout her life that her child had been fathered by Thaw during a rendezvous at Matteawan.

Thaw was enmeshed in another legal dispute in 1916, when he was charged with horsewhipping a teenage boy whom he was believed to have coerced into accompanying him on a cross-country trip from California. The case, which received considerable press coverage, was settled by the Thaws and the boy's parents for an undisclosed sum of money. After a 1917 suicide attempt, Thaw once again found himself in a mental hospital, where he spent the next seven years of his life. After his release in 1924 from this, his last extended stay in state custody, accusations of abusive treatment of women and boys persisted. With his mother's financial support, Thaw typically responded with offers of monetary compensation to his alleged victims.

In 1926 Thaw published *The Traitor*, his own version of the most note-worthy events of his earlier life, including his relationship with Evelyn Nesbit and his trials for the murder of Stanford White. In the 1930s he sought intermittently to work as a film producer. Lacking any particular expertise in this realm, he was unsuccessful in his efforts. Thaw spent the last years of his life in Pennsylvania, New York, California, Virginia, and Florida, where he died in Miami Beach.

L.C.

Joseph Valachi appeared before a Senate Investigations subcommittee in1963.

JOSEPH VALACHI
[22 SEPTEMBER 1904–3 APRIL 1971]

Joe Valachi was a lifelong professional criminal, a soldier in an organized crime family. Yet we know his name not for the crimes he committed but because of his role as a witness, the first large-scale public informant on the inner workings of the Mafia—or, as he himself taught us to call it, La Cosa Nostra.

Ironically enough, Valachi got into organized crime by holding his tongue. While imprisoned at Sing Sing, he was the target of a knife attack ordered by a gangster named Ciro Terranova. He survived, and refused to name his attacker; this brought him to the attention of gangland higher-ups and led, upon his release, to his admittance into Salvatore Maranzano's gang. While the leadership changed over the years, in coups bloodless and otherwise, Valachi remained a low-level soldier and survived in that capacity for more than thirty years.

Then, back in prison, he committed a murder in an effort to avoid being killed himself, and finally found his true calling as a witness, spewing out reams of testimony that made not merely law enforcement officials but the entire American public privy to the inner workings of organized crime. However high the price on his head, Valachi managed to outlive Vito Genovese and die of a heart attack.

Nowadays he looks like a pioneer. Omerta, *the Sicilian code of silence, is these days honored in the breach, if at all, and the Witness Protection Program is jammed full of former gang members who, after taking a long look at the prospect of a life sentence, decided they'd rather rat than rot.*

Joseph Valachi, career criminal and Mafia informer, was born Joseph Michael Valachi in New York City, the son of Dominick Valachi, a vegetable peddler and garbage scow laborer, and Marie Casale. Some sources give his year of birth as 1903. One of seventeen children, Valachi grew up in abject poverty in Manhattan's East Harlem. The Valachi family was so poor that they had to store stacks of stolen coal for winter heat in the filthy room that Valachi slept in, and his mother used old cement bags for sheets. When he was eleven, Valachi was sent to reform school. His formal education ended at that point, and he remained functionally illiterate for most of his life until he made the momentous decision to write his "memoirs," which became Peter Maas's famous *The Valachi Papers* (1968).

By the time Valachi was eighteen, his petty thievery had led to full-fledged membership in a Manhattan gang, where he soon became an expert "wheelman," or driver of getaway cars. In 1923 Valachi went to federal prison for burglary. He spent nine months in Sing Sing and was again incarcerated there for burglary in 1925. When he was released in 1928, he noted, "I didn't learn much in that [prison] school, but at least I could read something. . . . Before I went to Sing Sing, I could hardly make out street signs. But the real education was being worldly wise."

After his "educational" prison sentences, Valachi's apprenticeship in the criminal world was complete, and his initiation into the Mafia's secret society, which he called "La Cosa Nostra," or "this thing of ours," came in 1930. In *The Valachi Papers* he vividly relates the details of the ceremony, performed entirely in Italian by Salvatore Maranzano, the most powerful Mafia don in New York. The initiation, which ushered in some forty new members, or "soldiers," involved much violent symbolism and swearing of oaths. The central points, according to Valachi, were that the Cosa Nostra "comes before everything—our blood family, our religion, our country," and that "to betray the secret of Cosa Nostra means death without trial."

Since Valachi was a low-level soldier in a Mafia "family," he had to follow a rigid chain of command from crew chief to lieutenant to underboss (*subcapo*) and ultimately to the ruling boss of the family, the *capo*. All members of this highly structured Mafia family were united by one common bond: they had to be Italian. However, Valachi revealed that the Cosa Nostra is a closed society only within a much larger framework involving an ethnically diverse spectrum of American gangsters: Irish, Jewish, African American, and Puerto Rican, among many others.

According to Valachi, the loose Mafia confederation existed in most major American cities, with resort centers such as Miami, Las Vegas, and pre-Castro Havana designated "open" territory where any family could operate. About a third of the Cosa Nostra membership was in New York City, which was unique in having five families. Valachi began as part of the Maranzano family, which in 1930 was in the middle of the "Castellammarese War," an internal Mafia struggle for power between Maranzano and Joseph Masseria for the position of *càpo di tùtti I càpi* (boss of all bosses). Masseria, whose top lieutenants were Lucky Luciano, Vito Genovese, and Carlo Gambino, had sentenced all Cosa Nostra from the Italian village of Castellammarese to death. This group included Maranzano and many of his loyalists. During the bloody years of 1930 and 1931 Valachi was assigned to the palace guard of Maranzano himself. He was given many "contracts," or sanctioned Mafia murders, and carried them out to the letter.

Throughout this violent period Valachi was at the fringes of some of the most famous events in Mafia history. With the defections of Luciano, Genovese, and Gambino, the Maranzano faction won the Castellammarese War when Luciano arranged the murder of Masseria in April 1931. Five months later, as part of an intricate plan to exterminate virtually all important Mafia old-timers, Luciano guaranteed his ascension to power by setting up Maranzano's murder. Valachi, who was warned of this "hit," escaped unscathed and was established as a soldier in good standing in the Luciano family.

In 1932 Valachi, newly affluent with income from slot machine rackets granted him by Luciano himself, married Mildred Reina, the daughter of a murdered gangster. They had one child. Now a family man, Valachi made a good living in New York City as a loan shark, as a numbers racketeer, and eventually as a restaurateur and part-owner of a dress factory.

During World War II Valachi maintained his lifestyle by dealing in black market ration stamps. After the war he followed the fashionable flow of gangsters to the suburbs and bought a home in Yonkers. This period of Valachi's life in crime was relatively tranquil, but it ended abruptly with the last violent episode of his career.

In 1959 Valachi, who disliked the illegal drug trade, was sentenced to fifteen years in prison on a narcotics violation. For the rest of his life he said that he received a "bum rap" on this charge. Meanwhile Vito Genovese, who had supplanted the deported Lucky Luciano as boss of Valachi's family, outmaneuvered rival boss Frank Costello in a bid to become boss of all bosses. Within a year, however, Genovese was also convicted of a narcotics charge and was sent to the same federal prison in Atlanta where Valachi was incarcerated. For a time the two shared the same cell.

The beginning of the end came for Valachi when, through the machinations of the prison grapevine, Genovese got the mistaken impression that Valachi was working for the Bureau of Narcotics. Genovese began to shun Valachi, and one night in classic Mafia style, he planted a "kiss of death" on his one-time soldier. Valachi, now fearful of being beaten to death or poisoned, was sent to solitary confinement and refused to eat. After returning to the general prison population, Valachi became justifiably paranoid and was certain he was going to be killed. On 22 June 1962 he noticed a sinister inmate lurking in the prison shadows. In a panic, he picked up a pipe and beat to death an innocent man whom he had mistaken for Joseph Di Palermo, a Genovese henchman. Valachi was charged with first-degree murder.

During negotiations to reduce the charge to murder in the second degree, Valachi agreed to cooperate with FBI agent James P. Flynn, partly to expiate his criminal past, partly for revenge, and partly as a calculated bid for survival. For the next year Valachi was interrogated in a series of federal jails under tight security, since the Mafia had placed a $100,000 "contract" on his life. The FBI discovered that Valachi possessed almost total recall and cross-checked his story meticulously with their own crime files. He never contradicted their records.

Soon Valachi expressed a desire to testify in public. In September and October 1963 Valachi held a large portion of the United States in thrall as he described the lurid history of organized crime in America in televised hearings of Senator John McClellan's Senate Subcommittee on Investigations. Overnight the Valachi name became as recognizable as that of Capone, Luciano, and Genovese. Because of his importance, he was now asked to put his recollections in writing. For the next thirteen months he produced some 300,000 words in an exhaustive recounting of a thirty-year period of the inner workings of the Mafia. In 1965, with Valachi's consent, author Peter Maas was named to edit these memoirs. The manuscript eventually became the unique social document called *The Valachi Papers*. It demystified the closed world of organized crime and exposed it as a reflection of the dark side of American subculture.

Joseph Valachi, an obscure thug and murderer, with one extended outpouring of firsthand information, seriously undermined the effectiveness of the American Mafia by exposing it as a multimillion-dollar national crime cartel. By revealing its structure in great detail and by naming names, he showed American justice the face of the enemy. Valachi died of a heart attack in a federal penitentiary in El Paso, Texas.

B.L.J.

Some accounts of California bandit Tiburcio Vásquez have romanticized his criminal exploits.

TIBURCIO VÁSQUEZ

[15 AUGUST 1835–19 MARCH 1875]

"Tiburcio Vásquez was a native of early California, born in Monterrey in 1835. He was known as one of California's most clever and daring "Bandito" after fleeing to the hills at the age of 16 to escape a lynching party for allegedly committing a crime. . . . It is said that he made it possible for the Indians of the San Juan Bautista region to survive the winter months by supplying them with medical aid and food with money taken from various robberies.

"Tiburcio Vásquez was hanged at the age of 40 for a murder he swore he did not commit. Because his exploits came to symbolize the economic and political struggle between Mexican Californians and the Americans after the Gold Rush, Vásquez and his efforts personified those of an early Californian Robin Hood."

That's a not entirely objective view of Tiburcio Vásquez, but its bias is understandable when one considers the source—the promotional material of the Tiburcio Vásquez Health Center, a thriving facility providing health care in southern Alameda County, California. Immortality takes many forms and is visited upon the most unlikely recipients, but not even Robin Hood had a hospital named after him. Eat your heart out, Jesse James. . . .

Tiburcio Vásquez, bandit, was probably the son of another Tiburcio Vásquez, a soldier, politician, and cattleman, and Elvira Hernández. He stumbled into a criminal career about 1852 when he was a witness, and perhaps an accessory, to the killing of an Anglo constable in a dance hall brawl. Afraid of being implicated, Vásquez fled the scene and drifted into an apprenticeship in small-time crime, mostly stealing horses and cattle. He later said that he first secured his mother's blessing to go out and take his chances on "living off the world"—and suffering at its hands.

Arrested for the first time in 1857 for stealing horses, Vásquez was sentenced to five years in San Quentin. He escaped in the general prison break of 1859 but was rearrested that same year for rustling horses; returned to his cell, he was not released until 1863. Vásquez was next a suspect in the murder of an Italian butcher. He brazenly volunteered to serve as interpreter for the coroner's inquest before suspicion was fixed on him as the culprit. He then "skipped," but because there was no hard evidence of his guilt, no murder charge was filed against him.

Vásquez returned to stealing livestock—and other men's wives. He was quite the philanderer and is believed to have been shot, possibly more than once, by irate fathers or husbands of his *enamoradas*. He risked capture when he stole the wife of one of his gang members, a Chileno named Abdon Leiva. The cuckold turned state's evidence, and Vásquez only narrowly escaped when a posse raided his hiding place. In 1867 he was subsequently captured by another posse for stealing cattle and sent back to San Quentin.

His three terms of "graduate study" in San Quentin made Vásquez a more ambitious criminal. In 1871 he organized a gang and robbed a stage at Soap Lake, near San Felipe on the Pacheco Pass Road. To this point his crimes had not resulted in violence, and he simply tied up his victims after robbing them. Shortly thereafter, however, he robbed a traveler who recognized him and informed the sheriff of Monterey County and the state's best-known lawman, Sheriff Harry Morse of Alameda County. The peace officers' pursuit of Vásquez, a splendid horseman, failed, but a Santa Cruz constable found him and shot him.

Even though he was wounded in the chest, Vásquez made a remarkable sixty-mile ride to safety at Joaquín Murieta's old hideout of Arroyo Cantua in the Coast Range. After he recovered, he held up the San Benito stage and again evaded pursuing officers. Most Mexican-Californians admired the brave bandit and many sheltered him and observed a code of silence when questioned by peace officers (almost always Anglos) about his whereabouts. For his part, Vásquez did not molest the quicksilver miners of New Almadén and New Idria; even their employers looked the other way in a tacit truce.

In the spring of 1873 Vásquez and his right-hand man, Clodovio Chávez, invaded a little settlement, Firebaugh's Ferry, and robbed its general store.

He next planned to halt a Southern Pacific payroll train, but word of his plot was leaked so he struck the 21 Mile House, below San Jose, instead. This raid was a warmup for his raid on the San Benito County village of Tres Pinos, later renamed Paicines. On 26 August 1873 he and a few men ransacked the general store after tying up clerks and customers. But a sheepherder, variously described as a Portuguese and a Frenchman but apparently a Basque with a name resembling Bernard Berhurri, blundered into the holdup. When he was ordered to halt, the shepherd panicked and ran. Either Vásquez or one of his lieutenants, Moreno (later given a life sentence for the crime), or both of them, shot the shepherd dead. Then Vásquez ordered a hostler and a teamster to lie down to be tied. When the hostler hesitated, Vásquez knocked him out with the butt of his pistol. The teamster, George Redford, was deaf but seeing that something was wrong, ran. Vásquez shot him through the heart. A small boy also tried to make a dash to safety and was brutally bludgeoned by Chávez. Finally, the hotel proprietor, Leland Davidson, took refuge in his hotel, but Vásquez fired through the closed door with his Henry rifle and killed him.

Peace officers, the press, and the Anglo public all demanded vengeance for what was called the Tres Pinos Massacre, but the outlaws, as usual, evaded pursuit and robbed Jones's Store near Millerton in November. On the day after Christmas 1873, they raided the village of Kingston in Fresno County. Vásquez robbed perhaps thirty-five men as he plundered two stores and a hotel of provisions, goods, and $2,000 in coin, watches, and jewelry.

In January 1874 Governor Newton Booth proclaimed a $3,000 reward for the arrest of Vásquez, $2,000 for his corpse. (The bounty on Vásquez, if taken alive, was later raised to $8,000.) As if defying the governor, Vásquez held up two more stagecoaches in February and got away. This led Booth to fund one of the longest manhunts in western history. Harry Morse trailed the bandit for 2,700 miles, crisscrossing backwoods California, but came up empty-handed, while the *bandido* robbed an Italian sheepman near San Gabriel. Nonetheless the tireless Morse bribed a Mexican-Californian into betraying the outlaw's hiding place, the adobe of a Greek named George "Allen" (actually Charalambo), a former driver in the army's camel experiment. Because the hideout was located in Los Angeles County, Morse yielded the glory of capture (and the reward) to that county's sheriff, William R. Rowland, who sent a posse with Undersheriff Albert Johnson. Also in the posse was San Francisco *Chronicle* reporter George A. Beers. When the bandit leader jumped out of a window and ran for cover, it was Beers who brought him down with a charge of buckshot.

After he recovered in the Los Angeles jail, Vásquez was transferred to the San Jose jail to await trial. There he was visited by crowds of people, who brought him presents of flowers, food, and wine. Most of his visitors were sentimental women who romanticized him as a Robin Hood despite the fact that his victims included Italian immigrants and a Basque sheepherder—hardly American *ricos.*

Vásquez admitted he was a robber but insisted that he had killed no one, and he claimed to have been driven to crime by California's *yánquis.* "The Americans heaped wrongs upon me in Monterey, and the officers of the law hounded me," he complained. Found guilty of the Tres Pinos murders, Vásquez was sentenced to death, and his appeal was denied. In the figurative shadow of the gallows, he dictated two messages. One, correctly, assured his surviving gang members that he had not betrayed them. The other was an attempt to win more sympathy for himself as a vulgar celebrity. Role-playing the "gallant outlaw" to the hilt, he urged parents to keep their children aloof from "the degrading companionship of the immoral and the vicious." He asked the pardon of everyone he had injured and the prayers of all good Christians. His last words on the scaffold were "Pronto!—Make it quick!"

Unlike his legendary predecessor and mentor, Joaquín Murieta, who may actually have been a composite of several *bandidos* named Joaquín, Vásquez, the last of California's notorious Hispanic bandits, was very much a figure of history, not myth.

R.H.D.

JOHN WHITE WEBSTER

[20 MAY 1793–30 AUGUST 1850]

I hadn't heard of John White Webster until I began editing this volume. Then, even as I was in the process of deciding which criminals would make the cut, PBS's American Experience *series dramatized the Webster case, with a co-writer/producer declaring it "the O. J. Simpson case of its day." There were huge mobs around the courthouse, she said, with reporters in attendance from all over the country, and from as far away as Berlin, Paris, and London. "Back then," she added, "it was just truly shocking that someone of Webster's class and social standing would have committed such a crime." What's more surprising, I'd say, is that someone of Webster's class and social standing would have gone to the gallows.*

While the program worked to suggest that the case was still in some respects a mystery, the circumstantial evidence all by itself looks pretty convincing, and Webster's confession doesn't leave much room for doubt.

Even so, I can't avoid the feeling Johnnie Cochran could have gotten him off. . . .

John White Webster, university professor and murderer, was born in Boston, Massachusetts, the son of Redford Webster, an apothecary, and Hannah White. Soon after Webster's birth, his family moved to Amesbury, Massachusetts, where his father achieved great financial success in his business. Webster enrolled at Harvard College, where he was more mischievous than studious; still, he earned a bachelor's degree there in 1811 and a medical degree in 1815. That same year he continued his training at Guy's Hospital Medical School in London, where John Keats, also a student there, became his friend and fellow "dresser" for a hospital surgeon. Completing his course of instruction, Webster went on a scientific tour through England. On his way back to Boston during 1817 and 1818, he vacationed in the Azores, where he fell in love with Harriet Fredrica Hickling,

University professor John White Webster was convicted of murder in 1850.

the daughter of the American consul stationed at Fayal. They got married in May 1818, established their residence in Boston, and became the parents of four daughters.

After taking over the medical practice of one of his former instructors and finding it unprofitable, Webster in 1824 joined the Harvard faculty. He lectured there on chemistry until 1826, when he became an adjunct professor. The following year he became Erving Professor of Chemistry and Mineralogy. Webster made himself popular with the students less by his lectures than by establishing in 1838 the annual "Senior Spread"—an outdoor dancing and dinner event in the Harvard Yard on Class Day. He and his wife entertained lavishly, were guests of illustrious Bostonians, and often went to concerts. Webster also played whist and the flute.

Constantly living beyond his means, Webster was disappointed when his father died in 1833 and left much of his estate to Webster's four daughters. Webster compounded his financial troubles in 1835 by using his inheritance to build in Cambridge a house he could not afford (and was later forced to sell) and by investing in worthless land in the West. In 1842 Webster borrowed $400 from George Parkman, an acquaintance who was a wealthy Boston merchant and real estate speculator. After graduating from Harvard with an A.B. in 1809, Parkman, who was the uncle of the historian Francis Parkman, had obtained a medical degree at the University of Aberdeen in Scotland, studied psychiatry in Paris, and returned to Boston to pioneer in the treatment of the mentally ill. Inheriting money and property, however, he gradually devoted most of his time to collecting rents and to lending money privately. Even though the Parkman Professorship of Anatomy was established in his name after he had given in 1846 the land on which a new Harvard medical school was built, Parkman was widely regarded with disfavor because of his sharp land sales and eccentric behavior. Having repaid only a fraction of his original loan, Webster in 1847 again borrowed from Parkman. As collateral for a combined note of $2,432, Webster pledged his household furniture, books, and a collection of minerals. The next year Webster borrowed $1,200 from Parkman's wealthy brother-in-law Robert Gould Shaw (grandfather of the Civil War martyr Robert Gould Shaw), using the same minerals as security. When Parkman heard of this fraudulent transaction, he argued with Webster and agreed to discuss the situation further at Webster's Harvard laboratory on 23 November 1849. Parkman, who had been sighted near the medical college shortly before the interview, was never seen again.

A search of Webster's laboratory produced no evidence of Parkman. But on 30 November a Harvard janitor, suspicious of Webster's behavior, broke through masonry beneath his laboratory and into a privy separating it and the dissecting room. Finding human remains, he summoned the police, who removed parts of a pelvis, intestine, thigh, and leg. In or near the laboratory they also found a thorax, a lung, and another thigh in a tea chest and bone fragments and the remains of false teeth in the laboratory furnace. When Webster was arrested, he tried unsuccessfully to commit suicide by swallowing strychnine. Boston went into a frenzy, and the wheels of justice moved quickly.

On 13 December a coroner's jury concluded that the body parts were those of Parkman and that Webster had killed him. A grand jury indicted Webster, and, under Massachusetts law, the capital case had to be tried by a quorum of the supreme judicial court, the chief justice of which was Lemuel Shaw, a distinguished jurist and the father-in-law of Herman Melville. At his trial, which began on 19 March 1850, Webster professed his innocence and showed admirable composure; but the evidence against him, though only circumstantial, was overwhelming. The dentist who had made the false teeth, of gold, enamel, and "mineral," and with spiral springs, identified them as Parkman's; also, the efforts to destroy the remains and their location in Webster's laboratory pointed the finger of guilt at him. By law, Webster could not testify during the trial, and his wavering counsel, rather than presenting one seamless defense, presented alternative defenses.

After deliberating only three hours on 30 March 1850, the twelve-man jury returned a verdict of guilty. On 1 April 1850 Shaw sentenced Webster to hang. Later that month Webster wrote the governor a sworn avowal of innocence and asked for clemency. But suddenly on 23 May, after being visited in prison by George Putnam, a Unitarian minister from Roxbury, Massachusetts, Webster prepared and gave him a full written confession. In it, he described his argument with a heartlessly vindictive Parkman, his impulsively braining him with a grapevine trunk, his panic on finding Parkman dead, and his dismembering the body and disposing of parts— by potash, nitrate of copper, fire, and concealment. Although Putnam presented this petition to the appropriate committee on pardons, Webster was hanged as sentenced. He had wanted his body placed in his family vault at the Mount Auburn Cemetery, but—fearing body snatchers and without informing his widow or daughters—a couple of his friends and one of his defense attorneys buried him near Boston's Old North Church.

R.L.G.

Seth Wyman served time in the state prison in Charlestown, Massachusetts, shown here in an 1805 drawing.

SETH WYMAN

[4 MARCH 1784–2 APRIL 1843]

In and of itself, Seth Wyman's criminal career wouldn't have gotten him into this book—or indeed much of anywhere. He was nothing but a common thief, and his exploits as a shoplifter are hardly the stuff from which legends spring.

Wyman's chief pursuit seems to have been stealing cloth, and I don't suppose anybody does that anymore. But a fellow I know supported himself and his heroin habit for years by stealing clothing from the better stores, selling off his swag to a fence. As dope and drink took their toll, he became unequal to the task of shoplifting at Barneys, a pricey Manhattan menswear retailer. A resourceful improviser, he took to stealing labels from clothes at Barneys and sewing them into garments he filched from Lamston's, a budget chain store.

When his fence caught on, he was disconsolate. "But I trusted you," he protested. "I thought you were an honest man!"

It makes a good story, but it won't get my friend's name in the history books. Wyman owes his own enduring fame not to the crimes he committed but to the fact that he sat down and wrote about them. But for his autobiography, we wouldn't know a thing about the man.

And why should we believe a word of it? He was certainly no more an honest man than my shoplifting friend, so why should we trust him? According to him, every time he got into a fight he blackened his opponent's eye. Well, perhaps the hand was quicker than the eye, even as the pen has proved mightier than the sword. But I'd hate to take Wyman's word for it.

I believe him, though, when he tells of girdling his neighbor's trees. It's unlikely anyone would make up a story that shows him to be such a gratuitously mean-spirited son of a bitch.

Seth Wyman, thief and author, was born in Goffstown, New Hampshire, the son of Seth Wyman and Sarah Atwood, farmers. Wyman documented his life and career in his posthumously published autobiography, *The Life and Adventures of Seth Wyman, Embodying the Principal Events of a Life Spent in Robbery, Theft, Gambling, Passing Counterfeit Money . . .* (1843). His earliest attempts at what he would later term "roguery" began at a very early age, when he stole a silver dollar from a neighbor's house, explaining to his mother that he had found it in the street. Although Wyman later praised both of his parents in print as honest and upright individuals, he soon graduated to more serious crimes, gaining a sense of satisfaction and accomplishment with each theft. He also displayed a streak of misanthropy, killing a neighbor's trees by girdling them for no apparent gain other than the neighbor's distress.

Wyman's father, a wealthy and successful farmer, tried to set up his son in farming on a large tract on the Penobscot River in what is now Maine, but honest labor (at which Wyman would make occasional efforts, including stints at farming, shipbuilding, and sledmaking—usually with stolen tools) never held his attention for long. Early in his career Wyman specialized in shoplifting, at which he became quite adept. His normal modus operandi was to enter a store and engage the clerk or shopkeeper in idle conversation. When another customer entered the establishment or the clerk was otherwise sufficiently distracted, Wyman would quickly stuff some merchandise under a large cloak that he wore during his escapades. Watches and bolts of cloth held particular appeal for Wyman, but he did not disdain stealing any item of value. He usually worked alone but would occasionally use one or more assistants. Careful always to stash his booty in a meticulously selected hiding place, Wyman thus avoided detection when the inevitable suspicion generated by his activities led to searches of his dwelling place. According to his autobiography, Wyman enjoyed a long string of uninterrupted successful thefts.

Usually moving from place to place in order to avoid the detection of his crimes, Wyman generally indulged in life's pleasures. He was no stranger to hard liquor, often fortifying himself for his more daring crimes with brandy. Enjoying fine dining and card playing, he also paid consistent attention to women, often promising various potential mates the moon and the stars, promises which turned out to be worthless. A relationship with an unhappily married woman, Welthy Loomis Chandler, eventually culminated in marriage in Boston in 1808. The couple, who had already had a long-standing common-law relationship—Wyman's first stint in jail was on a charge of adultery, not theft—eventually had six children. While Wyman seems to have genuinely cared for his wife (and his parents), he seems to have formed no other lasting relationship with any other person.

During his years of activity, Wyman shuttled between Massachusetts, New Hampshire, and what is now Maine. He was incarcerated on several occasions, during which he attempted (several times successfully) to escape. His *Autobiography* is replete with tales of fist fights with other men (in which Wyman was inevitably triumphant) and woeful descriptions of the harsh conditions under which he was forced to live during his periods of imprisonment. Late in his career, Wyman took up the passing of counterfeit money (manufactured in Canada and drawn from a variety of banks), at which he seems to have been successful.

Wyman relocated to Maine about 1815, having finally worn out his welcome in Goffstown. Although he attempted farming one last time, his old habits proved difficult to leave behind. He was convicted of larceny in

June 1817 in Augusta, Maine, and received a three-year sentence to the state prison in Charlestown, Massachusetts. Pardoned after a year (which he spent composing verse), Wyman returned to New Hampshire. While the burden of supporting his wife and children (who had been living in a Boston almshouse) was lifted from the commonwealth of Massachusetts (a factor that helped him gain his early release), Wyman proved no more adept at remaining honest in his old surroundings. After once again stealing cloth (and again being caught), he was sent to the New Hampshire State Prison on 20 April 1820, where he served a full three-year sentence. Returning yet again to Goffstown following his release, he managed to live in relative peace (slowed by the effects of years of hard living as well as a serious injury to his back that he received from a fall from the third story of a factory while assisting in its construction). Plagued by poor health in his later years, he died in Goffstown after having apparently undergone an eleventh-hour conversion to religion.

While his lifestyle was hardly worthy of emulation, Seth Wyman's autobiography (published as a cautionary tale) provides a fascinating look at the social mores of the criminal element in early nineteenth-century American society.

E.L.L.

Bob, Jim, and Cole Younger (right) pose with their sister Rhetta.

COLE YOUNGER

[15 JANUARY 1844–20 MARCH 1916]

Cole Younger is often regarded as a man of principle, compelled by circumstance to take up arms, a reluctant participant in the ill-fated Northfield robbery, who spent the rest of his life maintaining a noble silence about his fellow robbers.

Whatever dignity and nobility he has attained is largely the result of his own efforts. In an interview he gave in prison, in the remarkably self-serving autobiography he published after his release, Younger does everything he can to create a positive image for himself. Given that the man never married and died without issue, you have to wonder why he cared all that much for posterity's judgment.

According to Younger, he saved some lives during the notorious massacre at Lawrence, Kansas. (He couldn't have saved many; of the town's male population, only one boy survived.) According to Younger, the Northfield debacle was the only time he ever robbed a bank, or rode with the James brothers after the war. According to Younger, he'd have been a clergyman but for the fact that Union troops murdered his father and burned his family home, leaving him set on vengeance.

Traditionally, the winners get to write the history, but sometimes the losing side manages to get its own in. Cole Younger started to do so when he began serving his life sentence at Stillwater, Minnesota. "We were victims of circumstance," he told a reporter. "We were drove to it."

Cole Younger, outlaw, was born Thomas Coleman Younger in Lee's Summit, Missouri, the son of Henry Washington Younger, an affluent plantation owner who served at one time as a county judge and also as mayor of Harrisonville, Missouri, and Bursheba Fristoe. Younger grew up experiencing at close hand the violent conflicts between antislavery factions in nearby Kansas and proslavery groups in Missouri prior to the Civil

War. The war intensified these conflicts, as the region experienced numerous atrocities carried out by rival guerrilla bands. Younger was a prominent lieutenant in William Clarke Quantrill's band of Confederate guerrillas
and participated in the massacre of about 150 unarmed pro-Union men
in Lawrence, Kansas. He later joined the regular Confederate army. Younger's
father opposed secession and remained neutral during the war. Nevertheless,
on 20 July 1862 he was ambushed, robbed, and murdered by Union soldiers. Cole Younger's family home was burned by Federal troops, and his
sisters were jailed.

After the Civil War, Younger and his three brothers, Jim, John, and Bob,
participated with former guerrilla comrades Frank and Jesse James in a
series of robberies. In March 1874 John Younger was killed in a gunfight
with Pinkerton agents. Cole Younger published a moving letter in the *St.
Louis Republican* proclaiming his brother's innocence and condemning the
Pinkertons who "hunted him down like a wild beast" (30 Nov. 1874).

For the next ten years the Youngers and other ex-Confederates were
lauded by the press and politicians of the Confederate wing of Missouri's
Democratic party. The prominence of the Younger family and injustices
done to the boys' parents by Union troops during the war were frequently
recounted. Newspaper editor John Newman Edwards was the prime force
in shaping a Robin Hood image for the James-Younger gang through
numerous editorials and in the book *Noted Guerrillas* (1877). In one essay
Edwards described the brigands as "men who might have sat with Arthur
at the Round Table, ridden in tourney with Sir Lancelot, or won the colors of Guinevere" (*Kansas City Times*, 29 Sept. 1872).

Edwards served as an able "campaign manager" for the James-Younger
gang, but these outlaws also had a shrewd sense of how to construct a
good public image. Besides writing letters to newspapers claiming innocence and condemning the ruling Radical Republicans, the bandits dramatized their robberies in meaningful ways, fostering a Robin Hood image
tinged with postwar politics.

All these public relations efforts culminated in an amnesty resolution
proposed by the Confederate wing of the Democratic party in Missouri

before the Missouri House of Representatives on 17 March 1875. The resolution described the James and Younger brothers as men who were driven into crime by Missouri Republicans and characterized them as men too brave to be mean, too generous to be revengeful, and too gallant and honorable to betray a friend or break a promise. It further suggested that most, if not all, the offenses with which they have been charged were committed by others, and perhaps by those pretending to hunt them. With every ex-Confederate in the legislature supporting it, the resolution narrowly missed the two-thirds majority needed to pass.

Attempts to revive the resolution were dashed by the attempted robbery of a bank in Northfield, Minnesota, on 7 September 1876, during which a cashier was killed and another wounded as he gave the alarm. In the confusion that followed, several robbers also were killed or wounded. The three Younger brothers wandered lost in the unfamiliar landscape for two weeks. On 21 September they were captured by a posse after a spirited gunfight. All the Younger brothers were severely wounded. Only two bandits escaped, presumably Frank and Jesse James.

The Younger brothers were taken by wagon through Madelia, Minnesota, where a crowd gathered. Cole Younger, despite eleven bullet wounds, managed to stand and bow to the women. Surprisingly, the captured bandits were treated kindly and regarded with curiosity. Numerous citizens and reporters met with the celebrities once they arrived at the jail in Faribault, Minnesota. The press interviewed the brothers at length and presented a picture of decent and courageous men united by bonds of love, honor, and compassion. These were also men who were quite adept at manipulating public sentiment. Younger told of his family and spoke of his religious background, often quoting from the Bible and expressing deep regret for his crimes. William Settle noted that Younger "was able to touch some of his audience, and when they wept, he allowed tears to roll down his cheeks. Then the visitor would usually reach a 'wipe' through the bars for him to use in drying the tears" (William A. Settle Jr., *Jesse James Was His Name* [1966, p. 93]). All three brothers pled guilty to robbery and murder and were sentenced to life in Stillwater Penitentiary.

Bob Younger died in prison in 1889. Cole and Jim Younger were paroled in 1901 but were required to live in Minnesota. Jim Younger committed suicide in 1902. Cole Younger received an official pardon in 1903 and eventually joined Frank James in a touring Wild West show. To his death in Lee's Summit, Missouri, Younger refused to reveal the identity of the two robbers who escaped from Northfield. He never married or had children.

Younger's fame was eclipsed by fellow gang member Jesse James, arguably America's most noted criminal. However, like James, Younger received widespread adulation both in his own lifetime and for following generations. His notoriety resulted from several factors. First, he was supported through the media and in other ways by powerful friends in Missouri politics. Second was his identity as an ex-Confederate soldier from a respectable Missouri family. And third was the social context that made extralegal symbols of justice marketable to a broad audience; in addition to the turmoil of Reconstruction politics, there was an economic depression in the 1870s throughout the West that was widely blamed on banks, railroads, and land monopolies—the victims of outlaws of the time such as the James-Younger gang, Billy the Kid, and Sam Bass. Newspapers and dime novels found outlaw tales to be quite profitable.

P.G.K.

A NOTE ON THE AMERICAN NATIONAL BIOGRAPHY

"How can I get into the *American National Biography*?"

As general editor of the *ANB*, I'm asked this question often. I look intently at the questioner and respond, invariably:

"Drop dead."

"But there's more," I say. "Being dead is the easiest criterion for inclusion. You also have to do something important. Compose a symphony. Paint a picture. Lead a social movement. Found a business enterprise. Invent a gizmo."

Few faces brighten at this, so I explain that the *ANB* defines "historical significance" broadly. One need not attain the stature of Eleanor Roosevelt or Andrew Carnegie or Thomas Alva Edison, though such people are of course included.

"The *ANB* includes people who have attained significance in all fields of endeavor, ranging from 'accordionists,' 'acrobats,' and 'actuaries' to 'yachtsmen,' 'Zionists,' and 'zoologists.'"

These words, too, are usually met with silence.

"But then," I add, lowering my voice, "there is yet another way."

I explain that the *ANB* is a historical tool, the result of a decade's labor of the nation's academic community. It is published under the auspices of the American Council of Learned Societies and Oxford University Press, the work of hundreds of associate editors, over 7,000 scholars, and a small army of copyeditors and fact-checkers. It was undertaken to help the nation understand its past. It is not a "hall of fame" of the great and good. It includes bank robbers as well as bankers, and assassins as well as astronauts.

"You mean, I can get in the *ANB* by robbing a bank or something?"

"Yes," I respond, "if you do it in such a way as to leave an imprint on the nation. But while undertaking your spectacularly antisocial actions, don't forget the part about dropping dead."

Those who have picked up this mischievously entitled volume can perhaps take guidance from among its sampling of con men, murderers, assassins, and rogues of all sorts who, in doing their worst, have become a part of the nation's history, and thus of the *ANB*. Lawrence Block, author of many a book about impressively wayward people, has dipped deep into the mire and muck from among the nearly 18,000 figures in the *ANB*, and ladled out a wonderfully malodorous brew of miscreants.

But after you have finished Block's splendid decoction, I encourage you to browse through the volumes of the *ANB*, available at nearly all libraries, or else to peruse the *Online ANB*, which can be accessed either through your local library or directly through a subscription service with Oxford University Press.

And if you happen upon someone worthy of note (for good or ill!) who is not in the *ANB*, I encourage you to write to me at Barnard College, Columbia University. But please check, first, to ensure that your figure is indeed deceased.

Mark C. Carnes
Ann Whitney Olin Professor of History, Barnard College
General Editor, *American National Biography*

AUTHORS OF ARTICLES
FROM THE *AMERICAN NATIONAL BIOGRAPHY*

S.M.A.   Stephen M. Archer (John Wilkes Booth)

D.B.   Dee Brown (Butch Cassidy)

D.R.B.   David R. Bewley-Taylor (Frank Costello)

A.C.   Albert Castel (William Clarke Quantrill)

J.C.   John Clendenning (Thomas Beer)

L.C.   Lisa Cardyn (Harry Kendall Thaw)

M.C.C.   Mark C. Carnes (Leon Czolgosz)

R.H.D.   Richard H. Dillon (Black Bart, Tiburcio Vásquez)

R.K.D.   Robert K. DeArment (Bob Dalton)

G.G.   Gilbert Geis (Gaston Bullock Means)

R.L.G.   Robert L. Gale (John Dillinger, Tom Horn, Machine Gun Kelly, John White Webster)

B.H.   Bruce Henstell (Mickey Cohen, Willie Sutton)

M.H.H.   Mark H. Haller (Al Capone, Meyer Lansky, Arnold Rothstein)

P.H.H.   Paul H. Hass (John F. Deitz)

S.H.   Stacey Hamilton (Ted Bundy, Joseph Anthony Colombo Sr., Carlo Gambino)

B.L.J.   Bruce L. Janoff (Joseph Valachi)

D.R.J.   David R. Johnson (Owen Victor Madden, Bugsy Siegel)

P.G.K.   Paul G. Kooistra (Jesse James, Belle Starr, Cole Younger)

E.L.L.   Edward L. Lach Jr. (Samuel Mason, Seth Wyman)

R.M.   Robert Muccigrosso (Nathan Freudenthal Leopold Jr. and Richard Albert Loeb)

W.H.M.   William Howard Moore (Vito Genovese, Dutch Schultz)

A.P.   Allan Peskin (Charles Julius Guiteau)

F.R.P.   Frank R. Prassel (William Doolin, Charles Arthur Floyd)

J.L.P.   James L. Penick (Railroad Bill, John Andrews Murrell)

W.P.   William Pencak (Ebenezer Mackintosh)
D.E.R.   David E. Ruth (Bonnie Parker and Clyde Chestnut Barrow)
S.A.R.   Steven A. Riess (Frankie Carbo)
W.W.R.   William W. Rogers (Stephen S. Renfroe)
H.S.   Harold Schechter (Edward Gein)
M.L.S.   Mary Lee Spence (Joseph Alfred Slade)
M.M.S.   Mary M. Stolberg (Lucky Luciano)
P.E.S.   Patricia E. Sweeney (Philip Mariano Fausto Musica)
R.M.U.   Robert M. Utley (Billy the Kid)
P.G.W.   Patrick G. Williams (John Wesley Hardin)

SOURCES AND FURTHER READING

THOMAS BEER
[1888?–1940]

The Beer Family Papers are at Yale University, Sterling Memorial Library, Manuscripts and Archives: MS 73. The discrepancy in the date of Thomas Beer's birth is clarified in the introduction to these papers compiled by Ruth Gay and Linda Wrigley. For criticism and bibliography, see Evans Burnham Harrington, "The Work of Thomas Beer: Appraisal and Bibliography" (Ph.D. diss., Univ. of Mississippi, 1968), and William Daniel Coyle, "The Short Stories of Thomas Beer" (Ph.D. diss., Univ. of North Carolina, 1977). The most influential critique of Beer's writing is in Alfred Kazin, *On Native Grounds* (1942). For recent discussions of Beer's *Stephen Crane*, see Stanley Wertheim and Paul Sorrentino, "Thomas Beer: The Clay Feet of Stephen Crane Biography," *American Literary Realism, 1870–1910* 22, no. 3 (1990): 2–16, and John Clendenning, "Thomas Beer's *Stephen Crane*: The Eye of His Imagination," *Prose Studies* 14, no. 2 (1991): 68–80.

BILLY THE KID
[1859–1881]

A vast body of literature focuses on Billy the Kid, but most of it is legend rather than history. The standard biography is Robert M. Utley, *Billy the Kid: A Short and Violent Life* (1989). The legend is expertly treated in Stephen Tatum, *Inventing Billy the Kid: Visions of the Outlaw in America, 1881–1981* (1982). For the Lincoln County War, see Frederick Nolan, *The Lincoln County War: A Documentary History* (1992), and Robert M. Utley, *High Noon in Lincoln: Violence on the Western Frontier* (1987). Important as both history and legend is Pat Garrett's own version, ghostwritten by a creative journalist named Marshal A. Upson, *The Authentic Life of Billy the Kid*; first published in 1882, it has reappeared in many editions.

BLACK BART
[fl. 1875–1888]
The best books on Black Bart are Richard H. Dillon, *Wells, Fargo Detective* (1969; repr. 1986), and William Collins and Bruce Levine, *Black Bart* (1993). Still useful are chapters in Joseph Henry Jackson, *Tintypes in Gold* (1939) and *Bad Company* (1949).

JOHN WILKES BOOTH
[1838–1865]
Archival materials on Booth include those in the War Department Records, the Kimmel collection in the Merl Kelce Library at the University of Tampa, and the Library of Congress. Other substantial Booth material appears in biographies of his brother Edwin or the Booth family in general, as in Stanley Kimmel, *The Mad Booths of Maryland* (1940; rev. ed., 1969), Eleanor Ruggles, *Prince of Players* (1953), and Gene Smith, *American Gothic* (1992). Booth's sister, Asia Booth Clarke, gave her brother individualized treatment in *The Unlocked Book: A Memoir of John Wilkes Booth* (1938), richly detailed if undeniably subjective. Less trustworthy is Izola Forrester, *The One Mad Act: The Unknown Story of John Wilkes Booth and His Family* (1937). See also Clarke, *The Elder and the Younger Booth* (1882), Francis Wilson, *John Wilkes Booth: Fact and Fiction of Lincoln's Assassination* (1929), and Philip Van Doren Stern, *The Man Who Killed Lincoln* (1939). William A. Tidwell (with James O. Hall and David W. Gaddy), *Come Retribution* (1988), speculates on the Confederacy's involvement in the assassination. John Lattimer, *Kennedy and Lincoln* (1980), offers detailed examinations of both assassinations. For Booth's theatrical career, see Gordon Samples, *Lust for Fame: The Stage Career of John Wilkes Booth* (1982). Also see Robert Silvester, *United States Theatre: A Bibliography from the Beginning to 1990* (1993), pp. 168–70.

TED BUNDY
[1946–1989]

Several books have been written about Bundy, the least sensational of which is Richard W. Larsen, *Bundy: The Deliberate Stranger* (1980); a television miniseries based on the book was released in 1986. Other accounts of Bundy include crime writer Ann Rule's *The Stranger beside Me* (1980; rev. ed., 1989), and Robert D. Keppel, *The Riverman: Ted Bundy and I Hunt for the Green River Killer* (1995), in which Keppel publishes excerpts of his conversations with Bundy and broaches the subject of Bundy's necrophilia. A transcript of Bundy's 23 Jan. 1989 interview with Christian broadcaster James Dobson in which Bundy rails against pornography is in the *St. Louis Post-Dispatch*, 25 Jan. 1989. Accounts of his execution are in the *New York Times*, the *Los Angeles Times*, and the *St. Petersburg (Fla.) Times*, all 25 Jan. 1989.

AL CAPONE
[1899–1947]

There are two important manuscript sources for studying Capone. One is the extensive files of the Chicago Crime Commission, which assembled newspaper clippings and investigative files on Capone and his associates through the 1920s and after. The other is the raw investigative file (no. SI 7085-F) assembled by the Intelligence Bureau of the IRS during its income tax investigation. This file—containing grand jury testimony, informants' reports, records seized from gambling houses, and other materials—has been closed since 1973.

The most thoroughly documented biographies of Capone are Robert J. Schoenberg, *Mr. Capone* (1992), and Laurence Bergreen, *Capone: The Man and the Era* (1994), both of which also include lists of primary sources. A careful earlier study is John Kobler, *Capone: The Life and World of Al Capone* (1971). All three books deal chiefly with the beer wars and assassinations rather than with Capone's business activities. Capone's life has also been the subject of numerous popular and journalistic studies that helped create his notoriety. Among these are Fred D. Pasley, *Al Capone: The Biography of a Self-Made Man* (1930); James O'Donnell Bennett, *Chicago Gang Land: The True Story of Chicago Crime* (1929); Walter Noble Burns, *The One-Way Ride: The Red Trail of Chicago Gangland from Prohibition to Jake Lingle* (1931); and Edward D. Sullivan, *Rattling the Cup on Chicago Crime* (1929). While these books contain inside information based on the reporters' knowledge, none are footnoted.

There have also been works looking at Capone from the point of view of law enforcement. Best known is Eliot Ness, with Oscar Fraley, *The Untouchables: The Real Story* (1957). One of the IRS agents described the income tax investigation in Elmer L. Irey, as told to William J. Slocum, *The Tax Dodgers: The Inside Story of the T-Men's War with America's Political and Underworld Hoodlums* (1948), chap. 2. For an analysis by a reporter who had access to the IRS files, see Hank Messick, *Secret File* (1969), chap. 2. Robert Ross, *The Trial of Al Capone* (1933), provides excerpts and summaries of Capone's trial and appeal. For an analysis of the official investigations, see Dennis E. Hoffman, *Scarface Al and the Crime Crusaders: Chicago's Private War against Capone* (1993), and James Calder, *The Origins and Development of Federal Crime Control Policy* (1993).

Some scholarly studies place Capone in a historical context. Most important is David E. Ruth, "Inventing the Public Enemy: The Gangster in American Culture, 1918–1934" (Ph.D. diss., Northwestern Univ., 1992), which uses Capone as the chief example in an incisive exploration of the mythology that surrounded the criminals of the 1920s. Humbert S. Nelli, *Italians in Chicago, 1880–1930: A Study in Ethnic Mobility* (1970), places Capone's activities in the context of the Chicago Italian community. Mark H. Haller, "Illegal Enterprise: A Theoretical and Historical Interpretation," *Criminology* 28 (May 1990): 215–23, briefly analyzes the structure of Capone's business operations.

FRANKIE CARBO
[1904–1976]

On Carbo's career, see U.S. Senate, Judiciary Committee, *Professional Boxing, Hearings before the Subcommittee on Antitrust and Monopoly*, 86th Cong.,

2d sess., 1960 (1960–1961). For Carbo's place in boxing history, see Steven A. Riess, "Only the Ring Was Square: Frankie Carbo and the Underworld Control of American Boxing," *International Journal of the History of Sport* 5 (May 1988): 29–52; Jeffrey T. Sammons, *Beyond the Ring: The Role of Boxing in American Society* (1988); and Barney Nagler, *James Norris and the Decline of Boxing* (1964). On Carbo and the International Boxing Club, see Robert Coughlin, "How the IBC Runs Boxing," *Sports Illustrated*, 17 Jan. 1955, pp. 47–48. Carbo's relations with LaMotta are described in Jake LaMotta, with Pete Savage, *Raging Bull* (1970). On Carbo's legal problems, see the *New York Times*, 25 July 1958, 31 Oct. 1959, 15 Mar. and 31 May 1961, and 31 Mar. 1962. For his obituary, see the *New York Times*, 11 Nov. 1976.

BUTCH CASSIDY
[1866–1908? or 1937?]
See Larry Pointer, *In Search of Butch Cassidy* (1977); Lula Parker Betenson, as told to Dora Flack, *Butch Cassidy, My Brother* (1975); C. Bruce Chatwin, *In Patagonia* (1977).

MICKEY COHEN
[1913–1976]
There are, of course, innumerable newspaper stories from 1945 to the early 1960s in which Mickey Cohen's name appears. Few are illuminating beyond the immediate events of the day. One of the few lengthy contemporary pieces on Cohen is Dean Jennings, "Mickey Cohen: The Private Life of a Hood," *Saturday Evening Post*, 20 Sept. 1958. At the end of his life Cohen published an autobiography, *Mickey Cohen: In My Own Words*, with John Peer Nugent (1976). The book is not more than a series of transcribed interviews. What it lacks in background regarding the period it makes up for in the authenticity of Cohen's language. Obituaries are in the *Los Angeles Times*, the *Los Angeles Examiner*, and the *New York Times*, all 30 July 1976.

JOSEPH ANTHONY COLOMBO SR.

[1923–1978]

Information on Colombo is limited. Some background can be found in John H. Davis, *Mafia Dynasty: The Rise and Fall of the Gambino Crime Family* (1993). See also Carl Sifakis, *The Mafia Encyclopedia* (1987), for a short biography. Reports of his shooting are in the *New York Times*, 29, 30 June 1971. An obituary is in the *New York Times*, 24 May 1978. An account of his funeral is in the same newspaper, 27 May 1978.

FRANK COSTELLO

[1891–1973]

The best sources on Costello remain the biographies by Leonard Katz, *Uncle Frank* (1973), and George Wolf and Joseph Dimona, *Frank Costello: Prime Minister of the Underworld* (1974). For an accurate portrayal of Costello's place within organized crime in America, see Michael Woodiwiss, *Crime Crusades and Corruption: Prohibitions in the United States, 1900–1987* (1988). An insight into Costello's popular image can be found in Estes Kefauver, *Crime in America* (1952). An obituary and follow-up article can be found in the *New York Times*, 19 and 22 Feb. 1973.

LEON CZOLGOSZ

[1873–1901]

Newspaper accounts and other materials on the assassination can be found at the Buffalo and Erie County Public Library, the Buffalo and Erie County Historical Association, and also the Courthouse Archives of Erie County, N.Y. (*People v. Leon F. Czolgosz* [1901], repr. in *American State Trials*, ed. John D. Lawson [1923]). The major biography is A. Wesley Johns, *The Man Who Shot McKinley* (1970). For the official report positing Czolgosz's sanity, see Joseph Fowler et al., "Official Report of the Experts for the People in the Case of the *People v. Leon F. Czolgosz*" (1901), repr. in *American State Trials*. On the posthumous claim that he was insane, see Walter Channing, "The Mental State of Czolgosz, the Assassin of President McKinley," *American Journal of Insanity* 59 (Oct. 1902); and L. Vernon

Briggs, *The Manner of Man That Kills* (1921). See also Robert J. Donovan, *The Assassins* (1952), and Sidney Fine, "Anarchism and the Assassination of McKinley," *American Historical Review* 60, no. 4 (July 1955).

BOB DALTON
[1869–1892]
Ben Dalton, a law-abiding brother, recounted the history of his outlaw siblings in an interview in the *San Francisco Chronicle*, 27 Oct. 1892. *The Dalton Brothers and Their Astounding Career of Crime, by an Eyewitness,* published anonymously in 1892, contains many errors of fact. Emmett Dalton, with professional help, wrote two books on the outlaws, *Beyond the Law* (1918) and *When the Daltons Rode* (1931). Frank F. Latta, *Dalton Gang Days* (1976), deals primarily with the brothers' troubles in California. Nancy B. Samuelson, *The Dalton Gang Story* (1992), sets straight many previously published inaccuracies in the Dalton story and is the best source on the Dalton family.

JOHN F. DEITZ
[1861–1924]
Information on Deitz can be found in two rich collections in the Wisconsin State Archives, State Historical Society of Wisconsin: the *Executive Department Pardon Papers*, ser. 1/1/10–7, and the Deitz Family Scrapbook (microfilm). The best sources for Deitz's colorful career are Paul H. Hass, "The Suppression of John F. Deitz: An Episode of the Progressive Era in Wisconsin," *Wisconsin Magazine of History*, 57 (Summer 1974): 255–309; Malcolm Rosholt, *The Battle of Cameron Dam* (1974); and *Dictionary of Wisconsin Biography* (1960).

JOHN DILLINGER
[1903–1934]
The John Dillinger Historical Museum in Nashville, Ind., has Dillinger memorabilia. Alanna Nash, "Maybe I'll Learn Someday, Dad, You Can't Win in This Game," *New York Times*, 7 Mar. 1976, describes the museum.

G. Russell Girardin, with William J. Hemler, *Dillinger: The Untold Story* (1994), is the definitive biography. Athan G. Theodoris and John Stuart Cox, *The Boss: J. Edgar Hoover and the Great American Inquisition* (1988); Anthony Summers, *Official and Confidential: The Secret Life of J. Edgar Hoover* (1993); and William W. Turner, *Hoover's F.B.I.* (1993), detail activities, carelessness, blunders, and cover-ups of the FBI under Hoover in connection with Dillinger. Richard Gid Powers, *G-Men: Hoover's FBI in American Popular Culture* (1983), traces permutations in the Dillinger legend. Jay Robert Nash, *Dillinger: Dead or Alive?* (1970), presents evidence that Dillinger was not killed in Chicago in 1934. A long obituary, with portrait, is in the *New York Times*, 23 July 1934.

WILLIAM DOOLIN
[1858–1896]
Leading sources include Bailey C. Hanes, *Bill Doolin: Outlaw O. T.* (1968); Glenn Shirley, *West of Hell's Fringe* (1978); and Paul Wellman, *A Dynasty of Western Outlaws* (1961).

CHARLES ARTHUR FLOYD
[1904–1934]
Leading sources include Michael Wallis, *Pretty Boy* (1992); Merle Clayton, *Union Station Massacre* (1975); and Paul Wellman, *A Dynasty of Western Outlaws* (1961). An obituary is in the *New York Times*, 23 Oct. 1934.

CARLO GAMBINO
[1902–1976]
As is true with most organized crime figures, reliable information on Gambino is limited. See John H. Davis, *Mafia Dynasty: The Rise and Fall of the Gambino Crime Family* (1993), and Carl Sifakis, *The Mafia Encyclopedia* (1987). An obituary is in the *New York Times*, 16 Oct. 1976. An account of his funeral is in the same newspaper, 19 Oct. 1976. An analysis of the effect of Gambino's death on organized crime is in the *New York Times*, 18 Oct. 1976.

EDWARD GEIN
[1906–1984]
For a complete account of Gein's life, crimes, and impact on American popular culture, see Harold Schechter, *Deviant: The Shocking True Story of the Original "Psycho"* (1989).

VITO GENOVESE
[1897–1969]
The only biography is David Hanna's brief *Vito Genovese* (1974). Peter Maas provides details from the exposés of the 1960s in *The Valachi Papers* (1968). A useful corrective to the popular literature on organized crime is Dwight C. Smith Jr., *The Mafia Mystique* (1975). An obituary is in the *New York Times*, 15 Feb. 1969.

CHARLES JULIUS GUITEAU
[1841–1882]
The indispensable source for Guiteau's life and crimes is the official three-volume transcript, *Report of the Proceedings in the Case of the United States vs. Charles J. Guiteau...* (1882). This should be supplemented with a journalistic account by H. G. and C. J. Hayes, *A Complete History of the Trial of Guiteau* (1882), which includes Guiteau's "Autobiography" and a narrative of his married life by his onetime wife. Useful secondary works include Allan Peskin, *Garfield* (1978), and Charles Rosenberg, *The Trial of the Assassin Guiteau* (1968), which places Guiteau's trial in the context of Gilded Age psychiatry and law.

JOHN WESLEY HARDIN
[1853–1895]
A collection of Hardin papers, chiefly letters written and received in prison, is in Special Collections, Albert B. Alkek Library, Southwest Texas State University in San Marcos. Papers related to Hardin's pardon are in the records of the secretary of state (RG 307), Archives Division of the Texas State Library, Austin. An autobiography, *The Life of John Wesley Hardin As*

Written by Himself, uncompleted at the time of his death, was published in 1896 and has been reprinted in paperback. Certain commentators have asserted that Hardin lacked the education to have written the work himself. His prison letters, however, demonstrate that he was quite capable of having done so. The most complete biography is Lewis Nordyke's essentially sympathetic *John Wesley Hardin: Texas Gunman* (1957); unfortunately, it lacks both bibliography and notes. The motives and circumstances of Hardin's murder have been debated over the years. See Leon Metz, *John Selman, Gunfighter* (1980). Following Hardin's murder, Texas newspapers carried often unreliable accounts of his life and death. See, for instance, the *Gonzales Inquirer,* 22 Aug. 1895.

TOM HORN
[1860–1903]
Documents by and relating to Tom Horn are in the First Judicial District of Wyoming, Laramie County Courthouse, Cheyenne; the Archives and Western History Library of the University of Wyoming, Laramie; and the James Covington Hancock Papers and the John Pleasant Gray Papers at the Arizona Pioneers' Historical Society Collections, Tucson. *Life of Tom Horn, Government Scout and Interpreter, Written by Himself Together with His Letters and Statements by His Friends: A Vindication* (1904) is fictitious in many parts. The following works concern Horn centrally or tangentially and often contradict one another: Britton Davis, *The Truth about Geronimo* (1929); Joe LeFors, *Wyoming Peace Officer: The Autobiography of Joe LeFors* (1953); Dean F. Krakel, *The Saga of Tom Horn: The Story of a Cattlemen's War, with Personal Narratives, Newspaper Accounts and Official Documents and Testimonies* (1954), with many photographs; John Rolfe Burroughs, *Where the Old West Stayed Young* (1962); Lauran Paine, *Tom Horn, Man of the West* (1963); Dan L. Thrapp, *Al Sieber: Chief of Scouts* (1964); "'No Cure, No Pay,' a Tom Horn Letter," ed. Larry D. Ball, *Journal of Arizona History* 8 (1967): 200–202; *Chasing Geronimo: The Journal of Leonard Wood, May-September 1886,* ed. Jack C. Lane (1970); Doyce B. Nunis Jr., *The Life of Tom Horn Revisited* (1992); "Tom Horn's Second

Chance," *Economist*, 25 Sept. 1993, p. 37; Chip Carson, *Joe LeFors: 'I Slickered Tom Horn': The History of the Texas Cowboy Turned Montana-Wyoming Lawman—A Sequel* (1995); and William Hafford, "The Life and Legend of Tom Horn," *Arizona Highways* 72 (May 1996): 18–23. An obituary is in the *New York Times*, 21 Nov. 1903.

JESSE JAMES
[1847–1882]
The definitive biography of Jesse James is William Settle Jr., *Jesse James Was His Name* (1966), which includes a twenty-page chapter analyzing works related to the outlaw and a twenty-page comprehensive bibliography listing relevant public documents and manuscript and newspaper collections as well as articles and books related to the outlaw's career. The State Historical Society of Missouri (Columbia) and the Kansas State Historical Society are major sources for manuscripts, letters, and newspaper clippings. Other books of note include Eric Hobsbawm, *Bandits* (1981), and Paul Kooistra, *Criminals as Heroes: Structure, Power, and Identity* (1989), an explanation of how certain mass murderers and habitual criminals, like Jesse James, came to be glorified rather than uniformly condemned. Also useful are Robertus Love, *The Rise and Fall of Jesse James* (1926); Kent Steckmesser, *The Western Hero in History and Legend* (1965); Frank Triplett, *The Life, Times, and Treacherous Death of Jesse James* (1882); and T. J. Stiles, *Jesse James: Last Rebel of the Civil War* (2002).

MACHINE GUN KELLY
[1895–1954]
Details of Machine Gun Kelly's life are available in Carl Sifakis, *The Encyclopedia of American Crime* (1982); George C. Kohn, *Dictionary of Culprits and Criminals* (1986); Susan L. Stetler, *Almanac of Famous People* (1989); and Michael Kurland, *A Gallery of Rogues: Portraits in True Crime* (1994). Two books with especially revealing evidence concerning Hoover and the Kelly case are Jay Robert Nash, *Citizen Hoover: A Critical Study of the Life and Times of J. Edgar Hoover* (1972), and Anthony Summers, *Official*

and Confidential: The Secret Life of J. Edgar Hoover (1993). An obituary that includes an early photograph of Kelly is in the *New York Times,* 18 July 1954.

MEYER LANSKY
[1902–1983]

The most thoughtful and thoroughly researched biography is Robert Lacey, *Little Man: Meyer Lansky and the Gangster Life* (1991). The footnotes and bibliography of Lacey's biography provide a full guide to the secondary works, government documents, and archival materials on Lansky's career. Also of interest because it is based in part on interviews with Lansky is Dennis Eisenberg et al., *Meyer Lansky: Mogul of the Mob* (1979). Hank Messick, *Lansky* (1971), is useful for understanding Florida gambling because Messick, a reporter, was knowledgeable about the Florida scene. Mark H. Haller, "Bootleggers as Businessmen: From City Slums to City Builders," in *Law, Alcohol, and Order: Perspectives on National Prohibition,* ed. David E. Kyvig (1985), places Lansky within the context of his bootlegging associates. An obituary is in the *New York Times,* 16 Jan. 1983.

NATHAN FREUDENTHAL LEOPOLD JR.
[1904–1971]
RICHARD ALBERT LOEB
[1905–1936]

Helpful accounts of the crime, trial, and personalities can be found in Hal Higdon, *The Crime of the Century: The Leopold and Loeb Case* (1975); Maureen McKernan, *The Amazing Crime and Trial of Leopold and Loeb* (1924); Maurycy Urstein, *Leopold and Loeb: A Psychiatric-Psychological Study* (1924); Richard Loeb, *The Leopold-Loeb Case: With Excerpts from the Evidence of the Alienists and Including the Arguments to the Court by Counsel for the Defense* (1926); Clarence Darrow, *Clarence Darrow's Sentencing Speech in* State of Illinois v. Leopold and Loeb (in the *Classics of the Courtroom* series, foreword by Irving Younger, 1988); Elmer Gertz, *A Handful of Cases* (1965); Frederick Arthur Mackenzie, *Twentieth Century Crimes* (1927); Clarence Darrow, *The Story of My Life* (1932); and Irving

Stone, *Clarence Darrow for the Defense* (1941). *Swoon* (1993), a film treatment of the Leopold-Loeb story, is distributed by New Line Home Video/Columbia Tristar Home Video. An obituary for Leopold is in the *New York Times*, 31 Aug. 1971, as is one for Loeb, 29 Jan. 1936.

LUCKY LUCIANO
[1897–1962]
A number of films have been made and two anecdotal and unreliable biographies have been written about Luciano. See Sid Feder and Joachim Joesten, *The Luciano Story* (1960), and Martin Gosch and Richard Hammer, *The Last Testament of Lucky Luciano* (1974). More credible evidence can be found in Mary M. Stolberg, "Political Justice" (Ph.D. diss., Univ. of Virginia, 1991), and Robert Lacey, *Little Man: Meyer Lansky and the Gangster Life* (1991). An obituary is in the *New York Times*, 27 Jan. 1962.

EBENEZER MACKINTOSH
[1737–1816]
Two articles by George Pomeroy Anderson, "Ebenezer Mackintosh: Stamp Act Rioter and Patriot," and "A Note on Ebenezer Mackintosh," in Colonial Society of Massachusetts, *Publications* 26 (1924–1926): 15–64 and 348–61, constitute remarkably thorough pieces of historical detective work. A surprisingly sympathetic sketch appears in Peter Oliver, *Origin and Progress of the American Rebellion*, ed. Douglass Adair and John A. Schultz (1961). See also Dirk Hoerder, *Crowd Action in Revolutionary Massachusetts, 1765–1780* (1977), and, for the Stamp Act riots, Edmund S. Morgan and Helen M. Morgan, *The Stamp Act Crisis: Prologue to Revolution* (1953).

OWEN VICTOR MADDEN
[1891–1965]
Madden has not received as much attention as several of his contemporaries. A full-length study of his career, Graham Nown, *The English Godfather* (1987), is a very sympathetic portrait that needs to be used cautiously. Madden is mentioned in Stephen R. Fox, *Blood and Power:*

Organized Crime in Twentieth-Century America (1989). An obituary is in the *New York Times,* 24 Apr. 1965.

SAMUEL MASON

[c. 1750–1803]

Some of Samuel Mason's correspondence has survived and is held with the papers of Samuel Draper at the Wisconsin State Historical Society, Madison, and a manuscript in French of his trial at New Madrid is held by the Mississippi Department of Archives and History, Jackson. The best secondary source of the life and career of Samuel Mason remains Otto A. Rothert, *The Outlaws of Cave-in-Rock* (1924).

GASTON BULLOCK MEANS

[1879–1938]

A full-length biography of Means is Edwin P. Hoyt, *Spectacular Rogue: Gaston B. Means* (1963). Among others, Andrew Sinclair, *The Available Man: The Life Behind the Masks of Warren Gamaliel Harding* (1965), pp. 285–87, provides an accurate portrayal of Harding's death from natural causes. The story of Means's involvement in the Lindbergh case is told in Evalyn Walsh McLean and Boyden Sparkes, *Father Struck It Rich* (1936), pp. 296–300, while his association with the Bureau of Investigation (later the FBI) is detailed in J. Edgar Hoover, "The Amazing Mr. Means," *American Magazine,* Dec. 1936. Obituaries are in the *St. Louis Post-Dispatch,* 12 Dec. 1938, and the *Concord* (N.C.) *Daily Tribune,* 15 Dec. 1938.

JOHN ANDREWS MURRELL

[1806?–1844]

The view of Murrell as an archcriminal originated in August Q. Walton, Esq., *A History of the Detection, Conviction, Life and Designs of John A. Murel, the Great Western Land Pirate* (1835), written by·Virgil A. Stewart or by a ghost-writer acting for Stewart; in either case, Walton is a pseudonym. Stewart was also responsible for H. R. Howard, comp., *The History of Virgil A. Stewart and His Adventure* (1836), which contains the Walton pamphlet, revised to reflect events of the panic of 1835; in it Murrell is made to express more explicit antislavery views. Two works that contributed additional details to the legend are *National Police Gazette*, eds., *The Life and Adventures of John A. Murrell, the Great Western Land Pirate* (1847), and Robert M. Coates, *The Outlaw Years: The History of the Land Pirates of the Natchez Trace* (1930). Coates as well as writers before and after him made uncritical use of Stewart's pamphlet and the *National Police Gazette* account as their main sources. The only scholarly treatment to date is James L. Penick, *The Great Western Land Pirate: John A. Murrell in Legend and History* (1981).

PHILIP MARIANO FAUSTO MUSICA
[1884–1938]
The most complete report on the personal life and business career of Musica is Robert Shaplen, "The Metamorphosis of Philip Musica," *New Yorker*, 22 and 29 Oct. 1955. "McKesson & Robbins: Its Fall and Rise," *Fortune*, Mar. 1940, pp. 72–75, focuses primarily on Musica's years there. The Dec. 1938 issues of the *New York Times* cover in detail the last events of his life. An obituary is in the *New York Times*, 17 Dec. 1938.

BONNIE PARKER
[1910–1934]
CLYDE CHESTNUT BARROW
[1909–1934]
E. R. Milner, *The Lives and Times of Bonnie and Clyde* (1996), is the most reliable biography. David E. Ruth, *Inventing the Public Enemy: The Gangster in American Culture, 1918–1934* (1996), explores the values promoted in mass media portrayals. The duo's ambush was widely reported in the press.

WILLIAM CLARKE QUANTRILL
[1837–1865]
John N. Edwards, *Noted Guerrillas; or, The War on the Border* (1877), describes Quantrill's career from a pro-Confederate standpoint and contains many exaggerations and falsehoods. William E. Connelley, *Quantrill*

and the Border Wars (1910), is the most detailed biography of Quantrill and contains many primary source materials not available elsewhere but is strongly biased from a Union standpoint. Albert Castel, *William Clarke Quantrill: His Life and Times* (1962), seeks to present an objective view of Quantrill and his career.

RAILROAD BILL
[?–1896]
A more or less complete listing of the literature on Railroad Bill is in A. J. Wright, comp., *Criminal Activity in the Deep South, 1700–1933* (1989). For a codification of the folk ballads, see Howard W. Odum, ed., "Folk-Song and Folk-Poetry as Found in the Secular Songs of the Southern Negroes," *Journal of American Folklore* 24 (1911): 289–93. The Brewton newspapers *Pine Belt News* and *Standard Gauge* are the best places to follow the story. For a fuller discussion of the identification question with citations, see James L. Penick, "Railroad Bill," *Gulf Coast Historical Review* 10 (1994): 85–92.

STEPHEN S. RENFROE
[1843–1886]
The only biography of Renfroe is William Warren Rogers and Ruth Pruitt, *Stephen S. Renfroe, Alabama's Outlaw Sheriff* (1972). An inaccurate sketch of Renfroe, based on the Renfroe legend, is in Carl Carmer, *Stars Fell on Alabama* (1934), pp. 126–33. The book is worthwhile for evoking the mood and atmosphere of Alabama during Reconstruction. The most recent work is Ruth Rogers Pruitt, *Wind Along the Waste* (1991), a work of fiction whose central character is based on Renfroe. See also Louis Roycraft Smith Jr., "A History of Sumter County, Alabama, through 1886" (Ph.D. diss., Univ. of Ala., 1988).

ARNOLD ROTHSTEIN

[1882–1928]

The standard source for Rothstein's life is Leo Katcher, *The Big Bankroll: The Life and Times of Arnold Rothstein* (1958). Another book is Donald Henderson Clarke, *In the Reign of Rothstein* (1929). After Rothstein's death his wife, Carolyn Greene Rothstein, wrote a memoir, *Now I'll Tell* (1934). Rothstein's role in the 1919 World Series fix is described in Eliot Asinof, *Eight Men Out: The Black Sox and the 1919 World Series* (1963); and in the biography of one of the players naively involved in the fix, Donald Gropman, *Say It Ain't So Joe: The Story of Shoeless Joe Jackson* (1979). The scandal is also referred to in the histories of baseball; see particularly Steven A. Riess, *Touching Base: Professional Baseball and American Culture in the Progressive Era* (1980), chap. 3; and Harold Seymour, *Baseball: The Golden Age* (1971), pp. 294–339. A number of histories of crime mention some aspects of Rothstein's career. See, for instance, relevant parts of Jenna Weissman Joselit, *Our Gang: Jewish Crime and the New York Jewish Community, 1900–1940* (1983); Albert Fried, *The Rise and Fall of the Jewish Gangster in America* (1980); and Stephen Fox, *Blood and Power: Organized Crime in Twentieth-Century America* (1989). An obituary is in the *New York Times,* 7 Nov. 1928.

DUTCH SCHULTZ

[1902–1935]

In *Kill the Dutchman! The Story of Dutch Schultz* (1971), veteran reporter Paul Sann advanced the argument that Schultz was murdered because he ran afoul of an Italian-American criminal cartel. Thomas E. Dewey, *Twenty Against the Underworld* (1974), and Richard Norton Smith, *Thomas E. Dewey and His Times* (1982), are especially useful on the prosecutor's investigation of Schultz's underworld operations. J. Richard "Dixie" Davis wrote "Things I Couldn't Tell Till Now," a colorful but not entirely reliable series of articles for *Collier's* in 1939. See also the *New York Times,* 24, 26, and 29 Oct. 1935.

BUGSY SIEGEL
[1906–1947]
Siegel's notoriety has attracted the attention of two biographers: David Hanna, *Bugsy Siegel: The Man Who Invented Murder, Inc.* (1974), and Dean Jennings, *We Only Kill Each Other: The Life and Bad Times of Bugsy Siegel* (1967). Both need to be read with care. Robert Lacey, *Little Man: Meyer Lansky and the Gangster Life* (1991), contains much useful information about Siegel and is essential for anyone seeking to place Siegel in the context of his times. An obituary is in the *New York Times*, 22 June 1947.

JOSEPH ALFRED SLADE
[1829 or 1830–1864]
John B. McClernan, *Slade's Wells Fargo Colt* (1977), best documents Slade's career and includes a good bibliography. Lew L. Callaway, "Joseph Alfred Slade: Killer or Victim?," *Montana: The Magazine of Western History* 3 (1953): 4–34, gives details about the violent episodes, real and legendary. In *Roughing It* (1872), Mark Twain devoted two chapters to Slade, one recounting his meeting and reaction to Slade on the overland stage, and the second quoting Thomas J. Dimsdale's description of the arrest and execution of Slade in his *The Vigilantes of Montana* (1866).

BELLE STARR
[1848–1889]
Much of the work done on Belle Starr is of dubious accuracy. Probably the best work is Glenn Shirley, *Belle Starr and Her Times* (1982), which contains a 25-page chapter that discusses books, poems, and movies about her. Richard Fox, *Belle Starr, the Bandit Queen* (1889), is the earliest biography. Samuel Harman, *Hell on the Border, He Hanged Eighty-Eight Men* (1898), also contains an account of Belle Starr and has been reprinted in various abridged versions. Another important source is *The Story of Cole Younger, by Himself* (1903), which debunks the often-held myth that Belle Starr had an illegitimate child by the famous outlaw. Burton Rascoe, *Belle Starr, "Bandit Queen"* (1941); Anton Booker, *Wildcats in Petticoats* (1945); Paul Wellman, *A Dynasty*

of Western Outlaws (1961); and Carl Breihan and Charles Rosamond, *The Bandit Belle* (1970), are among the better biographies. Movies include *Belle Starr* (1941), starring Randolph Scott and Gene Tierney; *Belle Starr's Daughter* (1948); *Son of Belle Starr* (1953); and *The Long Riders* (1980). In 1980 *Belle Starr*, a television movie, featured Elizabeth Montgomery in the title role.

WILLIE SUTTON
[1901–1980]
The chief published sources for Sutton's career outside contemporary newspaper reports are his biographies: *I, Willie Sutton*, written with Quentin Reynolds (1942), and the more familiar *Where the Money Was*, with Edward Linn (1976). Also of value are Erle Stanley Gardner, "The Case of Willie Sutton," *Look*, 6, 20 May 1952, and Robert M. Yoder, "Someday They'll Get Slick Willie Sutton," *Saturday Evening Post*, 20 Jan. 1951. A lengthy obituary appears in the *New York Times*, 19 Nov. 1980.

HARRY KENDALL THAW
[1871–1947]
A modest collection of Thaw's surviving papers is at the Harry Thaw Collection of the New York State Historical Association in Cooperstown. Other primary source materials dealing with the life of Harry K. Thaw, all of which focus almost exclusively on his relationship with Evelyn Nesbit and his trials for the murder of Stanford White, include F. A. Mackenzie, ed., *The Trial of Harry Thaw* (1928); Benjamin Atwell, *The Great Harry Thaw Case* (1907), authored by the Thaw family publicist; Harry K. Thaw's own account, *The Traitor: Being the Untampered with, Unrevised Account of the Trial and All That Led to It* (1926); and Mary Copley Thaw, *The Secret Unveiled* (1909). Another perspective on Thaw's character may be found in Evelyn Nesbit's autobiographies, *The Story of My Life* (1914) and *Prodigal Days* (1934). Among the secondary sources discussing the Thaw-White episode are Paul Baker, *Stanny: The Gilded Life of Stanford White* (1989); Kevin Brownlow, *Behind the Mask of Innocence* (1991); Frederick Collins, *Glamorous Sinners* (1932); Gerald Langford, *The Murder of Stanford White* (1962); and Michael Mooney, *Evelyn*

Nesbit and Stanford White: Love and Death in the Gilded Age (1976). Obituaries appear in the *New York Times*, 23 Feb. 1947; the *Pittsburgh Press*, 23, 25 Feb. 1947; and the *Pittsburgh Sun-Telegraph*, 24, 26 Feb. 1947.

JOSEPH VALACHI
[1904–1971]

There is a complicated publication history behind Valachi's memoirs. Originally the Justice Department hoped that his 1,180-page manuscript would be published under his own name. However, the Bureau of Prisons barred federal inmates from publishing anything about their crimes, and the Italian-American lobby argued that the book would slur all Italian Americans. Valachi's manuscript was therefore suppressed. However, after a long court battle, Peter Maas was given permission to use all of Valachi's material in addition to extensive interviews with Valachi to publish a third-person book that would be the basis for *The Valachi Papers* (1968). This book in particular, and Maas in general, are by far the most important sources on Valachi. In 1963 Maas was the first to publish an article breaking the news of Valachi's story, "Joseph Valachi: The Killer Who Told on the Mob," *Saturday Evening Post*, 23 Nov. 1963, pp. 21–23. Valachi is also featured in Maas, *The Canary That Sang* (1969), and Maas, "Joe Valachi's Big Contract," is a chapter in Nicholas Gage, *Mafia, USA* (1972). Valachi also rates a prominent place in Carl Sifakis, *The Mafia Encyclopedia* (1987), pp. 331–33. See also P. D. Zimmerman, "Hit Parade," *Newsweek*, 6 Jan. 1969, pp. 54–56. An obituary is in the *New York Times*, 4 Apr. 1971.

TIBURCIO VÁSQUEZ
[1835–1875]

There is no satisfactory full-scale biography of Vásquez. The preferred version of his life is Robert Greenwood, comp., *The California Outlaw: Tiburcio Vásquez* (1960), which includes George A. Beers's account, *Vásquez: Or the Hunted Bandits...* (1875). See also Charles H. Shinn, *Graphic Description of Pacific Coast Outlaws* (1958), Joseph Henry Jackson, *Bad Company* (1949), and Eugene T. Sawyer, *Life and Career of Tiburcio Vásquez* (1944).

JOHN WHITE WEBSTER

[1793–1850]

George Bemis, Webster's main prosecutor, thoroughly chronicles the events in *Report of the Case of John W. Webster* (1850); this book-length treatment is considered one of the finest and most complete concerning any criminal case in American court history. Robert Sullivan, *The Disappearance of Dr. Parkman* (1971), is a long, scholarly account, with illustrations and a bibliography. Helen Thomson, *Murder at Harvard* (1971), concentrates in more narrative form on the evidence, the trial, the verdict, the execution, and the aftermath—also with illustrations. The books by Sullivan and Thomson contain much identical material. Leonard W. Levy, *The Law of the Commonwealth and Chief Justice Shaw* (1957), offers succinct comments on legal aspects of the death sentence Lemuel Shaw pronounced on Webster. In narrating the crime from conflicting points of view, Simon Schama in his fascinating *Dead Certainties (Unwarranted Speculations)* (1991) deliberately mixes fact and fiction, jumbles chronology and details, and leaves the reader wondering. Eleanor M. Tilton, *Amiable Aristocrat: A Biography of Dr. Oliver Wendell Holmes* (1947), incidentally places Webster in the social and professional environment of Oliver Wendell Holmes, a distinguished Boston brahmin. Holmes, one of Webster's chemistry students, at the time of the murder and the trial ironically occupied the Parkman Chair of Anatomy at Harvard and was an expert medical witness against his former professor. See also Cleveland Amory, *The Proper Bostonians* (1947); Richard B. Morris, *Fair Trial* (1952); and Edmund Pearson, *Murder at Smutty Nose and Other Murders* (1926).

SETH WYMAN

[1784–1843]

No organized collection of Wyman papers is known to exist. His life and career have received little attention; the best sources remain his *Autobiography* and G. P. Hadley, *History of the Town of Goffstown, 1733–1920* (2 vols., 1922). His incarceration records are held at the Massachusetts and New Hampshire state prisons.

COLE YOUNGER

[1844–1916]

A good place to begin examining the life of Younger is his autobiography, *The Story of Cole Younger, by Himself* (1903). Other books of note on the subject include John Newman Edwards, *Noted Guerrillas* (1877), and Augustus Appler, *The Guerrillas of the West; or, the Life, Character, and Daring Exploits of the Younger Brothers* (1875). William A. Settle Jr., *Jesse James Was His Name* (1966), provides the definitive account of the James-Younger gang and includes a twenty-page descriptive bibliography analyzing works about the outlaw band. Paul Kooistra, *Criminals as Heroes: Structure, Power, and Identity* (1989), explains how certain mass murderers and habitual criminals like Younger have come to be glorified rather than uniformly condemned. The most recent work is Carl Breihan, *Ride the Razor's Edge: The Younger Brothers Story* (1992). Younger's life has been dramatized in several films, including *Cole Younger, Gunfighter* (1958), *The Great Northfield Raid* (1972), and *The Long Riders* (1980).

INDEX

PICTURE CREDITS

Photos are identified by the page number on which they appear.